RAISING YOUR SPIRITED CHILD

RAISING YOUR SPIRITED CHILD

A GUIDE FOR PARENTS WHOSE CHILD IS <u>MORE</u>

INTENSE • SENSITIVE • PERCEPTIVE
• PERSISTENT • ENERGETIC

Mary Sheedy Kurcinka

HarperCollins*Publishers*

FIRST EDITION

Designed by Joan Greenfield

Library of Congress Cataloging-in-Publication Data

Kurcinka, Mary Sheedy, 1953—
  Raising your spirited child : a guide for parents whose child is more intense, sensitive, percep-tive, persistent, energetic / by Mary Sheedy Kurcinka.—1st ed.
      p. cm.
  Includes index.
  ISBN 0-06-016361-5
  1. Child rearing. 2. Parent and child. 3. Aggressiveness (Psychology) in children. 4. Personality in children. I. Title.
HQ769.K867 1991
649'.1—dc20   90-56376

---

91 92 93 94 95 AC/HC 10 9 8 7 6 5 4 3 2 1

Dedicated to:
My husband, Joseph Michael Kurcinka—
without your insight, wit, and organizational eye I couldn't have done it.
My children, Joshua Thomas and Kristina Leah Sheedy Kurcinka—
without you I wouldn't have known.
My parents, Richard and Beatrice Sheedy—
without you I wouldn't be . . .

CONTENTS

PART THREE
LIVING WITH SPIRIT

PART FOUR
SOCIALIZING WITH SPIRIT

PART FIVE
ENJOYING SPIRIT

ACKNOWLEDGMENTS

The creation of a book is an amazing project, completed because of the contributions of many. To them I am very grateful and must say thank you.

In random order as always . . .

ALL OF THE PARENTS, teachers, and children who have shared their stories with me, you've asked me not to share your names and I won't, but I have learned so much from you!

Kim Cardwell, my friend and colleague who has been with me through every word and with it every moan, groan, and moment of elation.

Heide Lange, my agent, the "dream maker" as I refer to her—she put this project together.

Janet Goldstein, my editor, the emotional support and thoughtful insight she has given me have been incredibly important.

Peternelle van Arsdale, Janet's assistant editor, who has taken care of the details and stepped in to help me during Janet's maternity leave.

Ken Green, my attorney, whose daughter is a writer and provided not only legal advice but fatherly advice too.

JoAnne Ellison, my supervisor, thanks to her support and flexibility I was able to get the time to write.

Cal Zwiefel, not my boss, but a friend, a mentor, and an educational administrator who has always believed in me.

Tim and Pat Francisco, friends, fellow writers, artists who taught me what to expect and assured me I wasn't crazy when I experienced the range of a writer's emotions!

My entire ECFE staff, especially, Barbara Dopp, Shannon Dufresne, Beth Hersman, Marietta Rice, Jenna Ruble, Leta Fox, and Joan Kane, who have let me pick their brains.

Vicki Cronin, friend, colleague, and mother of the other original spirited children, we taught the first spirited child class together, she served as acting director for me while I was on leave writing and has shared her stories with me.

Red Rehwaldt, the superintendent of my school district, he supported my leave to write.

The members of the Rosemount, Apple Valley, Eagan Area Schools' Board of Education, who granted my leave of absence.

Deanne Haugen, my child-care person, my kids love her, she played with them, bought my groceries, washed our clothes, and kept us together while I wrote and wrote and wrote!

Sue Olson, house cleaner and budding author, my house has a semblance of order thanks to her efforts. Her interest and encouragement have been a wonderful boost.

Janey Whitt, secretary and friend, who typed my first book proposal and would *not* let me pay her.

LeeAnn McCarthy, writer, editor of the ECFE newsletter, has helped me to hone my skills over the years, and has always been ready with a hug when I needed it.

Jim Rogers, parent of a spirited child and radio announcer, who heard me speak, liked what he heard, invited me on his show, and helped this book to become a reality.

Pat Gardner, *Minneapolis Star Tribune* columnist, who nudged me to get going by writing in her column that my book was in process before it was started.

Susan Perry, writer and teacher, who taught me how to write a book proposal.

Joanne Burke, friend and creator of my "keep inchin' along" worm, that kept me going on the tough days.

Kerry Reif, parent of spirited children and reader of my rough drafts; her feedback helped me keep a "parent's" perspective.

Jeanne Isley Clarke, author, who took the time to teach me the ropes of publishing.

Dr. Stella Chess, originator of the temperament research, who let me call her at home and took the time to answer my questions.

Joe and Mary Kurcinka, my in-laws, who patiently endured short visits when my attention was focused on "the book."

Barbara Majerus, Kathy Kurz, Helen Kennedy, and Sue Nelson, my sisters, who each in her own way encouraged and helped me and who all taught me not to write anything that I haven't experienced or firmly believe to be true—otherwise they'll make sure I eat my words!

Ada Aldan, friend and colleague; her wit and support have been appreciated.

Brian Newhouse, Bonnie White, Marge Barrett, and Brian Cabalka, members of my writer's group who let me know in a tactful way when my writing was dry and boring or incomprehensible and made the writing process much less lonely.

Julie Olson, colleague, an elementary school principal whose input on the school chapter was very helpful.

Shirley Gilmore, colleague and friend who gave me pink socks for the days I got "cold feet."

Norm Wallace, my high-school English teacher, who told me I could write . . .

THANK YOU! THANK YOU! THANK YOU! THANK YOU! THANK YOU!

GREETINGS!

Welcome to *Raising Your Spirited Child.* I'm Mary, your guide, licensed teacher of parents and young children, fellow parent of a spirited child. I have been teaching classes for parents through Minnesota Public Schools since 1976. In 1984 I developed a new curriculum titled Raising Your Spirited Child. I have to admit I did it for selfish reasons. I *needed* to talk with other parents who understood what it was like to live with a child who could scream for forty-five minutes because his toast had been cut in triangles when he was expecting rectangles. The kind of kid who would rather die than take no for an answer and knew the perfect trigger to "push my button." The kind of kid the existing parenting books either failed to address or did so in terribly negative terms—terms I wasn't willing to accept.

To my amazement and delight the class was an immediate success. Meeting together, we shared our feelings, concerns, and challenges. I brought in the latest research reports and studies of child development, communication, personality, temperament, and type. We hashed them over, tore them apart, and figured out ways to use them to help us get resistant little bodies dressed, fed, into bed, or through the grocery store with a little less hassle. By sharing our stories we allowed each other to peek into our homes, schools, and neighborhoods. We discovered similarities in the things we worried about and screamed about. We shared the rules that prevailed in our families, the discipline techniques that worked and those that didn't. We learned what each of us was doing to build a healthy relationship with our spirited child.

1

Over the years some of those who enjoyed and benefited from the classes moved away. Soon my mailbox was brimming with letters from New York, New Jersey, Kansas, and California seeking more information or one more reassurance that other parents of spirited children were alive and well. Others who stayed asked for information for their sister in Georgia, their brother in Colorado, their friend in Texas. The result is this book. A portable Raising Your Spirited Child class.

Although I couldn't package a dozen parents to send along for you, hundreds have been willing to share their questions, worries, favorite techniques, horror stories, and meaty moments. All the anecdotes are true, the ages accurate, but all the names, places, and descriptive details are those of a storyteller. People, I have found, don't mind us looking in their window as long as we don't share their address.

The stories are included here, not so much in the genre of how-to books but more in what Dolores Curran, author of *Stress and the Healthy Family*, calls the "how-they" books. Let the tales reinforce what you are already doing well or point out qualities in your child you might never have imagined. Listen carefully and they just might teach you new tricks or divulge deep, dark, secret emotions that you were sure only you had ever felt. You'll hear about kids' antics that yours hasn't even thought of yet, allowing you to count your blessings for the one you've got. They'll share with you the challenging, frustrating, exhilarating journey of building a joyful relationship with a spirited child.

Raising Your Spirited Child is based on the most recent personality development research. The verdict is still out as to how much of our personality is the result of genetics and how much is due to environmental influences. The soundest approach is a combination of both. What I've done is taken the most credible, the most renowned work and "tested" it in my classes with parents. Not in a scientific, theoretical approach but in a practical, "what makes the most sense" style. What helps us to understand our children better and to focus on their strengths? What eases the daily demands we face? The theories and techniques that were most applicable are included here. Use them as guidelines rather than givens. Take what fits for you. Use it and enjoy it. Leave the rest. Only you can truly know what you and your child need.

Finally you need to know the motto for *Raising Your Spirited Child:*

PROGRESS NOT PERFECTION

Being a parent, building a healthy relationship with a child is a never-ending process. There are good days and there are lousy days. With progress as our goal we don't have to wait for an obscure finale. We can count every second of understanding gleaned, every power struggle fizzled, every hug held tight as a success. We can be kind to ourselves, rejoicing in moments of peace and hours of "parenting greatness," even if the entire day is not perfection. We can forgive ourselves the times we huff in frustration or flare in anger, recognizing that although we cannot be abusive, we are human. Progress takes time. The first spirited child class met for two and a half hours each week for six weeks. It wasn't long enough. We extended it to eight, then ten, and finally twelve weeks. It could still be longer. Changing attitudes, strengthening old skills, and learning new ones doesn't happen quickly. That's why we need to count each tiny success. Fortunately those teeny, tiny successes are like wet, sticky snowflakes: they can snowball. Rolled together they can build a happy, healthy relationship. So grab a cup of coffee, tea, or whatever you prefer and begin to discover the "secrets" of raising a child with "spirit." And remember, progress not perfection is our goal.

PART ONE

UNDERSTANDING SPIRIT

1

WHO IS THE SPIRITED CHILD?

An opportunity to fall in love, fodder for frustration, source of anxiety, and an unending puzzle—this is my spirited child.
—Diane, the mother of two

THE WORD THAT DISTINGUISHES spirited children from other children is *more*. They are normal children who are *more* intense, persistent, sensitive, perceptive, and uncomfortable with change than other children. All children possess these characteristics, but spirited kids possess them with a depth and range not available to other children. Spirited kids are the Super Ball in a room full of rubber balls. Other kids bounce three feet off the ground. Every bounce for a spirited child hits the ceiling.

It's difficult to describe what it is like to be the parent of a spirited child. The answer keeps changing; it depends on the day, even the moment. How does one describe the experience of sliding from joy to exasperation in seconds, ten times a day. How does one explain the "sense" at eight in the morning that this will be a good day or a dreadful one.

The good ones couldn't be better. A warm snuggle and sloppy kiss awaken you. He captures you with his funny antics as he stands in front of the dog, a glob of peanut butter clinging to a knife hidden in the palm of his hand, and asks, "Is Susie a rotten sister?" The dog listens attentively. The hand moves just slightly up and down like a magical wand. The dog's nose follows the scent, appearing to nod in agreement. You can't help laughing.

Profound statements roll from his mouth, much too mature and intellectual for a child of his age. He remembers experiences you've long since forgotten and drags you to the window to watch the raindrops, falling like diamonds from the sky. On the good days being the parent of a spirited child is astounding, dumbfounding, wonderful, funny, interesting, and interspersed with moments of brilliance.

The dreadful days are another story. On those days you're not sure you can face another twenty-four hours with him. It's hard to feel good as a parent when you can't even get his socks on, when every word you've said to him has been a reprimand, when the innocent act of serving tuna casserole instead of the expected tacos incites a riot, when you realize you've left more public places in a huff with your child in five years than most parents do in a lifetime.

You feel weary, drained, and much too old for this even if you were only in your twenties when your child was born. It's hard to love a kid who keeps you up at night and embarrasses you in shopping centers.

On the bad days being the parent of a spirited child is confusing, frustrating, taxing, challenging, and guilt inducing. You may wonder if you are the only parent with a kid like this, scared of what is to come in the teen years if you don't figure out what to do now, in the early years.

THE DISCOVERY OF SPIRIT

You might have known since pregnancy that this child was different from other kids, normal but different. She might have kicked so hard during pregnancy that you couldn't sleep from six months on. Or it might not have been until birth, when the nurses in the nursery shook their heads in dismay and wished you luck. It could have been years later. At first you might have thought all kids were like this. Your "awakening" might have come with the birth of a second child—one who slept through the family gatherings instead of screaming and let you dress her in a frilly dress instead of ripping at the lace. Or it could have been the birth of your sister-in-law's child, the one who could be laid down anywhere and promptly went to sleep. Your sister-in-law proudly beamed as though she had done something right, while your child continued to fume and fuss, causing all the eyes in the room to turn to you, silently accusing, "What's wrong with yours?" Your intuition has fought the stares and the indictments brought against you, knowing, believing that this child was tougher to parent, but not quite sure if you were right, and if you were, you didn't know why.

WHY "SPIRITED"

You probably haven't heard the term *spirited children* before. That's because it's mine. In 1979 when my son, Joshua, was born there weren't any spirited child classes or books. In fact the only information I could find that described a kid like him used words such as *difficult, strong willed, stub-*

born, mother killer, or *Dennis the Menace.* It was the "good" days that made me search for a better word to describe him. On those days I realized that this kid who could drive me crazy possessed personality traits that were actually strengths when they were understood and well guided.

My Webster's dictionary defines *spirited* as: lively, creative, keen, eager, full of energy and courage, and having a strong assertive personality. *Spirited*—it feels good, sounds good, communicates the exciting potential of these kids, yet honestly captures the challenge faced by their parents. When we choose to see our children as spirited, we give them and ourselves hope. It pulls our focus to their strengths rather than their weaknesses, not as another label but as a tool for understanding.

THE CHARACTERISTICS

Each spirited child is unique, yet there exists distinct characteristics in which *more* is very apparent. Not all spirited children will possess all of the following five characteristics, but each will exhibit enough of them to make her stand out in a crowd.

1. INTENSITY   The loud, dramatic spirited children are the easiest to spot. They don't cry, they shriek. They're noisy when they play, when they laugh, and even when they take a shower, singing at the top of their lungs while the hot-water tank empties.

But quiet, intently observant children may also be spirited. They assess each situation before entering it as though developing a strategy for every move; their intensity is focused inward rather than outward.

No matter where their intensity is focused, the reactions of spirited children are always powerful. There is rarely a middle of the road. They never whimper, they wail. They can skip into a room, smiling and laughing only to depart thirty seconds later inflamed. Their tantrums are raw and enduring.

2. PERSISTENCE   If an idea or an activity is important to them, spirited children can "lock" right in. They are committed to their task, goal oriented, and unwilling to give up. Getting them to change their minds is a major undertaking. They love to debate and are not afraid to assert themselves.

3. SENSITIVITY   Keenly aware, spirited kids quickly respond to the slightest noises, smells, lights, textures, or changes in mood. They are easily overwhelmed in crowds by the barrage of sensations. Getting them through a shopping center, long religious service, fair, or family gathering without losing them to a fit of tears is a major achievement. Dressing can be a torture. A wayward string, or a scratchy texture can render clothes unwearable.

Every sensation and emotion is absorbed by them, including your feelings. They'll tell you that you are having a rotten day before you realize it yourself and even scream and sulk for you.

4. PERCEPTIVENESS Send them to their room to get dressed and they'll never make it. Something along the way—perhaps a commercial on the television—will catch their attention as they walk by and they'll forget about getting dressed. It can take ten minutes to get them from the house to the car. They notice everything—the latest oil spill, the white feather in the bird's nest, and the dew in the spiderweb. They're often accused of not listening.

5. ADAPTABILITY Spirited children are uncomfortable with change. They hate surprises and do not shift easily from one activity or idea to another. If they're expecting hot dogs on the grill for supper, heaven forbid if you come home and suggest going out to a restaurant. Even if it is their favorite restaurant,, they'll say, "No, I want hot dogs."

Adapting to change, any change is tough: ending a game in order to come to lunch, changing clothes for different seasons, sleeping at Grandma's instead of at home, getting in the car, and getting out of the car. All of these activities signal a struggle for slow-to-adapt spirited children.

WHILE EACH spirited child is unique most are more intense, persistent, sensitive, perceptive, and uncomfortable with change. Many, but not all, possess four additional "bonus" characteristics: aspects of their personality that can make being their parent even more challenging.

6. REGULARITY Figuring out when they will sleep or eat is a daily puzzle for parents of spirited kids who are irregular. It seems impossible to get them on to any kind of schedule. An eight-hour night of undisturbed sleep is a mere memory lingering in your mind from the days before their birth.

7. ENERGY The tales of spirited kids I hear from parents are truly amazing, like that of the two-week-old baby that "crawled" the entire length of a queen-size bed and was about to land on the floor when his father found him. Or the baby who *in utero* kicked so hard he triggered the keys of a typewriter pressed against his mother's womb.

Not all spirited kids are climbers and leapers. But they do tend to be busy—taking things apart, exploring, and creating projects—from the time they wake up until they finally fall asleep. Although sometimes viewed as "wild," their energy is usually focused and has a purpose.

It may surprise you that not all spirited children have a high energy level because for those who do it is often the energy that first catches a parent's attention, and why I have included it in the title of this book. However, with closer scrutiny it is usually the intensity of that motion or the persistence of it rather than the energy itself which is at issue.

8. FIRST REACTION   A quick withdrawal from anything new is typical of many spirited kids. Any unfamiliar idea, thing, place, or person may be met with a vehement *no*. They need time to warm up before they're ready to participate.

9. MOOD   The world is a serious place for some spirited kids. They're analytical, picking apart experiences, finding the flaws, and making suggestions for change. Their smiles are few and far between and they may be prone to whining.

THE "BONUS" characteristics are not common to all spirited kids, but if your child possesses any of them you will need to be even more enterprising. You're not only living with a child who is more, but you're also faced with the exhaustion of life with a kid who is energetic, needs little sleep, expresses a strong resistance to new situations and things, and shares fewer rewarding smiles. Don't despair, these too have their potential.

All children possess these characteristics to a certain degree, but the distinguishing factor for spirited children is more. They are not, however, experiencing Attention Deficit Hyperactivity Disorder (ADHD). Children experiencing ADHD, even if they want to, are unable to focus their energy and attention. Spirited behavior falls within the range of normal human behavior.

YOU'RE NOT ALONE

Being the parent of a spirited child can be lonely. Because they are "more," much of the advice that works for parenting other children is ineffective with spirited kids. To ignore your child's tantrums is ridiculous. He can rage for an hour because you opened the door when he was expecting to do it himself. Send him to his room for a "time out" and he is liable to tear it apart. There is no distracting him from something that he wants. Even if the stereo is off limits, he'll climb over, under, or around the barriers to return to the shiny dials. As a result you can feel crazy, wondering what you are doing wrong and thinking that you are the only parent in the world with a kid who acts this way.

Suzanne felt like that before she had met other parents who understood what it was like to have a child who is "more." Suzanne is one of the thousands of parents I have worked with in my family education classes. She smiled to herself as she told me about the first time she had seen the words *spirited children*. They had been written in big, blue letters on the whiteboard as she entered the family center where I work. The one with a lobby filled by a big wooden jungle gym that begs to be climbed, a bouncy blue trampoline, and oversized pink pillows.

On that first day she had rushed through the door with her three-year-old son, Peter, in tow. They were late for their class. She told me later that on that particular day they had been waylaid by a string in Peter's sock which had turned the simple task of pulling on tube socks into a fifteen-minute ordeal, carefully removing all the loose strings and twisting the sock until it felt just right. That was followed by tears and screams because his sweater itched through two cotton shirts, the tags on the back scratched his neck and the wristbands were too tight.

Now, two months later, her speculation has been confirmed—it does take "more" to parent the spirited child. But today she can appreciate Peter's sensitivity, predict his "triggers," and avoid the blowups. She has learned that managing spirit well takes understanding, skill, and patience, but it is possible. In fact, it can even be enjoyable.

Like Suzanne I have found myself learning from other parents. Laughing with them and worrying with them, too. I have appreciated their understanding of life with spirit and valued their support. Over the years I've saved my notes and journal entries and now I have set for myself the task of capturing the information and techniques that can make living with spirit more rewarding and fun.

As we go along together, there are a few things I'd like you to remember. I've written them in the form of a credo. To me they are the essentials of living with spirited children and most important to building healthy relationships with them. I suggest you hang the credo on your refrigerator for the lousy days—the days when you feel like you are alone—and share it with a friend on the good ones.

A CREDO FOR PARENTS OF SPIRITED CHILDREN

1. *You are not alone.* According to the personality research, 10 to 15 percent of all children living in this country fit the description of the spirited child. That means that there are millions of parents who empathize with you and understand the challenges you face. Your child is not an oddity or a freak. You are not the world's worst parent. You are not the only one. You are among friends.

2. *You did not make your child spirited.* You are but one of many influences in your child's life. Other parent(s), relatives, siblings, teachers, neighbors, friends, life experiences, and the world at large all play a part. You make a big difference but not the only difference.

3. *You are not powerless.* There is information in this book to help you understand your spirited child. You can read it and use it. You can strengthen skills you already have and learn new ones. You can reduce the hassles and live peacefully with your spirited child—most days. Progress not perfection is your goal.

4. *You have permission to take care of yourself.* Your own need for sleep, quiet, uninterrupted adult conversation, lovemaking, a leisurely bath, a walk around the block, and time to complete your own projects is real and legitimate. It is not a sign of failure to ask a friend for help, to hire a sitter, or to allow relatives the opportunity to build a relationship with your child while you take a break. When you fulfill your needs you generate the energy to meet your child's needs.

5. *You may celebrate and enjoy the delights of your spirited child.* You can concentrate on her strengths, appreciate her tender heart and tickle your fancy with her wild stories and crazy creations. It is appropriate and right to tell her when she is good, instead of when she is bad, to teach her the right way to behave rather than to punish her for innocent errors. Your spirited child possesses personality traits that we value in adults. It is never too early to begin proclaiming her virtues.

WHEN SPIRITED CHILDREN GROW UP

As I have learned to focus on the strengths of spirited children, I have realized that I am surrounded by spirited children grown up. Adults I admire and enjoy: intense, dramatic people—perhaps even actor-comedian Robin Williams. That man is more of everything. Is he spirited? Only he and his parents know for sure, but I do know that today he is a very famous and successful adult who makes us laugh and cry because of his perceptiveness, an individual who fascinates us with his energy.

There are figures from history, I strongly suspect were spirited too. Minnesota Public Radio recently paid tribute to Thomas Edison. I remember chuckling to myself as I heard the announcer say, "Thomas Edison invented the phonograph, the electric light bulb, the quadruplex telegraph, and the motion picture camera and projector. He was a man who didn't know when it was time to quit."

I thought of his mother. I wondered how many meals had gone cold when he forgot to come home for dinner or how many times his dad had yelled at him to stop taking apart everything in the house. Today we enjoy his inventions when we relax in front of a movie or read a good book any time of the day. We celebrate his persistence, single-mindedness, perceptiveness, and drive.

Then there are the regular people, not those that we see on television or hear about on the radio, but those we live with each day, like my husband, who notices the little things in life and makes me laugh. My friend, who has the energy to help me out, even after taking care of all her own responsibilities. My coworker, who sends me cards on the days I need them the most. And my niece, who won't give up on the Monopoly game, beating all of us, when the rest of us would have filed bankruptcy three rounds back.

These are individuals who have learned to understand themselves, to manage their strengths, and to minimize their weaknesses. They are normal. They are more than normal. They are spirited.

2

A DIFFERENT POINT OF VIEW: BUILDING ON THE STRENGTHS

When I was a little boy, they called me a liar, but now that I am grown up, they call me a writer.
—Isaac Bashevis Singer

I LIKE TO collect labels. Any kind of labels, the kind that stick to cans and the kind that stick to people too. At lunch today, I studied the label on my can of soup. It's brilliant red against a sharp contrasting white. Bright and cheery, it makes me feel kind of happy. There are splashes of yellow that announce to me this is "Chicken ALPHABET with vegetables SOUP." I like how they hide the vegetables, the yucky stuff, and highlight the AL-PHABET, the fun stuff. On the back side the label tells me the ingredients, and a stamp verifies that the U.S. government has inspected this soup and found it fit and proper.

The label tells me a lot. Even before I open it, I know what's inside and that the government approves. Companies spend thousands, even millions, of dollars designing these labels to ensure that we find them enticing and desirable.

LOOKING AT OUR LABELS

The labels that stick to people are not always as captivating. They come in many shapes and forms, nicknames like Grumpy and Whiner, titles like Lord Know It All and The Boss, and tags like pokey and dreamer. Some are bright and colorful and make me feel good when I hear them, like scooter and love. Some, like nitpicky and crabby, are drab and dreary and taste sour when they cross my lips. Each highlights a distinctive quality, an identifiable characteristic. They tell me what's inside of the person even if

I've never met him. Unfortunately, these names are not presented in any particular order, so I never know when I hear *crabby* if it means the person is a little crabby or a lot crabby. There isn't any government regulation either, so some names are true and some are not.

Spirited kids seem to beg for labels—and not very positive ones. All kids get called a few names, but spirited kids manage to garner an over-abundance of awful, miserable, and poorly designed labels that seem to stick like a Minnesota mosquito on the back of your neck, leaving welts on tender, smooth skin. It can happen in any family, just as it happened in Diane's.

"My husband says we should have named her Helen because she's 'hell' on wheels!" Diane laughed, as we listened to her three-year-old daughter, Alexia, "organize" her buddies in the sandbox. "But, seriously, I never realized how easy it is to label her, and I'm beginning to see the impact it has on her. She's the youngest, the surprise baby in our family. She is so different from the other two that we have always referred to her as 'Wild Woman.' Yesterday, my mother reprimanded her for jumping on the couch. Alexia excused herself by saying, 'Grandma, it's okay. I'm supposed to be the wild one.' "

In *The Art of Sensitive Parenting,* Katherine C. Kersey wrote, "Children come into the world not knowing who they are. They learn who they are from those around them." Think about the spirited children you know. What words do you use to describe them? Do they sound like the million-dollar words created by advertising companies, words that can make you wish you could have even more children who are spirited? Are they the kind of descriptors that would make others envy you the opportunity of raising a spirited child? Tags that create warm, tender feelings? Labels that make you puff with pride, smile in appreciation and chuckle with enjoyment? Positive words that focus on what's right instead of what's wrong? To be perfectly honest, it's unlikely.

Most of us find ourselves facing an array of labels spoken and unspoken that affect how we think, feel, and act toward our spirited children. If we are going to build a healthy relationship with them, we must lay the labels out on the table, dissect them, and then redesign those that make us and our kids feel lousy. The ones that cloud our vision and hide the potential within.

THE TOPIC IS LABELS

The labels are always slightly different for each family. You'll need to dissect and redesign your own, but let me allow you to join one of the spirited child classes and hear a few of the dreadful labels other parents have composed. Just to let you know you're not the only parent ever to harbor a few horrid impressions of a spirited child.

It's the commotion that strikes you first—a collage of sound. Happy sounds: squeals of excitement, laughter, and calls to moms and dads to "watch this" as agile little bodies leap from the top of the slide and bounce on the trampoline. Sounds of fear: cries of protests and declarations of "I won't do it" as kids wrap their arms around their parents' legs forcing the adults into a "Gunsmoke Chester" stiff-legged walk across the room. The start of a spirited child class is a rowdy event. Fourteen parents and eighteen kids arriving at the same time.

Each child has his or her own style. Some come leaping into the room, their gestures big and wide like dancing puppets on a string. Others slide along the wall watching, listening carefully, and taking it all in before they venture out.

They're followed by the parents who are talking, always talking. Loud voices, hurried words, and excited exclamations dominate, almost drown out, the soft, hesitant ones—the quiet parents who like to listen more than they like to talk.

The families spend the first thirty minutes together and then separate. The children continue in their program while the parents move to a discussion group.

Today the topic is labels. Everyone is given three cards. The parents are asked to write on each card a word or phrase that describes something their child does that drives them crazy. A few immediately ask for more cards insisting that three is not nearly enough. Everyone laughs. It feels good to know that other people might also entertain a few unpleasant thoughts. The cards are completed in seconds.

"Who would like to share their words or phrases?" I ask.

Dead silence. Bodies shift in the chairs, they look at each other and cough. The thought of publicly admitting these horrible thoughts is almost unbearable.

It's Mike, low-key, observant Mike, the father of two—one spirited, one not—who breaks the silence. "Argumentative," he announces. "John will argue about anything. Yesterday he tried to tell me the sun wasn't shining. I'm not blind, the sun was shining. 'Look out the window,' I told him, 'the sun is shining.' Do you know what John's answer was? 'Well it isn't in China.' "

The others laugh, nodding in recognition, remembering their own dead-end debates. As the laughter dies down, Nancy flips one of her cards over.

"Never stops," she reads. "I've got four kids, and this one keeps me on duty twenty-four hours a day. I'm on call from the minute she wakes up until she falls asleep. Even then I'm busy developing the strategies I need in order to make it through the next day. I'm beat. I need a break."

"Me too," Pattie agreed. "Elizabeth is two years old and I'm still waiting for her to sleep through the night. *Unpredictable* is my word. I never know when she'll fall asleep and when she'll be awake." Pattie sheepishly glanced around the group and added. "Sex. What's that? I think I remember making love. I must have at least once."

The others roar and once again heads nod knowingly.

"We're going to get a break," Joni offered, weariness draining her voice. "My parents have offered to take our two kids so John and I can have a weekend alone. I know the youngest one will be fine, but Stephanie will make us miserable when we come back. She gets so angry. That's my word—*angry*. It makes me angry! Why should we have to 'pay' when we come back? Tara doesn't do that to us."

"I can't believe I'm telling anyone this," Suzanne admitted as she flipped her card over. *Aggressive* was written there in big bold letters. "We invited a friend over yesterday afternoon. Peter was so excited to see him, but within five minutes he had tackled him in a bear hug and bit him! I don't know why he has to be so rough. We don't act like that with him. You can't imagine how horrible I felt calling the other mother to tell her that her son had been bitten. I'm sure she'll never let him come over again."

"If it helps any," Bill added, "you're not the only one with *aggressive* written down. I've got it and *explosive*. The daily blastoffs are almost more than I can endure. I'm beginning to feel like a career astronaut."

"Well maybe my kid isn't as bad as I thought," Laura said, joking. "I get frustrated because she's so 'picky.' The pancakes have to be the same shade of brown on both sides. Her clothes have to feel right."

The list grows, filling one sheet of newsprint and then another:

demanding	argumentative
stubborn	never stops
noisy	unpredictable
nosy	angry
loud	aggressive
whiny	explosive
easily frustrated	picky
wild	single-minded
disruptive	easily bored
self-critical	obnoxious
manipulative	up/down extreme

It's a sobering list, one that catches us by surprise. Each is a label and describes something "inside." When we hear these words, we are not enticed and definitely not filled with desire. We are not confident that socially approved standards of behavior are being met.

WHAT THE LABELS DO TO US

The labels can be devastating to the kids they are stuck on. Just looking at the list makes us realize what an impossible task they face attempting to build a healthy sense of self-esteem with words such as *stubborn, explosive,* and *argumentative.* Yet children are not the only victims. Parents too feel the pain. Reacting to the labels, their emotions are raw and real and have names like:

Fear: "Tell me I didn't screw up. That I'm not a terrible mother."

Confusion: "On the days when I am absolutely overwhelmed my husband says, 'Call your mother. She raised six kids. Ask Dot how she did it.' All I can say is, I don't know how Dot did it, but she cried a lot."

Resentment: "Some days I think, why me? What did I ever do to deserve this. My mother just laughs. She says there is justice and sighs deeply!"

Shame: "I wonder if I am doing something wrong. I see a lot of me in him. My bad points. I'm stubborn and impatient and so is he. My parents were very involved in community affairs so I got dragged to lots of different places. They let me know in no uncertain terms 'good kids' were not stubborn and impatient. It sets me off when he acts that way."

Embarrassment: "I can't even get through the grocery store un-scathed with this intense, demanding child. I find myself glaring at other patrons, snapping at them to mind their own business as I struggle with John over who is going to push the cart. I do my best to ignore them but I can imagine what they are thinking. 'What kind of dad can't even control his kid in public.' "

Exhaustion: Asked if she ever gets tired, Anna, the frazzled mother of three children under the age of four, responded, "Every day I think, 'How long before he drives me nuts?' I tell myself I can hold on for another thirty minutes until my husband gets home, then he calls and tells me he is going to be late!"

Anger: "Since day one Matthew has demanded attention. The more you give, the more he wants. The other kids don't need it. Why does he?"

It's very likely that if you too have experienced these emotions, you have not found a friend to share them with. You've kept them to yourself, suffering alone. Thinking that your child was the only one who could be demanding, stubborn, picky, nosy, noisy, and all those other rotten names, making you wonder what you were doing wrong. You might find the labels so uncomfortable that you have never spoken them, not even to yourself. But they lurk in your subconscious, influencing how you feel and how you act. They undermine your confidence as a parent and your feelings toward your child.

It's easy to fall into the trap of labeling kids. Even if you tend to be an incredibly positive person, you might have gotten yourself caught in a swirl of negative labeling when it comes to dealing with your child. You may not be sure how it happened, maybe just the pressures of life. At least that's what happened to Peg.

"I've got three other children besides Cassie. We are in transition, moving from one place to another. Cassie is starting kindergarten. There has just been more to do than I can possibly accomplish. I have no patience and as a result *everything* she does drives me crazy. I see myself in all of those negative words. I see how I talk about my daughter and I know I have to change."

Unknowingly, unwittingly, we can create labels for our spirited children that highlight the yucky stuff and hide the neat stuff. Labels that embarrass us, their parents, and make us feel lousy.

Starting today, you can choose to stop using words that project a negative image of your child. It really isn't that far of a leap from *picky* to *selective,* or from *obnoxious* to *dramatic.* By merely changing your vocabulary you can alter how you and others perceive your child. You can create a new image that feels good, looks good, and meets socially approved standards. The first step to enhancing your spirited child's strengths comes with the words you use. It's as simple as that.

REDESIGNING THE LABELS

Grab a piece of paper and on the left side of your sheet, write down all the words that you can think of that describe the crazy, obnoxious things your spirited child does. Be sure to include the worst ones. The ones you believe to have the least possibility of possessing any redeeming qualities. Include in your list words that you've heard relatives, friends, and teachers use to describe your child that made you flare in anger or shrink in embarrassment. Squeeze them all out.

Now take a deep breath, relax your shoulders, wiggle your toes, and pull from your memory your favorite image of your spirited child. The one that includes the snappy eyes, the infectious grin, the agile body, or the astounding question. Hold on to that image as you look at the list of lousy labels—it will help you to discover the hidden potential in each of the words. If you look closely, you'll see that the lousy labels often reflect strengths that are being overused. Find that strength and name it. For example, with a little guidance, aggression can become assertiveness. Obnoxious behavior well managed may be dramatic. The possibilities are limitless.

Your list may look like this:

Old Negative Labels	*New Exciting Labels*
Demanding	Holds high standards
Unpredictable	Flexible, a creative problem solver
Loud	Enthusiastic and zestful
Argumentative	Opinionated, strongly committed to one's goals
Stubborn	Assertive, a willingness to persist in the face of difficulties
Nosy	Curious
Wild	Energetic
Extreme	Tenderhearted
Inflexible	Traditional
Manipulative	Charismatic
Impatient	Compelling
Anxious	Cautious
Explosive	Dramatic
Picky	Selective
Whiny	Analytical
Distractible	Perceptive

You can teach yourself to use your new labels when you talk about your kids and when you discipline them. As you pull your toddler out of the stereo cabinet you can say, "You really are curious. Let's see what you can discover over here in the kitchen cupboard instead." To the five-year-old who won't wear the new outfit Grandma just sent, "You certainly are selective." And to the eight-year-old who refuses to go to bed until he has finished one more chapter in his book, "You are very persistent."

The feelings and images the new labels create are totally different from those of the lousy labels. It feels good to be the parent of a child who is assertive, committed, selective, dramatic, analytical, enthusiastic, and charismatic. These words may even describe the child you dreamed of having.

After completing this exercise in class Nancy acknowledged, "I looked at the new labels and realized they made sense. I saw a sparkle of hope. All the qualities my son possesses are not bad. I always thought they were. It made me step back and realize he is who he is. I can work *with* him instead of against him."

GOOD LABELS ARE CONTAGIOUS

Not only are the new labels helpful to parents, they're great for kids. It is easy for a child to build a healthy sense of self-esteem when the words used to describe him are ones like *compelling, zestful,* and *perceptive.*

"As my vocabulary changed, so did my perspective," Rose reported. "I began to notice John's good qualities instead of focusing on the bad. For the first time, I could appreciate his intensity as a quality that merely needed direction. John noticed the difference. His attitude and behavior improved. Today he is in kindergarten. He is at the top of his class, has friends, and is loved by his teacher. John beams. He likes himself and we like John."

Words that create positive images wrap our kids in a protective armor, giving them the strength they need to make the behavior changes that actually turn the inappropriate behavior into acceptable actions. Research done by Kate Cauley at Iona College and Bonnie Tyler at the University of Maryland shows that there is a strong link between a child's positive self-image and her willingness to cooperate. In other words, kids who like themselves behave themselves.

The exciting thing about changing the vocabulary we use to describe our spirited children is that it is contagious. Rose learned that when she used positive words to describe John, so did her relatives and John's teachers.

"Whenever someone would say, 'John is awfully loud,' I would respond, 'He really is dramatic isn't he? Let's get him outside where we can appreciate that more.' They'd be taken aback, but after a few minutes of reflection they would agree he really can be spectacular. After I'd done it a few times I overheard my mother say, 'John, your dramatic side is coming out again. Let's turn on the stereo and sing together.'

"Even at school when his teacher told us he was stubborn, I nodded my head in agreement but said, 'We find him to be very tenacious at home too.'

" 'I never thought of it in that light,' the teacher responded. 'I guess it isn't all bad is it?' It really changed the way she saw him and they seem to have now developed a much better relationship."

Don't let others intimidate you with hurtful labels. Teach them to use words that reflect your child's potential by using them yourself. You don't even have to argue with them. Merely reflect their thoughts in more positive terms.

Building a healthy relationship with your spirited child begins with the labels, the words you use to describe what's inside. When you drop the negative images and introduce to yourself and others the new words and labels that focus on strengths and potential instead of weaknesses, you change not only your vocabulary but your perceptions and, as a result, your actions as well.

You may be thinking right now that the leap from aggressive to assertive, or explosive to dramatic, is much too great for you to make. A feat beyond your ability. Keep reading, more information can help you make that leap.

3

WHAT MAKES KIDS SPIRITED: WHY THEY DO WHAT THEY DO

*This was a person who had come into my life. A real person,
not a robot to be programed, or a blank slate to write on, but
a person who in his own way talked to me and told me what
he liked and what he hated—usually in a very loud and
demanding voice.*
—Sue, the mother of three

THE WINDOWS THAT wrap around the room on two sides let in the
autumn sunset, giving the entire room a rosy hue. Before the families
arrive for class I like to write our agenda for the night on the whiteboard,
but today all I write is one question.

WHAT MAKES KIDS SPIRITED?

The parents meander into the discussion room, chatting with one another, grabbing a cup of coffee and finding a chair. Moans, groans, and
nervous laughter erupt as they read the words written on the board.

"I've been trying to answer that question for three years," Pam exclaimed not even waiting for everyone to sit down. "I've lain awake more
nights than I care to remember reviewing my pregnancy. What did I eat?
What did I do? Chastising myself for going water skiing when I was two
months pregnant. So what if I didn't even *know* I was pregnant. I never
should have gone."

Bill added, "I keep thinking about Seth's birth. How long and difficult it
was. Maybe we should have asked for a cesarean."

"I thought it *was* the cesarean," Sherry piped in.

"I've been thinking it might be due to Melanie's prematurity," Mike
remarked thoughtfully. "She arrived six weeks early and was quite ill the
first few days."

Nancy grimaced. "I've always blamed it on the fact that I nursed the
older kids, but I didn't nurse her. With four kids I just couldn't do it."

I raised my hand to grab their attention. "Wait a minute!" I almost shouted above the clamor. "You didn't do it." All heads turned to me. An audible sigh of relief escaped in the room.

WHAT IS TEMPERAMENT?

Your actions have not made your child spirited. The most recent personality research demonstrates that there does exist a genetic influence on personality, but being spirited has nothing to do with a difficult pregnancy or birth, or whether you breast or bottle fed. It appears that children are born with a tendency to act and react to people and events in their lives in specific ways that can be identified and predicted. The reactions are relatively consistent for each child in different situations and at different times. *This "preferred style of responding"—a child's first and most natural way of reacting to the world around him—is called his temperament.*

Today, temperament has become a major focus of research for pediatricians, psychologists, psychiatrists, infancy researchers, cultural anthropologists, and behavioral geneticists. In the 1950s Stella Chess and Alexander Thomas, professors of psychiatry at New York University Medical Center, were among the first to describe temperament. The prevailing theories of the time insisted that all children arrived as "blank slates." Their personality was determined by the parenting they received—specifically the influence of their mother. Nurture, not nature, made the difference. Comments such as "You must be doing something wrong" and "Give him to me for a week and I'll fix him" stem from this theory. The significance of individual differences in behavior style was either ignored or minimized.

As a result of their clinical practice, Chess and Thomas saw too many cases in which the one-sided nurture approach could not adequately explain the child's personality. As important as the mother's and family's influences were, there was still something missing.

It was this "gap" in understanding that led them to conduct the now-famous New York Longitudinal Study. Chess and Thomas observed 133 children eat, dress, and play with friends and also interviewed the children's parents and teachers. From the results of this study, Chess and Thomas identified distinct differences in how children respond to the world around them. These differences reflect their temperament.

Temperament describes a range of different characteristics that include not only our typical energy level but also our speed in adjusting to new situations; the intensity of our emotions; our sensitivity to sights, sounds, smells, feelings, and tastes; and more. A child who is temperamentally active not only likes to move but *needs* to move. Telling this child to sit still for extended periods of time, and that he could do it if he really wanted to, is like telling you to ignore a full bladder. The pressure builds. Your child's temperament signals a need to act in a particular way—a need that is inside and real.

Children are seemingly born with their own temperament just as they are born with black hair or with blond. This isn't to imply, however, that temperament is rigid or unchanging. Like hair, which can be styled, trimmed, or colored, but remains hair, temperament may change in appearance according to how it is "managed," while remaining fundamentally the same. The temperamentally active child will always be an energetic individual. How that looks, however, will change over time. The toddler who has climbed on top of the counters will have learned not to do so by the age of thirty, but it's very likely that he'll be the one in the office who paces around his desk while he talks on the phone or hand delivers his memos rather than routing them through interoffice mail. He styles his energy differently, but he is still active.

YOU DO MAKE A DIFFERENCE

You don't get to choose your child's temperament nor does your child, but you do make a big difference. It is you who helps your child understand his temperament, emphasizes his strengths, and provides him with the guidance he needs to express himself appropriately.

The temperamentally active child will *never* be the quiescent kid playing quietly for hours, but with good guidance from you he can learn to channel his energy. Instead of jumping on Grandma's couch he may be jumping on a diving board. The slow-to-accept-change kid will *never* jump from one activity to another easily, but you can help him learn to cope with change. With forewarning and preparation, he can be ready to go to the store, but his temperament must be considered. By adapting your parenting techniques to fit his temperament and his style, you can help him to live cooperatively with others and to be all that he can be. To deny him his energy or any of his other temperamental traits is to tell him "don't be"— don't be who you are.

Until Jim, the father of two, discovered this "secret," there was an undeclared war raging in his home. The lines had been drawn and the battles were being fought every single day.

"To tell you the truth," he told me, "the 'war' frightened me. Usually I'm a low-key, quiet kind of guy. Competent—little things don't rile me. How my four-year-old could send me to the moon totally baffled me, but he could and he did.

"Then I learned about temperament. All of a sudden I realized he wasn't doing this just to get me. He had a reason, he needed to move, or he needed more time to accept the change. When I recognized that, I could work with it. Little things as simple as calling his day care from work to inform him that we'd be stopping at the store on the way home, rather than just surprising him with it when I got there, really seemed to help.

"I can't believe how much more I enjoy my son when I'm not fighting with him all the time. You know, he's a pretty neat kid."

Identifying your child's temperamental traits is like taking an X ray. It helps you to understand what's going on inside of your child so you can understand how he is reacting to the world around him and why. Once you understand the reasons behind his responses, you can learn to work with them, ease the hassles, teach new behaviors where they are needed, and, most important, help your child understand and like himself.

GETTING A PICTURE OF YOUR CHILD'S TEMPERAMENT

There are nine different temperamental traits. Each of these traits can be placed on a continuum from a mild reaction to a strong reaction or from high to low. Everyone has her own temperament, her own unique style. Spirited children tend to fall on the strong end of the continuum, but others may fall on that end in one or more traits as well. It's the overall picture that helps us understand the spirited child.

Remember, there isn't a perfect temperament. There are positive and negative aspects of all the temperamental traits. Parents make the difference by helping a child to shape her particular qualities in the most advantageous way.

As you review the traits, think about your child's typical, most natural reaction. What response have you come to predict?

1. INTENSITY

HOW STRONG ARE YOUR CHILD'S EMOTIONAL REACTIONS? DOES HE LAUGH AND CRY
LOUDLY AND ENERGETICALLY OR SOFTLY AND MILDLY?

1	2	3	4	5
MILD REACTION				INTENSE REACTION
"SQUEAKS" WHEN CRIES				NEVER JUST CRIES—WAILS
IT'S ALMOST A SURPRISE WHEN HE GETS UPSET				A LIVING STAIRCASE OF EMOTION, UP ONE MINUTE DOWN THE NEXT
REACTIONS ARE MILD				EVERY REACTION IS DEEP AND POWERFUL
SMILES WHEN HAPPY				SHOUTS WITH GLEE
USUALLY WORKS THROUGH A PROBLEM WITHOUT BECOMING FRUSTRATED				EASILY FRUSTRATED

Daniel Goldman wrote in the *New York Times* in 1987:

Some people find themselves in emotional tumult even in reaction to
mundane events, while others remain unperturbed under the most
trying of circumstances. These levels of feeling characterize a person's entire emotional life: Those with the deepest lows also have the
loftiest highs, the research shows. And differences between people
seem to emerge early in childhood, if not from birth, and remain a
major mark of character.

Even in the hospital nursery the differences in emotional intensity are
apparent. Some babies "squeak" when they're hungry. Others wail, their
cries echoing down the corridor. Spirited kids are born intense. Inevitably
for the parent of a spirited child, one of those squeakers belongs to a
relative. At the family gatherings the squeaker whimpers while the spirited
one screams!

But there's nothing wrong with the spirited screamer. He is temperamentally more intense. That isn't all bad. It means he is also more enthusiastic, exuberant, and zestful.

Spirited kids experience every emotion and sensation deeply and pow-
erfully. Their hearts pound, the adrenaline flows through their bodies.
There is actually a physical reaction that occurs more strongly in their
bodies than in less intense individuals. They are not loud because they
know it irritates people; they are loud because they really feel that much
excitement, pain, or whatever the emotion or sensation might be. Their

intensity is real. It is their first and most natural reaction. If you have circled a 4 or a 5, you can predict that your child will be easily excited, frustrated, and emotional. When you know your child is intense, you can expect a strong reaction and develop a plan to help your child express it appropriately or diffuse it.

2. PERSISTENCE

IF YOUR CHILD IS INVOLVED IN AN ACTIVITY AND YOU TELL HER TO STOP, DOES SHE STOP EASILY OR FIGHT TO CONTINUE?

1	2	3	4	5
EASILY STOPS				**"LOCKS IN"**
CAN BE REDIRECTED TO PARTICIPATE IN ANOTHER ACTIVITY QUITE EASILY				STICKS TO HER GUNS, DOESN'T EASILY LET GO OF AN IDEA OR ACTIVITY
WILL CRY FOR A FEW MINUTES AND THEN STOP				LOCKS IN, CAN CRY FOR HOURS
ACCEPTS "NO" FOR AN ANSWER				NEVER TAKES "NO" FOR AN ANSWER

In their studies, Chess and Thomas have observed that some children can easily stop an activity, whereas others continue despite major obstacles (see *Know Your Child: An Authoritative Guide for Today's Parents,* New York: Basic Books, Inc., 1987). Spirited kids "lock in." If they want to do something, they want to do it now and can't easily give up on it. I remember visiting friends in Colorado. We had gone out for dinner and found ourselves returning to the house in the dark. It was a cold November night, with the wind blowing in gusts, whipping our scarves in our faces and pushing us down the driveway. Without thinking, I picked up their two-year-old daughter and carried her into the house and out of the cold wind. Once inside she turned around and slugged me! I had spoiled her plans. She had every intention of walking up the steps herself. I tried to cajole her out of her coat, but she wouldn't give it up. A less persistent child might have, but not Anne. She stood screaming at the door, pounding on it with her bare fists. It was obvious that *nothing* other than opening that door and letting her go out was going to be acceptable to her. I stood back and let her go. The wind nearly knocked her off the landing but she marched down those steps and then determinedly back up them. Only after shutting the door herself was she ready to take off her coat. She wasn't about to be distracted from her goal!

The advice to stop a persistent child's cry by ignoring it is worthless, a frustrating joke. Although other children may fall asleep within minutes of being lain in their crib, this child can scream for hours unless Mom or Dad finds a way to soothe her and help her stop. Ignoring doesn't work. Persistent kids only cry louder and longer.

Cleaning up may be another situation where persistence comes into play. This determined child wants to use every block in the bucket before she can stop playing and come to dinner.

Persistent kids are committed to their tasks. If they want a cookie, they'll keep coming back until they get one. They are goal oriented, unwilling to give up easily.

Many parents of spirited kids are baffled by the fact that spirited kids can be both persistent and perceptive. They wonder how spirited kids can forget two directions from their parents, yet remember the Kentucky Fried Chicken stand fifty miles back and insist on going there. The answer is simple. Spirited kids are persistent when they are motivated and personally interested in the idea or activity. If it's their idea, they won't let go of it. If it's yours, they are much more interested in what else is going on in the world around them. The world needs people who are persistent, but as their parent you can expect to expend more energy and skill to win their cooperation.

3. SENSITIVITY

HOW AWARE IS YOUR CHILD OF SLIGHT NOISES, EMOTIONS, AND DIFFERENCES IN TEMPERATURE, TASTE, AND TEXTURE? DOES HE REACT EASILY TO CERTAIN FOODS, TAGS IN CLOTHING, IRRITATING NOISES, OR YOUR STRESS?

1	2	3	4	5
USUALLY NOT SENSITIVE				**VERY SENSITIVE**
SLEEPS THROUGH NOISY ROUTINES				HAS TO HAVE QUIET TO SLEEP
ISN'T AFFECTED BY SCRATCHY TEXTURES				HAS TO HAVE A SOCK SEAM LINED UP JUST SO
ISN'T BOTHERED BY FUNNY SMELLS				GAGS EASILY FROM SMELLS
EATS ANYTHING				A PICKY EATER
UNAWARE OF YOUR STRESS				ACTS YOUR STRESS OUT
NOT OVERLY CONCERNED WITH HOW THINGS FEEL				STRONG REACTION TO HOW THINGS FEEL—WHETHER PLEASANT OR UNPLEASANT

Researchers have observed great differences in how children react to the sights, sounds, and smells around them. Some children seem unperturbed by scratchy clothes, loud noises, or funny smells, whereas others are extremely sensitive.

Spirited children are born with a super set of sensors. Although many other kids can fall asleep in a room full of people, the spirited child stays wide awake taking in every sound and sight. Sleeping in a hotel or Grandma's house may be a difficult task. The sheets smell weird and the pillow doesn't feel right. Sensitive kids also respond to emotions, serving as the family's stress gauge. When you feel the worst, they'll act the worst.

To the sensitive spirited child, every experience is a sensual bombardment. He sees, hears, and smells things that others—including his parents and siblings—might miss or is sensitive to a degree that can't even be imagined by most of us. In class one day, Mike illustrated this phenomenon with the following story of an outing with his daughter.

"It was to be a great father-daughter experience—just Melanie, me, and *Sleeping Beauty* at the local theater. I let her skip supper and bought her popcorn and candy. What more could she need? The minute the lights went out she started to scream."

" 'Daddy,' she gasped, 'it's too dark I can't see. It makes my skin crawl!'

"She leapt into my lap just as the film began.

" 'It's too loud,' she complained, pressing the palms of her hands against her ears. 'It's hurting my ears.'

"I could see she was going to lose it, I've seen it hit before, so I took her out into the lobby. 'Melanie, it's all right. We can go home. I don't need to see *Sleeping Beauty*,' I told her.

" 'No! No!' she protested. 'I can handle it. I want to stay.'

"We slid back into our seats, crawling over the family sitting next to us, the kind of family where everyone has a barrel chest. She pulled her sweatshirt up over her mouth and ears to help deaden the sound. All seemed to be going well until the family next to us started munching and crunching their popcorn and salted peanuts.

" 'Daddy, they're chewing too loudly,' she complained. 'Tell them to close their mouths.'

"I shot a glance at the guy. One look and I knew he was at least two hundred and fifty pounds and counting. I'm one forty-five on a stretch. There was no way I was going to tell him to shut his mouth. I decided I couldn't hear anything and refused to intervene.

"For once she accepted my refusal and buried her head deeper into her sweatshirt. Suddenly she grabbed her stomach.

" 'Yuck, Daddy, I can smell popcorn and peanuts and somebody's got *bad* breath. It's making me sick, Daddy.'

"I grabbed our popcorn container and stuck it in front of her face, but she found her own solution, pulling the sweatshirt right up over her nose. Now only her eyes showed above the pink collar. I turned to the film, thinking maybe I'd get to watch it now.

"Melanie sat hunched in her seat, head buried in the sweatshirt, hands still clamped over her ears. She sighed, and I wondered what was coming next.

" 'I'm *hot*,' she whispered, in a Melanie whisper that echoed through the theater.

"I still had my coat zipped. I wasn't hot.

" 'I'm dying,' she protested.

"She wanted to get her sweatshirt off but it was protecting her nose. Have you ever seen anyone struggle out of a sweatshirt while trying to protect her nose? Her elbow caught me in the eye as she twisted in her seat to tie the sweatshirt over her mouth and nose. I wondered if people would realize she'd done it herself or if they would think I had.

"Through the sweatshirt, she demanded, 'What's going to happen next? Where did the witch go? Do you think the prince will find her? When the doctor pricks my finger will I fall asleep for a long time?'

"She kept a running dialogue going through the entire film. The big guy next to us sent searing glares our way. I slunk farther down into my seat. 'Shhh,' I reprimanded. She lowered her voice but the questions continued.

" 'Did the needle prick hurt her? Would you be sad if I fell asleep for a long time?' (I was beginning to think it might be nice.)

"The family next to us moved away, the entire row of seats reverberating as they struggled out. I was surprised she didn't complain about that.

"It seemed like hours, maybe even days before the credits finally appeared. I was exhausted. She skipped out the door, arms flying.

" 'Let's do that again!' she exclaimed.

"Never, I thought. Never!"

MELANIE WAS not trying to get to her father, to intentionally ruin their special night out. Melanie is temperamentally sensitive. She notices and absorbs all of the sounds, smells, bright lights, and textures around her and reacts to them. As Mike shared, "The level of stimulation necessary to get a response from her is almost indiscernible." Add intensity, and she reacts very, very strongly.

If your child is temperamentally sensitive—hearing, smelling, and feeling things that you may not even discern—you can expect that he will be easily triggered by food, clothing, crowds, noisy celebrations, and other sensorially loaded activities. Now when it happens, instead of worrying that he is being obnoxious or naughty on purpose, you can recognize it for what it is: his first and most natural reaction, a reaction you can help him learn to manage.

4. PERCEPTIVENESS

DOES YOUR CHILD NOTICE PEOPLE, COLORS, NOISES, AND OBJECTS AROUND HER? DOES SHE FREQUENTLY FORGET TO DO WHAT YOU ASKED BECAUSE SOMETHING ELSE HAS CAUGHT HER ATTENTION?

1	2	3	4	5
HARDLY EVER NOTICES				**VERY PERCEPTIVE**
STAYS ON TASK, ISN'T WATCHING BIRDS OUTSIDE THE WINDOW				NOTICES THINGS MOST PEOPLE MISS
WALKS PAST THE RAINBOW THAT IS REFLECTED IN THE NEW OIL SPILL				SPENDS FIVE MINUTES WATCHING THE LIGHT IN THE NEW OIL SPILL
CAN REMEMBER AND COMPLETE MULTIPLE DIRECTIONS EASILY				FORGETS MULTIPLE DIRECTIONS

Researchers have found stark differences in how aware individuals are of the world around them. Spirited kids are not only more sensitive they are also more perceptive. They notice *everything*. Drive down the freeway with them, and they'll point out the hawk sitting forty feet up in the air on top of the light post. Take them for a walk, and they'll notice the shiny dime hidden in the grass.

Their perceptiveness can get them into trouble because it sometimes might appear as though they aren't listening. Ask a spirited child to get dressed and she'll disappear. Thirty minutes later you can find her still in her pajamas staring out the window at the cloud formations or playing with the ball she tripped over on the way to her room. The ten-second journey from your neighbor's yard to yours may take the perceptive child twenty minutes. On her way, she'll notice the dew in the grass, the new bird's nest in the apple tree, and the delicate spiderweb woven in the flowers; she'll stop to enjoy the rainbow reflected in the fresh oil spill on the garage floor.

The keen observations of perceptive kids feed a rich imagination. They'll point out the king's crown left in the carpet by the strokes of the vacuum and the letter *B* formed by the spaghetti sauce on their plates. They'll act out stories and design crazy costumes.

It may be impossible to nurse the perceptive baby in a room full of people. There's a standing joke among nursing mothers in my spirited child groups—you may become known for your elongated breasts if you attempt to nurse your baby during the discussion because every time someone speaks or walks past, the baby will turn to look or listen, taking the nipple with her. It's a painful stretch!

It is this trait that is most often confused with children experiencing Attention Deficit Hyperactivity Disorder (ADHD). Unmanaged perceptiveness may be perceived as distractibility. The difference between a perceptive spirited child and a child experiencing ADHD is that a spirited child will notice everything going on around her, but will be able to process that information more quickly and ultimately be able to select the most important information to listen to. As a result she will be able to focus on and complete a task in which she is interested. A child experiencing ADHD will not be able to process information quickly. Despite her best efforts, she will be unable to figure out what is the most important information to listen to and will not be able to focus on and complete a task, even if she wants to.

Danny was diagnosed as ADHD in kindergarten. I had known him as a preschooler and wanted to observe him so I could understand more clearly the difference between a perceptive spirited child and a child experiencing ADHD. As I entered the room he and his classmates were just getting out their workbooks to practice their letter *C*. Danny started working immediately, getting out his pencil just as the teacher had requested. She drew a large circle on the board and filled in the numbers of a clock. Danny watched attentively. His tongue stuck between his teeth as he attempted to start his *C* at two o'clock just like his teacher said.

"Go up to the black line," the teacher directed the students. Her words followed the movement of her hand as she formed a big yellow *C* on the chalkboard. The movements were quick and so were her directions, delivered in a staccato fashion. "Through the dotted line—down to the black line—up just a little bit," she continued.

The directions flew at Danny. Every time the next one came he looked up, forgot where he was on the page, and had to start again.

"All right now, everyone finish your workbook page," the teacher directed.

Danny sat on the edge of his chair, its rear legs hung in the air, as he bent over his book. The teacher began whipping around the room trying to get to each of the twenty-one children to help where needed and reward their efforts.

"Good job!" she exclaimed to Tommy.

Danny looked up.

"Perfect *C*, Jennifer!"

Danny looked up again.

"Hold your pencil in your right hand," she reminded Rachel.

Danny checked his. Every time the teacher spoke, Danny's concentration was broken. He got three C's done then his progress stopped. His head continued to bob up and down with each exclamation of praise. The other children finished while his work remained incomplete.

Danny loved his teacher and was excited to learn but he was unable to sort out which information was the most important for him to listen to. He could not focus and was not able to complete his task, even though he wanted to. Danny is experiencing ADHD.

A spirited child in the same situation would have been aware of her teacher's movements, directions, and affirmations, but would have been able to process the information more quickly, stay tuned in to the most important directions, and ultimately complete the worksheet. She might be slower than the other children because she is processing so much information but she would be able to finish.

Both the child experiencing ADHD and the perceptive spirited child would benefit from a slower presentation of directions and less stimulation. With that help, the perceptive child will be very successful. The child experiencing ADHD will still be struggling, but her efforts will be more effective.

According to Dr. Elsa Shapiro, director of Pediatric Neuropsychology at the University of Minnesota, distractibility is a symptom of a multitude of physical and psychological problems in children, including childhood depression, epilepsy, allergies, and thyroid disease.

"Distractibility is like experiencing a headache," she says. "If you go to the doctor and tell her that you are experiencing headaches, you expect that she will check for brain tumors, migraines, and stress-related causes before prescribing medication. It is critical that parents of children who are experiencing distractibility to a debilitating degree make sure their children have a complete workup that looks at all possibilities, both physical and emotional, before allowing the doctor to prescribe medication such as Ritalin."

If you have marked a 4 or 5 for your child's perceptiveness, you know that your child is engaging more of the world around her than the average person. She will need your help learning how to tune in to the most important messages.

5. ADAPTABILITY

HOW QUICKLY DOES YOUR CHILD ADAPT TO CHANGES IN HIS SCHEDULE OR ROUTINE?
HOW DOES HE COPE WITH SURPRISES?

1	2	3	4	5
ADAPTS QUICKLY				**ADAPTS SLOWLY**
EASILY STOPS ONE ACTIVITY AND STARTS ANOTHER				CRIES OR FUSSES WHEN ONE ACTIVITY ENDS AND ANOTHER BEGINS
IS FLEXIBLE WITH MEALTIMES AND NAP TIMES				NEEDS A SET SCHEDULE FOR MEALS AND NAPS
IS NOT UPSET BY SURPRISES				MAY BE VERY UPSET BY SURPRISES

Chess and Thomas have found major differences in how individuals adapt to changes in their lives. Some children take little notice of changes or transitions. For others, transitions or changes of any kind are stressful. Spirited children usually adapt to change very slowly. They hate surprises and need time and forewarning in order to shift from one activity to another.

You may find the concept of adaptability is new to you and may have not really noticed how your child reacts. Yet adaptability may be one of the major reasons why you and your child are finding yourselves in daily hassles. It's the slow-to-adapt child who loses it because you cut his toast in triangles when he wanted rectangles or you stopped at Burger King when he was expecting McDonald's. Nap time, lunchtime, bedtime, drop-off-at-day-care time, and pick-up-from-school time are all daily transitions that are challenging for this child. If there's a substitute bus driver, teacher, or day-care provider, you can bet the spirited child will have a tough day. Traveling can be stressful, adjusting to a new hotel room and bed may take until well past midnight. A move from one home to another can be very upsetting. Changing to daylight savings time is a hassle. A new season, and the inevitable change in clothing, may prove to be a major source of contention. Stopping a game in order to eat dinner can be a significant intrusion. Even having another child unexpectedly attempt to join a slow-to-adapt child and his friend can lead to tears. Spirited kids honestly do shift this slowly. They are not trying to be stubborn and make life miserable for you. They *need* time to adjust.

Alice realized it was Sara's slow adaptability to adjust that turned the task of running errands into a struggle.

"I couldn't understand why Sara would start screaming every time I put her in the car and took her out to go in the store. My older child loved to run errands with me. It was a special time, just me and one child. I wanted to share that special time with Sara. But Sara hated it. She couldn't stand going in and out of places. It was a fight to get her in the door and then a bigger battle to get her out again. Now I realize she can't stand it because there are too many transitions, too close together. She just can't adapt that quickly. Running errands is *not* a special time with Sara!"

Understanding how your child reacts to transitions and changes is a key to winning his cooperation. If your child is slow to adapt, you need to know it so you can help him prepare.

6. REGULARITY

IS YOUR CHILD QUITE REGULAR ABOUT EATING TIMES, SLEEPING TIMES, AMOUNT OF SLEEP NEEDED, AND OTHER BODILY FUNCTIONS?

1	2	3	4	5
REGULAR				**IRREGULAR**
FALLS ASLEEP AT THE SAME TIME ALMOST EVERY DAY				NEVER FALLS ASLEEP AT THE SAME TIME
IS HUNGRY AT REGULAR INTERVALS				IS HUNGRY AT DIFFERENT TIMES EACH DAY
ELIMINATES ON A REGULAR SCHEDULE				ELIMINATES ON AN IRREGULAR SCHEDULE

In Chess and Thomas's study, it was observed that some children fall easily into regular sleeping and eating schedules, whereas others never do. Some days these children would nap for four hours, the next they would not nap at all. They were hungry at different times of the day.

Many, but not all, spirited kids never fall into a schedule, leaving their parents exhausted. It seems impossible to predict when they will be awake, when they'll need a nap, or when they'll be hungry, and it can take years to get an irregular child to sleep through the night or at least teach her not to disturb you when she wakes. Sleep deprivation is used as a method of torture and parents of kids who are irregular in their sleep patterns understand why.

Irregularity can also affect how children handle mealtime, bedtime, and toilet learning; get up in the morning; travel; and "prowl" the house at night. We live in a culture that likes schedules, and putting a child on a schedule seems to be a mark of good parenting. But for the parent of the irregular child this can be a very frustrating expectation.

Spirited kids who are irregular by nature are not intentionally trying to upset their parents. Their bodies are not easily scheduled into a predictable pattern or rhythm. If you have marked a 4 or a 5 you can expect to work much harder at establishing regular routines in your household. You can expect a child who isn't hungry at dinner but is hungry the moment you put the dishes away. It's her temperament that causes this behavior, not her disrespect for you. When you understand that, it is easier to work out a mutually acceptable solution.

7. ENERGY

IS YOUR CHILD ALWAYS ON THE MOVE AND BUSY OR QUIET AND QUIESCENT? DOES HE NEED TO RUN, JUMP, AND USE HIS WHOLE BODY IN ORDER TO FEEL GOOD?

1	2	3	4	5
QUIET				VERY ACTIVE
STAYS IN ONE PLACE WHEN SLEEPING				MOVES ALL OVER THE BED WHEN SLEEPING
SITS AND PLAYS QUIETLY FOR EXTENDED PERIODS OF TIME				ALWAYS ON THE MOVE; EVEN WHEN SITTING, IS MOVING IN PLACE

Individual differences in energy levels have also been found by Chess and Thomas. Some children have been observed to sit quietly for long periods of time. Other children are always on the move.

Many spirited kids are energetic; however, not all of them are climbers and leapers. Some merely seem to possess incredible energy. They are busy from the moment they wake up until they fall asleep. They don't walk, they run. They can't pass through a door frame without jumping up to touch the header. They fall out of their chairs at school and at the dinner table. Their milk is spilled at every meal as they wiggle and twist in their chairs. It isn't that they aren't paying attention or trying to follow the rules, they simply have a need to move. A long trip in the car can be a nightmare unless frequent stops are taken to let this child release the energy pumping through his veins.

According to Dr. Shapiro, energy levels are also a major factor in Attention Deficit Hyperactivity Syndrome. Actually, it is not the amount of activity or energy that is the concern, Dr. Shapiro states, but the focus of that action. For example, the six-year-old who wiggles around and jumps in and out of his chair while he completes his worksheet is a child with an active temperament. The child who pings around the room and never completes his worksheet may be experiencing ADHD.

It isn't possible for even seasoned professionals to make a diagnosis of ADHD simply by observing a child. If you are concerned that your child may be experiencing ADHD it is important that you have the child undergo a full physical and psychological review.

If your child is temperamentally energetic you can expect that he will *need* to move. You can predict it and use this information to plan for his success.

8. FIRST REACTION

WHAT IS YOUR CHILD'S FIRST REACTION WHEN SHE IS ASKED TO MEET PEOPLE, TRY A NEW ACTIVITY OR IDEA, OR GO SOMEPLACE NEW?

1	2	3	4	5
JUMPS RIGHT IN				**REJECTS AT FIRST OR WATCHES BEFORE JOINING IN**
DOESN'T HESITATE IN NEW SITUATIONS				HOLDS BACK BEFORE PARTICIPATING
SEEMS TO LEARN BY DOING				LEARNS BY WATCHING
OPEN TO NEW ACTIVITIES				IS DISTRESSED BY NEW ACTIVITIES OR THINGS
USUALLY COMPLIES WITH A NEW REQUEST WITH LITTLE FUSS				IMMEDIATELY SAYS NO WHEN YOU ASK HER TO DO SOMETHING

Researchers have found lifelong differences in how people initially respond to new situations. Some individuals do not hesitate and move right in. They seem to learn by doing. Others hold back and appear to learn by watching. They prefer to check out a new situation before joining in.

A group of spirited children will usually split right down the middle on this trait. Half of the children will jump in to new situations, which poses the problem of children *literally* jumping into trouble. They leap before they look. The other half hang back, often refusing to participate; they may cry and throw themselves on the floor, kicking and screaming the first time they are introduced to anything new. It is this half that poses the greatest challenge for most parents, because our culture tends to be more supportive of go-getters.

How a child responds to new situations can be spotted very easily and early. Pam remembers being nearly hysterical at Lisa's first bath.

"If you saw the picture of her first bath, you would think there was an error in the color processing because her skin looks purple. There was no error in the processing, she really was screaming that hard."

Whether it's the first bath, the first day of school, a new food, a new car seat, or the first try at swimming lessons, many spirited kids don't want to try it and insist that they don't like it. It's important to recognize this as a first reaction—not a final decision—because often, with time, the child will change her mind and really enjoy participating.

Suzanne realized it was Peter's first reaction that turned a family outing into a major disagreement.

"I had planned a day to visit Santa Claus. It was going to be a very special outing to downtown Minneapolis. Peter was two. I was so excited, because I just knew it was going to be a thrilling day, seeing all the decorations, talking with Santa, getting the traditional gingerbread cookie afterward, just like the one I had always gotten when I was a kid. I hadn't told Peter, and when I did he started crying. He refused to put on his coat and tore his mittens off as fast as I could put them on. I had to carry him kicking and screaming into the car. I kept saying, 'You're going to have a great time. We are going to go see Santa and *you are going to love it!*' I was furious. He was wrecking my special outing! He cried and pouted all the way, thirty minutes in the car. I just turned up the radio and let him scream. But I guess that time was what he needed to get used to the idea. When we got there, he walked through the display, then sat on Santa's lap and told him everything he wanted, so sweet and adorable. I later realized I was lucky, because there were other kids there who wouldn't even get on Santa's lap. Afterward we both took a two-hour nap. I was exhausted and swore I wouldn't do it again.

"This year he said to me, 'Mom when are we going to see Santa? That was so much fun.'

"I almost strangled him on the spot."

HOW DOES your child normally react to new situations and people? If you have circled a 4 or 5 you can expect that your child will balk at new situations. You can anticipate it will happen and avoid feeling disappointed, knowing that if you work with her, she may change her mind.

9. MOOD

HOW MUCH OF THE TIME DOES YOUR CHILD FEEL HAPPY AND CONTENT COMPARED WITH SERIOUS, ANALYTICAL, OR CRANKY?

1	2	3	4	5
USUALLY POSITIVE				**MORE SERIOUS AND ANALYTICAL**
USUALLY IN A GOOD MOOD				USUALLY SERIOUS
POSITIVE				SEES THE FLAWS, WHAT NEEDS TO BE FIXED

Finally, the ninth temperamental trait describes differences in mood. Many of the children observed by Chess and Thomas were generally happy, positive, smiley, and friendly. In contrast, other kids tended to be more serious, to cry and whine more, and to see the flaws in situations and people.

In my spirited child classes approximately half of the children will possess a generally positive, happy mood. The other half are definitely the most challenging for parents. They tend to be much more serious, to cry more, and to appear more negative, because they are always offering suggestions for improving an activity. We're used to adults telling us how to make things better, but it's a little tough to take advice from a three-year-old who tells you to read the story with more expression or to add a little more milk to the mashed potatoes.

Asked a general question such as "How was school today?" the more serious kids will respond with comments like "boring," "dumb," or "really stupid." They'll tell you they didn't do anything interesting, despite the fact they took a field trip to their favorite radio station. They really don't mean to appear unappreciative or uninterested. They see the world from a more analytical perspective.

If your child is temperamentally more analytical, you can predict that you will get evaluative responses from him. This child will not be the one to rave about an outing or event, but he will provide information on how to make it even better next time. When you recognize that he is responding because of a first and most natural reaction rather than intentionally being contrary, you can teach him to be more diplomatic and respectful of others' feelings.

Although some children are temperamentally more serious, a child who *never* expresses happiness or joy may actually be suffering from depression. Not all children, however, will appear sad when they are depressed. They may also be irritable and bad tempered, acting out rather than withdrawing. If you are concerned about your child, a complete medical checkup should be conducted to determine the cause of his unhappiness. Child psychologists and doctors now know that childhood depression is much more common than previously thought.

Now GO back through each of the temperamental traits and total your responses. Mark your total on the scale below.

Score:

9–18	19–28	29–45
COOL KID	SPUNKY KID	SPIRITED KID

Of course, this is not a scientific analysis, it is merely a sketch, the initial strokes in the total picture of your child's personality. You can use it as a guide, helping you to understand who your child is and what gifts and challenges your child brings to you. It's like a map, identifying your starting point, helping you to plan the best route to take, and predicting where the trouble spots may be. If your child is temperamentally intense, now you know it. You can expect strong reactions from her and teach her how to diffuse that intensity or to direct it appropriately. If your child doesn't like new situations you can predict her reaction, teach her the social skills she needs to express herself respectfully, and learn the techniques that help her feel more comfortable.

Temperament is real. It is inside. It is not the terrible twos, sixes, or thirteens. It doesn't go away. Your child doesn't get to choose his temperament and neither do you, but an understanding of temperament allows you to predict your child's first and most natural reactions and plan for success.

4

MATCHES AND MISMATCHES—PARENTS AND KIDS FITTING TOGETHER

*Each of us shines in a different way, but this doesn't make
our light less bright.*
—Unknown

PAT WAS ALWAYS the last parent to talk in the group. Her dark eyes drank in the words and gestures of others, but her comments were rare and far apart. Her daughter Lindsey was the kind of kid you "felt" before you heard her and heard before you saw her bursting into a room. The temperamental portrait Pat saw was not the dream child she had hoped for.

"I never imagined having a baby like Lindsey," she said. "I thought I would spend hours cuddling her, talking and singing with her. But Lindsey was born kicking. She never liked to be cuddled unless she chose it. As a baby she wanted to be carried looking out at the world. I remember when she was fourteen months old, holding her on my lap and sobbing, thinking, 'Why can't you be like the other kids? Why can't I do the right things to make you like the child I expected you to be?'

"I tried talking to my husband about it but he got angry when I told him. It just wasn't an issue for him but it was for me. I had this phantom child in my mind. I knew how she was supposed to look and act and what our relationship would be like. But our reality was so opposite."

LETTING GO OF THE DREAM CHILD

If you, like Pat, have held a preconceived perception of what your child would be like, the temperamental portrait your child presents to you may not be one you expected or wanted to see. For you, letting go of your "dream child" may be one of the most difficult tasks you face as a parent.

43

You might find yourself grieving, mourning the loss of the child that never materialized. The realization hits—there isn't a quick fix, ten easy steps to success, or a perfect punishment that will make your spirited child into that dream kid.

Your grief can blind you. It can prevent you from seeing the unique qualities of your child. It can force you to expend your time and energy desperately trying to change your child, to make her fit your expectations of the "perfect" child, the child that doesn't really exist.

In the December 1989 issue of *Parent's Magazine,* Julius Segal wrote, "To reject kids' distinctive natures is to deny one of the central facts of human development: the extraordinary range of individual differences that characterize children from the moment of their birth."

FOCUSING ON RELATIONSHIPS

A spirited child comes to us with not only distinct physical characteristics but a built-in predisposition to be spirited as well. We do not have control over our child's basic personality but we can choose to alter our response to him. We can stop thinking of our child as "the problem" and instead focus our energies on discovering more effective ways to relate, to work together, and to enjoy each other's company.

In a conversation with me, Jerome Kagan, a researcher from Harvard University, said, "We try to change our loved ones, and when we can't, we get friction and conflict. People are not really all that changeable. One of the greatest tragedies in human interaction is that we believe 'will' can change everything—it can't."

It is all right to shed your tears, to lament the fantasies that never materialized, but your child needs you to move on, to let go of that image of a dream child so that it does not interfere with your relationship with your spirited child. Now is the time to begin focusing on your child and discovering how to work with her particular temperamental style on an everyday basis. To find the beauty in her "portrait."

In the chapters that follow, I will help you to see the connections between everyday hassles and your child's temperament. Once you have identified the "connections" you can develop strategies which will work with each particular temperamental issue.

For example, in the past you may have thought your child was intentionally being disobedient when she didn't come to lunch when you called. By understanding her temperament you will discover that her reluctant response is actually the result of her slow adaptability. She is not deliberately being uncooperative in order to frustrate you.

A child who is slow to adapt needs time for transition and moving from one activity to another. There is a reason for her slow response and by learning techniques that respect her temperament, you can work with it and win her cooperation. You can forewarn her that lunch will be served in ten minutes and allow her the time she needs for transition. Or you can develop a consistent routine that includes watching *Sesame Street* and eating lunch immediately afterward. These techniques allow her the time and consistency she needs to shift from one activity to another smoothly and easily even though she is slow to adapt. She will be more cooperative. You will be relating better. The result will be a stronger and healthier relationship, because you are working with her temperament rather than trying to change it.

RECOGNIZING THE TWO-WAY STREET

As I talk about your spirited child's temperament, I'll also talk about yours. Building a healthy relationship with your spirited child is a two-way street. You have to understand your own reaction as well as your child's. Sometimes it isn't the strength of a spirited child's reaction that makes living with him challenging as much as how that reaction matches or mismatches yours. Understanding your own temperament can help you work with your child's.

In chapter 3 you reviewed the temperamental traits in order to create a picture of your child's temperament. Now I want you to complete a "self-portrait." Using the chart that follows, place yourself on the continuum for each trait. It is more difficult to distinguish temperamental traits in adults because they get mixed up with motivation and learned skills, but try your best to get to your typical response in each of the following situations. Remember there isn't an ideal.

When you have a picture of your own temperament you can compare yours with that of your child. How are you alike? How are you different? Where do you fit together easily and where do the sparks fly? It is from this information that you will begin to build a more effective relationship with your spirited child.

TAKING A LOOK AT YOUR OWN TEMPERAMENT . . .

1. INTENSITY
HOW STRONG ARE YOUR EMOTIONAL REACTIONS? DO YOU LAUGH AND CRY ENERGET-
ICALLY OR ARE YOU MORE QUIET AND RESERVED WITH YOUR REACTIONS?

1	2	3	4	5
MILD REACTION				INTENSE REACTION

2. PERSISTENCE
IF YOU ARE INVOLVED IN AN ACTIVITY AND YOU ARE ASKED TO STOP, CAN YOU DO SO
EASILY? IF YOU ARE ANGRY OR UPSET CAN YOU EASILY LET GO OF THOSE FEELINGS?

1	2	3	4	5
EASILY STOP				"LOCK IN" DON'T LET GO

3. SENSITIVITY
HOW AWARE ARE YOU OF SLIGHT NOISES, EMOTIONS, DIFFERENCES IN TEMPERATURE,
TASTE, AND TEXTURES. DO YOU REACT EASILY TO CERTAIN FOODS, TAGS IN CLOTHING,
OR IRRITATING NOISES?

1	2	3	4	5
USUALLY NOT SENSITIVE				VERY SENSITIVE

4. PERCEPTIVENESS
ARE YOU KEENLY AWARE OF PEOPLE, COLORS, NOISES, AND OBJECTS AROUND YOU?
DO YOU FREQUENTLY FORGET TO DO WHAT YOU WERE GOING TO DO BECAUSE SOME-
THING ELSE HAS CAUGHT YOUR ATTENTION?

1	2	3	4	5
HARDLY EVER NOTICE				VERY PERCEPTIVE

5. ADAPTABILITY
HOW QUICKLY DO YOU ADAPT TO CHANGES IN YOUR SCHEDULE OR ROUTINE? HOW
QUICKLY DO YOU ADAPT TO NEW FOODS AND PLACES?

1	2	3	4	5
ADAPT QUICKLY				SLOW TO ADAPT

6. REGULARITY
ARE YOU QUITE REGULAR ABOUT EATING TIMES, SLEEPING TIMES, AMOUNT OF SLEEP
NEEDED, AND OTHER BODILY FUNCTIONS?

1	2	3	4	5
REGULAR				IRREGULAR

7. ENERGY
ARE YOU ALWAYS ON THE MOVE AND BUSY OR QUIET? DO YOU NEED TO RUN AND EXERCISE IN ORDER TO FEEL GOOD?

1	2	3	4	5
QUIET				ACTIVE

8. FIRST REACTION
HOW DO YOU (USUALLY) REACT TO A NEW IDEA, ACTIVITY, PLACE, OR PERSON?

1	2	3	4	5
JUMP RIGHT IN				REJECT AT FIRST

9. MOOD
HOW MUCH OF THE TIME DO YOU FEEL HAPPY AND CONTENT COMPARED WITH SERIOUS AND DISCONTENT?

1	2	3	4	5
USUALLY POSITIVE				MORE SERIOUS AND ANALYTICAL

SCORE:

9–18	19–28	29–45
COOL PARENT	SPUNKY PARENT	SPIRITED PARENT

Now you have it! Your own temperamental portrait.

Compare your portrait with that of your child's. What does it tell you?

"I can see that Amy is very sensitive, but I'm not," John commented, after completing this exercise in class. "No wonder I'm not very understanding when clothes drive her crazy. I just can't imagine what she must be feeling."

"It looks like we are both sensitive," Sarah responded. "We really are tuned in to one another, but that also means that the noises that drive him nuts also get under my skin. He needs me to help him stay cool but I don't have any energy to spare. I need all I've got to keep myself under control."

"Beth and I are both very intense," Jill added. "We both lose it over the same things."

"Maybe it's temperament that is getting us into fights at the dinner table," Janet remarked. "In my family, sitting down to eat dinner together is a special part of the day. I really value it. But Paul," she said, jabbing an elbow toward him as he sat in the chair next to her, "and our son, Tyler, are constantly eating their meals strolling around the kitchen. Neither of them can stand to sit on the dining room chairs. I've been thinking that they did it on purpose to irritate me, but looking at this chart, they both score five on energy and I score one. We don't match. Maybe that's the problem."

Paul nodded his head. "After a stressful day at the office," he said, "I just can't sit there. I have to move. It's been hard for Janet to understand that."

Whether you are a spirited parent or a cool parent doesn't really matter. There are benefits and drawbacks to both. What is important is recognizing how you and your child or other family members are alike or different. What triggers set you off? When is it challenging for you to understand each other's reactions? This understanding allows you to respond in a more effective manner.

A week later, Janet and Paul arrived at class, beaming. "Guess what we did?" Janet laughed.

I shrugged. "I haven't the faintest idea."

"We bought new dining room chairs," she exclaimed. "They rock, roll, and swivel! Now Paul and Tyler move to their hearts' content, but they're still at the table and in their chairs. They're happy and so am I."

Understanding their temperamental differences allowed Janet and Paul to respect each other's needs and to respond in a way that felt good to both of them. What could have been a contest of wills became a creative problem-solving episode—a more effective way of relating.

You too can build a stronger relationship with your spirited child. You too can learn techniques that will allow you to relate better. As you do, you will be able to let go of the "phantom child" and enjoy the one who actually lives with you more.

(By the way, if you checked a 4 or a 5 on first reaction, you can expect it to take more effort for you to make changes in your relationship with your child. That's your style. You approach new ideas and new situations cautiously. Just remember to allow yourself time to reflect. Your first reaction may not be your final decision. Think about it, then decide.)

PART TWO

WORKING WITH SPIRIT

5

EXTRAVERT OR INTROVERT: FINDING THE ENERGY TO COPE

What really opened my eyes was realizing that, when I'm at home alone taking care of the kids, just one phone call, one opportunity to talk with another adult, can give me hours more of patience.
—Katrina, the mother of three, all under the age of four

THE SCHOOL BUS growled through the neighborhood, belching at each corner as it disgorged the neighborhood children. I walked to the door, unlocking it in anticipation of my spirited son and spunky daughter bursting through. Josh, bigger, older, and faster hit the door first. Flinging it open, he threw down his book bag in the hallway, ignored the hooks in the closet (as always), and shouted, "I got an autograph from WLOL disk jockey Denny Schaeffer," as he disappeared down the steps to the family room and Nintendo.

Kristina was inches behind him until she hit the front steps. Then she paused long enough to pull her papers out of her bag and thrust them in my face as she came through the door. "I got to go up on the roof today," she announced, following me back into the den.

"It was discovery day," Kristina said. "I was supposed to go to creative dramatics, but I changed my mind, so three of us got to go with Doug the engineer. We went up on the roof and saw the *thing* in the boiler room that has to be checked every day. Saturday and Sunday too, even when he's sick, or the whole school could blow up KABOOM!"

Without taking a breath, she pushed the papers closer to my nose. "I have math sheets to do and I have to read my book to you. Listen, Mom. I want to read my book to you, right now. Oh, Mom, can I play with Kellen? I told Kellen I'd come down to his house. Can I go to Kellen's? Mom, what's for snack?"

She didn't even wait for my answer before she started her next question. Fifteen minutes after she arrived home, I knew everything that had happened that day, including her teacher's mood, how she was feeling, and what her plans were for tomorrow.

I broke away to check on Josh. "What did you learn about radio?" I asked.

"Not much," he mumbled, glued to the Nintendo game in front of him.

"Am I going to hear about it or do I have to wait?"

"You'll have to wait, Mom," he responded, allowing me to kiss his cheek for "my" needs and returned to his Nintendo game. Silence. Nothing about his day. Two kids, two distinctive styles of recharging at the end of a busy day.

Kristina is an extravert. She isn't just chattering. She is drawing her energy from me. She prefers to engage the world around her "outside" of her body by talking with people, sharing ideas and experiences. If I don't take the time to talk with her, she gets cranky and even more demanding, because she is out of steam. If I allow her to recharge her batteries off of mine she's fine.

Joshua is an introvert. He isn't stubborn or antisocial. He prefers to interact with the world on the "inside" by reflecting on his thoughts and ideas before he shares them with others on the "outside." He refreshes himself by spending time alone. If he gets it, he plays well with the other kids and cooperates with me. If he doesn't get it, he gets surly and nasty.

HOW WE GET OUR ENERGY

Extraversion and introversion describe how we get our energy, an important dimension of personality development. Spirited kids need energy to manage their strong temperament. It takes a great deal of effort to express intensity as assertiveness rather than aggressiveness. It is an exertion to adapt to new situations and to make transitions smoothly. It's hard work to stay cool and calm in a noisy room full of people. When energy levels are low, spirited kids can't cope. They just don't have the strength to refine their behavior. When energy levels are high they have more power to demonstrate their strengths.

A spirited child can be either an introvert or an extravert. It doesn't matter which. But it does matter that you find out because, like Josh and Kristina, introverts and extraverts need to energize in different ways and at different times of the day. Identifying your child's preference helps you to understand where she gets her energy to cope and allows you to teach her to resupply before she becomes overwhelmed. The more your spirited child is allowed to tap into her "preferred" energy source the calmer and happier her day.

During class one day, Barb explained, "I never could understand why Leah would disappear into her room whenever people spent the day with us, until I learned about introverts and extraverts. Now I know she is an introvert—she needs time alone to recharge. Yesterday I put that information to work for us. I was taking care of a little girl, the same age as Leah. Leah had just gotten up and was not ready to talk or play. Normally I would have told her, 'We have a guest. It isn't good manners not to talk with her and play with her.' But this time I respected Leah. I told the friend that Leah had just woken up and would be ready to play in a little bit. Until then she could have breakfast with me. After thirty minutes I went to Leah's room and told her it was now time to play and talk to the friend. By then she was ready and they played beautifully together."

INTROVERTS

Introverts get their energy by being alone or with one or two special people. They prefer to interact with the world on the inside by reflecting on their thoughts and ideas before sharing them with others on the outside. They refresh themselves by spending time alone. If they get it, they'll play well with other kids and be more cooperative. If they don't get it they'll get surly and nasty.

Introverts are the babies who become overwhelmed at the family reunions. The toddlers who talk to their grandparents for a while and then "shut down." After a day at school they are worn out by people. They need a break, a chance to energize by being alone. Interaction with people, especially those who are not close friends, depletes their energy supplies. Playing video games and watching television are favorite energizers.

It probably will be nine o'clock at night before introverts are ready to tell you the highlights of the day. You have to ask questions in order to follow up on the events from yesterday and to find out the ending of a few old stories. They share their worries and concerns with you in bits and pieces. You have to listen well or you will miss them. If you only have to wait until bedtime to find out what's happening in their lives, you're doing well. Sometimes it takes days or even weeks.

EXTRAVERTS

Extraverts draw their energy from others. They prefer to engage the world around them outside of their bodies by talking with people, sharing ideas and experiences. If they don't have the opportunity to talk, they get crabby and more demanding because they are running out of steam. If they are allowed to recharge by being with other people they are fine.

Extraverts tend to be the babies who demand to be held up so that they can look around and "talk" to those around them. They are the toddlers who jabber endlessly even if the words don't make sense. They are the school-age kids who jump off the bus and immediately have to tell you about their day. They need to share their ideas with you while they are fresh in their minds. They follow you around the house demanding your ear, pulling energy from you. You may not even be able to go to the bathroom without them following you to continue the one-sided conversation. If you remind them that you'd like a little privacy, they seem surprised and step just outside the door, where you can still hear them as they continue sharing their day with you. They're not even breathless after a twenty-minute monologue. Fortunately for you they are probably ready to play with a friend. If a friend isn't available you may find yourself in a game of crazy eight's or Candyland as they continue to build their energy off of you.

Truly spirited extraverts can wipe their parents out. The minute they wake up they have something to say. Brothers and sisters may feel unloved and left out as the spirited "motor mouth" gobbles up Mom's and Dad's attention and time.

There isn't a right or wrong preference. Both extraverts and introverts have their strengths and weaknesses. Introverts, however, are outnumbered three to one in our society. It is frequently the introvert who is misunderstood and pressured to shape up. This is tough on the introverted spirited child. The pressure to be a part of the group can be especially detrimental to this child who isn't allowed to refuel by taking time alone. As his energy supply dwindles, his behavior deteriorates.

THE THEORY

The concepts of introversion and extraversion are drawn from the theory of Psychological Type and were first described more than sixty years ago by Carl Jung, a Swiss psychologist. He suggested that human behavior could be classified into predictable categories or preferences. His framework was developed separately from the temperament work completed by Chess and Thomas and describes different dimensions of personality development. Like Chess and Thomas, however, Jung believed we are born with specific preferences that reflect both genetics and early life experiences.

According to Otto Kroeger and Janet Thuesen in *Type Talk,* "Jung believed that healthy development was based on lifelong nurturing of these preferences, not on working to change them." Spurred by Jung's work, Katharine Briggs and her daughter Isabel Briggs Myers spent more than twenty years developing the Myers-Briggs Type Indicator to distinguish the preferences described by Jung. Their hope was to help people understand and appreciate differences in individuals. The Myers-Briggs Type Indicator describes four preference pairs:

Extraversion vs. Introversion: how we get our energy and how we choose to interact with the world.

Sensing vs. Intuition: how we prefer to gather information.

Thinker vs. Feeler: how we choose to make decisions.

Judger vs. Perceiver: how we prefer to organize and structure our lives.

For spirited kids and their parents, the most important preference is extraversion and introversion—how we get our energy. Every family probably has a mix of introverts and extraverts. Identifying our types and understanding our differences can help us to orchestrate the social activities the extravert needs and create the quiet retreats the introvert requires. Misbehavior disappears when energy levels are high and coping skills are working smoothly.

IDENTIFYING YOUR CHILD'S ENERGY SOURCE

For our purposes a formal study in Psychological Type is not necessary. Your children will give you the information you need, if you watch carefully and listen well. Read through the following lists. Check each of those statements you agree with in each group.

Your child may demonstrate both extravert and introvert tendencies, but you want to know which one she prefers (in other words, the preference you would see most frequently).

IF YOUR CHILD IS AN EXTRAVERT SHE PROBABLY:

_____ is quite gregarious and outgoing. (It's important not to confuse normal development with a preference for introversion or extraversion. It is normal for children to cry or protest when held by strangers, especially from nine months to two and a half years of age. An extraverted child will probably become calm more quickly than an introverted child in this situation, but both will cry.)

_____ enjoys being around people. She becomes energized by a group rather than overwhelmed by it.

_____ wants to tell you about her experiences and ideas immediately.

_____ thinks by talking. She'll walk around the house saying, "Where's my ball" or "I'm looking for my blanket," as she hunts for them. She needs to talk in order to make decisions.

_____ talks a lot and easily initiates conversations with other people.

_____ hates being sent to her room to sit alone.

_____ can't imagine why you would want to be alone in a room and always joins you to "cheer you up."

_____ lets you know what she's thinking and feeling.

_____ needs lots of approval. You may find yourself doubting the health of her self-esteem as she demands that you tell her what a good job she is doing or how much you like her gift.

IF YOUR CHILD IS AN INTROVERT SHE PROBABLY:

_____ prefers to watch or listen before joining into an activity.

_____ enjoys doing things by herself or with one or two special friends or family members.

_____ becomes grouchy if around people too long, especially after school.

_____ finds being with strangers more draining than being with family members or one close friend.

_____ refuses to discuss the day's events until later, even days or weeks.

_____ has a strong sense of personal space. Does not like people sitting too close or coming into her room.

_____ seems to enjoy being sent to her room to sit alone.

_____ may find it difficult to share what she is feeling.

_____ may find guests in your home "invasive."

_____ may talk a lot with family members but be quieter around outsiders.

Count how many statements you would agree with in each group.

TOTAL

_____ Extravert statements

_____ Introvert statements

If you are unsure after reading through the statements you may need to tune in and watch your child more closely in the next few days or weeks. Think about her past as well: Has she shown a pattern?

In reviewing each of the statements, you may find that your child is a very strong extravert or introvert or she may show only a slight preference. Either is fine. Each of us is capable of both extraversion and introversion, but we prefer one over the other. A friend whose daughter is a spirited introvert shared how she saw her daughter using both:

"Brenda asked to have a friend over. We've talked about introverts and extraverts so she knows the terms. Today she said, 'The extravert part of me says I want to be with a friend, but the introvert side of me says, only for a while.' "

Like Brenda, if your child is an introvert she can learn to utilize and enjoy aspects of her extraverted side; however, she will never become an extravert. The same is true of extraverts utilizing their introverted side.

Traditionally the term introvert has described someone who is shy and socially unskilled. It's important to remember that in Psychological Type introversion and extraversion do not describe social skills. They explain how we get our energy. Both introverts and extraverts can be very savvy interacting with people. The key is what happens afterward. The introvert will be drained and ready for a nap or a quiet, solitary activity whereas the extravert will be wound up and ready for more action.

The temperamental trait of first reactions can fool you too. Some introverts whose first reaction is positive will move into new social situations relatively quickly. Some extraverts who's first reaction is negative will hold back. The issue is how they get their energy, not how quickly they join a group.

The world needs both extraverts and introverts. Our differences create a healthy balance and can actually be fun. We just need to remember that introverts prefer to use the inside energy bank to conduct their recharging business, whereas extraverts go for the outside version.

ENERGY SOURCES FOR INTROVERTS

You can help your child be more successful by keeping her energy bank full. Although each individual will recharge differently, here are some common sources of energy for introverted spirited children.

1. TIME ALONE   Introverts are lonely in groups. Participating in a group forces them to act outside of themselves, which is difficult for them to do. Their energy is drained as they socialize. If your child is a quarrelsome curmudgeon after a day in school or day care, it may be that he is an introvert in need of time alone.

"I'm a family day-care provider," Karen explained in a group one night. "My daughter starts picking on the other kids the minute she walks in the door. It's as though she were begging to be sent to her room."

Introverts need their private time. It is often difficult for introverted children to tactfully pull out and play by themselves because of our social pressure to be part of the group. They don't understand that when they are feeling out of sorts they *need* time alone. All they know is that being around people bugs them and makes them feel grumpy. That's why they pick on the other kids until you send them to their rooms. That's why they'll suddenly stop playing with friends and scream, "I hate you! Go home!" *An unrecognized need for time alone is one of the major reasons spirited children have tantrums, fight with siblings, or get nasty.*

Seth is a five-year-old spirited introvert. During his Early Childhood Family Education (ECFE) class he played beautifully with the other children until the end. That's when he got tired and needed to dip into his "preferred" energy account. Unfortunately, when he first started the class, he didn't know how to accomplish this properly. As a result, he got his time alone by hitting. At first his teacher didn't understand what he was doing and got upset with him. Then, by watching him closely she realized that Seth needed a quick introvert "fix" at this time of the day. Now when she sees him start to misbehave she says, "Seth I think you need a break. Let's go out to the lobby and get your coat. You can help me gather the materials for the other kids."

That five-minute break from people and action recharges Seth and gives him the energy he needs to make it through the transition from school to home. Seth's teacher is hopeful that in the near future, he will be able to ask for a break instead of hitting to get one.

If your child is an introvert you have to help her understand that she needs time alone in order to recharge. When she starts to get agitated, tell her, "I think your body is telling you that you need some time alone." If she is playing with other children, teach her how to tactfully say, "I've enjoyed playing with you, but it's time for you to go home now," or something along that line. You have to help her find appropriate ways to pull out of the group.

Kids can take a break in many ways. Some do it by finding a quiet corner. Others pull themselves slightly out of the circle at school, allowing themselves more personal space. Reading a book, asking for a walk, taking a nap, or disappearing into their room to play quietly by themselves are all socially acceptable ways for introverted children to recharge.

Introverted children grow up to be introverted adults. The need to energize by being alone remains the same, but it may look different. Adults take a break by pulling a newspaper up around their face, lingering in the bathroom, or burying their head in a book in the middle of an airport. Being alone restores their energy bank and allows them to develop their reserves for interacting with the group again later. After Thanksgiving, a parent in my class shared the following.

"Tara went and played by herself. My mother watched her go, then said, 'What a good idea. Let's all go find a place to be alone.' "

Extraverts need to resist the temptation to pressure the introvert into staying with the group. A few minutes alone for the introvert can mean the difference between a reasonable, conversational human being and a living scrooge. Introverts are their own best friends. They can have a great time all by themselves. That's hard for an extravert to understand.

Just as you would plan for your child's nutritional needs, plan for her *energy* needs. Next time your neighbors invite you to go to the zoo and then for a picnic, stop and think about your introverted child. How will she be able to dip into her energy bank during this long, social day? Can you drive your own car and give her a break between the zoo and the park? Can you plan to separate at the zoo for a while and retreat with her to a quiet corner to watch the snow monkeys?

If it is impossible to create an opportunity for her to recharge, maybe you need to go to the zoo and forget the picnic this time. It is better to be successful at one activity rather than attempt both and end with a disaster. Remember your introvert isn't trying to be a party pooper. She gets her energy from time spent alone. As you plan your activities avoid starving her energy bank.

2. PHYSICAL SPACE Physical space is very important to introverts. Introverts are drained when their physical space is invaded. I recently had a phone call from the mother of a four-year-old. She said he was getting into trouble at nursery school for pushing in line and biting the kid next to him when they sat at the table. I asked her if he had told her why he was doing it.

She said, "All he'll say is he bit the little boy sitting next to him because he shouldn't be sitting there."

"Makes sense to me," I responded.

"What are you talking about?" the mother queried.

"Introverts need their space, and your son's was encroached on, so he bit. Biting is usually quite effective in clearing the place out—obviously not acceptable, but effective. Sharing space takes lots of energy from introverted spirited children. When they get tired, they don't do it very well. Your son needs to learn that he needs space. He can choose where to set his chair or where to stand in line to allow himself more space. He can learn to say, 'Please move over' or 'Stand back. I feel more comfortable if I have more room.' Simply realizing that sharing space is exhausting to him can help him recognize when his reserves are low and he needs to refuel."

You'll see the need for space in many ways: the child who has to have his own seat in the van, otherwise he grouses about someone touching his leg or breathing in his face; the two-year-old who throws a fit because you pulled off her hat or took off her sweater, not only because she wanted to do it herself—which is normal for two-year-olds—but because you invaded her personal space; and the six-year-old who lays a jump rope across the center of the couch to mark her half. Other signs might be the child who can't stand sharing his room with another or the one who posts a sign on his door that says "Republicans Only" to let you know how important space is to his well-being and energy stores.

This need for space can be hard for extraverts to understand. Extraverts like to be helpful and they like to be together. Space is not an issue for them. Extraverts need to know that sitting too close, standing too near, or walking into a private room unannounced will drive an introvert nuts and drain their energy. Introverts are not being selfish or rejecting others by asking for their space. Giving introverts space is giving them energy. You can teach your introverted children to be aware of their need for space and help them learn tactful ways to ask for it.

3. TIME FOR REFLECTION Introverts like to think about problems and then talk about them. When you demand immediate answers from introverts you are robbing them of energy. Extraverts like to talk about problems and usually have an immediate response. This can be a source of contention. The extravert who insists that the introvert "talk" about a problem will be frustrated by the introvert who backs off, trying to get the "thinking" space she needs to work through a problem. An introvert isn't ready to share her thoughts before she has had an opportunity to reflect. The more frustrated the extravert gets with the introvert's lack of enthusiasm for the discussion, the more energy the introvert burns trying to escape. Once introverts have time to think, they will be willing to talk about the issue.

Giving introverts time to think about a problem, however, isn't always easy for extraverts who think while talking and want to talk now!

A friend of mine shared her attempts to plan a fortieth birthday party with her introverted husband:

"I asked my husband how he would like to celebrate his birthday," she said. "He didn't answer me. I waited a few moments, then asked again, thinking that he must not have heard my question. No answer. 'Don't you want to do anything for your birthday?' I quizzed, incredulous at the thought of not celebrating a fortieth birthday in a very big way.

" 'I'm thinking,' he finally grumbled. 'Give me time to think.' "

Extraverts have to remember that an introvert's pause or delayed response does not mean "no thoughts." Allowing your introverted child time to pause and reflect before expecting an answer gives him energy. Don't expect him to tell you what happened at school or day care the minute he comes home. He needs to reflect on his experiences before sharing them. He is not being stubborn or withholding information. Introverts are bright. They do have answers. We simply have to wait a little longer for them.

If you find yourself getting frustrated because your child isn't answering your questions, it may be that she is an introvert. Try saying to her, "I'm really interested in hearing about your field trip. Let me know when you're ready to talk." If you are an extravert and can't stand leaving it so wide open, you might say instead, "Let's plan to talk after supper." It gives your introverted child time to think and you the extravert the knowledge that you will get to talk.

4. UNINTERRUPTED WORK TIME Interruptions rob energy from introverts. If you have ever wondered why your child never comes to greet you when you come home from work, it may be that he is an introvert, guarding his energy supplies. If an introvert is busy, he doesn't like it if you stop to say hello to him and expect him to talk to you. In fact, you won't find him to say hello to, unless you go looking for him. If you want your introvert to be socially respectful, teach him to say hello, then allow him to finish his task. By doing so, you respect his energy supply.

Helping your introverted spirited child to make deposits in his energy bank is a critical step to good behavior. A child who knows how to refuel has the energy to maximize his strengths. Next time your introverted spirited child starts to misbehave, make a mental check of her energy account. Has she been with lots of people? Has she had to share space? Was she required to give quick answers? Has her work been continuously interrupted? If the answer to any of these questions is yes, then allowing her to recharge by taking time alone may be all that's needed to bring out "the sunny side." Spirited kids behave themselves when their energy levels are *high*.

ENERGY SOURCES FOR EXTRAVERTS

Energy sources for your extraverted spirited child are very different from those of the introvert. As with introverts, extraverts are each unique individuals, but here are some common sources of energy you can help them learn to use.

1. TIME WITH PEOPLE Extraverts collect their energy on the outside. They not only like people, they need them. Allowing extraverts to talk, share their experiences, and air their feelings gives them energy. Extraverts talk their way through movies, television shows, and the newspaper. They like to discuss the action and ideas as they occur, either in person or by telephone. Extraverts will greet you the minute you come home from work. It doesn't matter if they're a block away, they'll come tearing home to give you a hello. They aren't blabbering. They're not acting "flighty." They are energizing themselves by interacting with others.

Spirited children who are extraverts are the happiest and the best mannered when they can be with others. Forcing them to stay home or expecting them to entertain themselves by playing alone can be exhausting to them. As the parent of a spirited extravert it's important to utilize all of your resources. There is no way one parent, especially an introverted parent, can keep up with the interaction needs of an extraverted spirited child.

You can teach your extraverted child to fill her energy bank by using the telephone to talk with friends and relatives or by inviting other children over to play. To give yourself a break you can also register her in nursery school or community activities, or join a baby-sitting co-op. Any activities that will allow your child to interact with others will build her energy supply.

Sometimes, because of their need to be with people, parents of extraverts worry that their extraverted children lack independence. That was true for Kathy.

"Sarah is the only extravert in our family. We could never understand why she always wanted friends over. I was worried about too much peer pressure. I began to wonder if we'd done something wrong, if we had damaged her self-esteem, because she seemed to need other people so much. We tried to 'toughen her up,' telling her she needed to play by herself, but she would just get grouchy and mean. Now I understand what she is doing and encourage her much more. She has been happier and *so much better behaved.*"

Extraverts have lots of friends, need friends, and can't imagine having a good time without them. Being with friends gives extraverts energy. Be sure to provide opportunities for your extravert to recharge by being with people.

2. FEEDBACK To keep their energy levels high, extraverts need feedback, love feedback, and can't get enough feedback. A few words of positive reinforcement and the extravert is flying high, ready to roll. Introverts may wonder why so much reinforcement is needed.

I am a strong extravert who needs lots of affirmation from my introverted husband. We had agreed to do something for Valentine's Day rather than exchange gifts. But my husband knows me well. Shortly after he left for work, I found a valentine card on the kitchen counter. It said he loved me. An hour later I found another card on the keyboard of my computer—a second confirmation of his love. Making lunch, I found still another card in the refrigerator. I was thrilled, but the best of all was the card I found laying on our bed. It's cover was one continuous rainbow-colored statement: "I love you I love you I love you I love you . . ." Inside, the card read: "There, now are you satisfied? Happy Valentine's Day," signed with Joe's scrawl. Four cards just about fulfilled my requirements!

Your spirited extravert needs feedback to recharge. She isn't just nagging when she asks for your reassurance or response. It isn't a sign of poor self-esteem when she needs your words of encouragement. Feedback refuels her energy bank.

Providing enough feedback for the spirited extravert can be exhausting. You need to teach your child to ask for attention and responses from her other parent, grandparents, friends, teachers, and neighbors as well as you. Protect yourself from overdrawing your own energy account.

3. PEOPLE TO HELP THEM THINK Extraverts "think by talking." To solve a problem or reduce their stress, they need to talk with someone who will listen to them. Many times they don't even need a response from their listener. The opportunity to express themselves is all they need to work through their issues. Tony Bouza, ex-Minneapolis police chief, was once overheard saying, "My mouth runs about eleven minutes ahead of my brain. I'm always amazed to hear what I have to say." Be sure to provide opportunities for your spirited extravert to tell you about her worries and concerns and to share her ideas with you. She isn't just chattering, she is thinking.

The need to think by talking sometimes gets the spirited extravert in trouble at school. He talks out of turn. The teacher asks the class a question, expecting the kids to raise their hands before answering. The spirited extravert however, simply hears a question and responds immediately. His thoughts spill out in words.

Making your child aware that it is difficult for an extravert to think without talking can help your child learn to hold on to his response. Applaud his good ideas, but explain that in the classroom he has to hold onto his ideas until the teacher calls on him. Better yet, find a teacher who frequently divides the children into small groups where everyone can talk. Then raising a hand isn't an issue. We'll talk about that more in chapter 19.

WORKING TOGETHER

Identifying your children's energy sources is critical to their well-being and good behavior. As you can see, however, kids can't tap into those sources by themselves. They need your help. That's why it is important for you to understand your preferences too. Then you can recognize your differences and similarities and work with them to keep everyone's energy levels high. If you don't recognize those differences you can run into a mismatch, which is what happened to Jill and her son.

It was eight A.M. when the phone rang. "Mary, have you got a minute? I need to talk," the voice on the other end responded to my hello. It was Jill, and I could tell by the tone of the voice that this was not a one-minute conversation. It was easy to recognize. I've heard it in my own voice frequently.

"Sure," I responded, knowing full well our minute would stretch.

"I can't figure out how to give Mark my attention," she said.

I found this an interesting comment from a woman I knew to be a very committed mother with a demanding spirited son.

"He always wants it at the wrong time. [This I understood.] When he comes home from nursery school I'm ready to talk. He's not. When he's ready to talk I'm making dinner. I'm not about to stop what I'm doing and read to him or play with him. I'm hungry and I want to eat! He starts revving up after dinner. By bedtime he's in full gear and I'm beat. 'Read to me, Mom!' he demands. 'Mom, let me tell you about my idea!'

"My only response is a dragged out, monotone, 'Go to bed, Mark.'

" 'You never read to me,' he complains. 'How about just one short book?'

"Then I start screaming, 'Stop stalling! Go to bed!' and so the day ends. I'm exhausted and he hasn't been read to or had a chance to share his stories. Our energies never mesh. Both of us are willing to share but not at the same time. It feels like we're never connecting. I'm not sure what to do."

Jill and her son were "missing" each other because they energized and shared information in different ways. As an extravert, Jill wanted to talk immediately after her son arrived home. Mark, the introvert, needed to recharge by taking time alone before he was ready to converse. Jill felt like Mark was ignoring her, refusing to share his day with her. Mark thought his mother was pushing him and it made him back even farther away. Later when Mark was ready to talk, Jill was drained by her anger. She was too tired and hurt to be a good listener.

During our conversation I explained to Jill the differences between introverts and extraverts. Once she understood their different energy sources she was able to work out a new approach. She decided that instead of demanding that Mark talk with her when he first arrived home, she would call a friend and chat. Talking would refuel her energy bank. Later, when Mark was ready for conversation, her energy level would be high from interacting with her friend. She wouldn't be drained by anger because now she understood Mark was recharging, not blocking her out.

If we lived alone, personality type wouldn't matter. It's because of our relationships that we need to understand each other's style, to figure out how to work *together*—sharing ideas, solving problems, and recharging—without draining each other.

IDENTIFYING YOUR OWN ENERGY SOURCE

As you work to understand your spirited child you also need to understand yourself. Where does your energy come from? What is your preference? When you have this information you can build a "match" into your day.

To help you identify your type I've included the following questions. Read through them. Check the statements you agree with in each group. You may find yourself agreeing with statements in both the introvert and extravert sections. That's because we are capable of using both preferences. Look closely and think carefully: Which feels the most comfortable to you? Which would be your *first* choice—not what you have been taught to choose, but which actually fits who you are. Many introverts do not realize they prefer introversion over extraversion because they have been told that to introvert is unsociable. Some have so repressed this preference to please others that they have almost lost touch with it. To keep your energies high as the parent of a spirited child, it's important that you find your *true* energy source.

IF YOU ARE AN EXTRAVERT, YOU PROBABLY:

_____ want to talk with someone at the end of a busy day.

_____ have an immediate answer for a question.

_____ want to invite friends over on Friday night.

_____ are comfortable repeating something already said by someone else.

_____ need and like to hear that others love you and like your work.

_____ start to invite a few friends for dinner and realize you've invited the entire neighborhood.

_____ find yourself telling your introverted child to get out of her room and call a few friends to play.

_____ solve a problem by talking through the solution with someone else.

_____ feel comfortable initiating a conversation.

_____ call for the baby-sitter.

_____ are comfortable revealing personal things about yourself.

_____ frequently leave a party chastising yourself for talking too much and not listening.

____ enjoy and need to interact with other people and feel exhausted when you have spent too much time alone or only with young children.

____ immediately share a new idea or experience with someone and find joy and energy in the telling.

IF YOU ARE AN INTROVERT, YOU PROBABLY:

____ sit down with the newspaper or zone out in front of the television after a hard day.

____ will do anything, even clean the toilets, if someone else will agree to call the sitter.

____ can't imagine wanting to invite a group over on Friday night.

____ find being in a large group for an extended period of time exhausting.

____ share personal information only with those who are very close to you. It may not be unusual for a long-term friend to exclaim, "I never knew that about you!"

____ think before answering a question, often berating yourself for not sharing an answer you knew.

____ frequently have extraverts ask you the same question twice because they interpret your pause to think as ignorance of the question.

____ prefer dinner with the family or one special friend rather than with the whole neighborhood.

____ find yourself hiding in the bathroom or back bedroom at large family gatherings.

____ solve a problem by thinking through it yourself before ever talking about it with anyone else.

____ get tired of telling extraverts what a wonderful job they're doing and how much you love and appreciate them.

Count how many statements you agreed with in each group. If you checked more extravert statements your energy comes from outside sources. If you checked more introvert statements your energy come from inside sources.

TOTAL

____ Extravert statements

____ Introvert statements

REFILLING YOUR ENERGY BANK

Understanding your own type helps you understand your reactions to your children and helps get your own needs met.

Recognizing she was an introvert gave Sarah permission to ask for her space.

"I couldn't understand why it was so upsetting to me when my daughter would crawl all over me and stick her face right in mine when she was talking to me. Now I realize she is an extravert. She likes to be close. I am an introvert and I need my space. I used to feel so mean pushing her away. Now I let her know I love her, but I need my space!"

For David, working with his type has reduced the guilt.

"This is the first time in my life I don't feel 'antifamily,' " David shared. "I am an introvert and I need time alone. I've always felt guilty taking it because it seemed so antifamily. Now we all have an explanation for why I need some time. My wife doesn't resent it anymore, because she understands that I'll come back and be happier and more attentive."

And Megan now understands why she felt so drained at the end of a day with her children even though she enjoyed being home.

"I am a very strong extravert. I *need* people. I didn't know that interacting with children wasn't fulfilling my needs as an extraverted adult. I like being home with my children and I didn't want to change that. I have started planning a lot more outings with other moms and I'm using the telephone to stay connected with others more. My energy is staying much higher. My husband has noticed the difference and appreciates it."

Donald Tubesing, in *Kicking Your Stress Habits*, wrote, "It would be nice if we could eat a side of beef, drink a barrel of water and have our nutritional needs met for a month, but that doesn't happen. We have to meet our needs on a daily basis." This is also true of our energy needs. If you are an introvert *plan* some time alone every day. Stop the car a block from day care and listen to your favorite song before you pick up the kids. Take a walk around the lake, alone or with a special friend; instead of rushing to the grocery store on Saturday afternoon, settle in for a nap, even if you end up with peanut butter sandwiches for dinner again.

If you are an extravert make sure you have other adults to talk with. During nap time choose to call a friend rather than folding one more load of clothes. Schedule a regular when-the-kids-go-to-sleep time to talk with your partner or another adult.

Each of these activities provides you with a few moments to rest your weary brain and body, to nurture yourself so you can nurture your child. It is a must for parents of spirited children.

If you can't remember the last time you had a twenty-minute bubble bath or left the kids with a sitter so you could go out with friends—it's time to recharge. If you find yourself absolutely unable to get up off the couch and follow through with your spirited child, your energy account is overdrawn. It is time to make a deposit!

APPRECIATING BOTH EXTRAVERTS AND INTROVERTS

An important step in refilling our energy levels is learning to appreciate both introverts and extraverts. When we appreciate who we are, we can more easily respect our style and that of others. Then we can give each other permission to recharge in our own way. Grab a piece of paper and try this exercise.

If you are an extravert answer the following question: What's good about being an extravert?

If you are an introvert answer this question: What's good about being an introvert?

Once you have written down your answers read on to what other extraverts and introverts have had to say.

In a class all the extraverts inevitably form one large raucous group and start writing pages and pages of responses. They fire comments at each other, laugh in agreement, and repeat them. They lean toward each other. Their hands dance in the air in front of them. Their voices squeal and they laugh loudly and frequently.

With encouragement the introverts form little groups, sometimes breaking into pairs and threesomes rather than one big group. Their voices are quieter and their lists shorter. They sit with thoughtful, puzzled expressions on their faces. The quiet demeanor is occasionally disrupted by a dry humorous comment.

This is what the extraverts' list looks like:

Extraverts are good at keeping the conversation going.

Without us, the world would be a dull place and nothing would get done.

We have a lot of energy.

We are impulsive and fun.

We can make quick decisions.

Others know our opinions.

We're easy to talk to.

We express our feelings.

We have lots of friends.

We're convincing.

The introverts' list looks like this:

Introverts are able to have deep, long-lasting relationships.

We have a good time when we're by ourselves.

We think before we speak.

We don't rush into decisions.

We learn more because we listen.

To quote Mary Poppins, "We're practically perfect in every way."

We're masters of the delayed minimal response.

We can make decisions without consulting others.

When you can recognize the strengths of both introverts and extraverts, it's easier to accept your style and your child's. You can tap into your energy bank more frequently and comfortably. It isn't a hassle. It isn't an intrusion. Energy levels stay high. The good days start to outnumber the bad.

INTROVERTS: A SUMMARY

Introverts get their energy by being alone or with one or two special people. They prefer to interact with the world on the inside by reflecting on their thoughts and ideas before sharing them with others on the outside. They refresh themselves by spending time alone. If they get it, they'll play well with other kids and be more cooperative. If they don't get it, they'll get surly and nasty.

Introverted spirited children need to hear:

You think before you talk.

You enjoy spending time by yourself.

You need time alone to recharge.

You form deep and lasting relationships.

Teaching tips:

Make sure your introverted child has an opportunity to pull out of the action and refuel by being alone.

Help your child to understand that she needs space and can ask for it without pushing others away.

Allow your introverted child time to think before you expect a response.

Avoid interrupting her when she is working.

If you are an introvert too:

Recognize your need for time alone in order to refuel.

Let others know you need time to think before you can respond.

Appreciate your observation skills.

EXTRAVERTS: A SUMMARY

Extraverts draw their energy from others. They prefer to engage the world around them outside of their bodies by talking with people, sharing ideas and experiences. If they don't have the opportunity to talk, they get cranky and more demanding because they are running out of steam.

Extraverted spirited children need to hear:

You're outgoing.

You share your thoughts and feelings easily.

You enjoy being with people.

You make others feel comfortable.

Teaching tips:

Your extraverted child needs other people to help her recharge.

Provide her with lots of feedback.

Spend time talking with her to help her think through problems.

Understand that her need for people and feedback is not a reflection of low self-esteem.

If you are an extravert too:

Avoid isolating yourself at home with small children. Plan outings with other parents and children. Recognize that you need time with other adults in order to refuel.

Take time to talk through problems and issues with others before making a decision.

Let others know you need feedback. You aren't nagging.

6

INTENSITY: DIFFUSING THE STRONG REACTIONS

*I don't know why I go to extremes, too high and too low,
there ain't no inbetweens.*
—Billy Joel

I REMEMBER SITTING on a beach in Wisconsin, watching the Fourth of July fireworks display. A deep thud then *whoosh* like an old jalopy backfiring and racing off, tingling my ears. My eyes were dazzled with the blaze of red, gold, and blue lights. "Ooooooohhh, ahhhhhhh," the crowd murmured. My skin prickled in excitement, awaiting the next burst of sensation. It was not what I had expected. A fury of explosions erupted and balls of fire flew into the crowd. Screams tore into the night as excitement twisted to panic. The warm, deep sand, launched by fleeing feet, scratched my face. The entire cache of fireworks had exploded on the ground. Energy—mistakenly triggered and poorly guided, transformed from beauty to destruction.

How like the intensity of spirited children. Intensity is the driving force behind your child's strong reactions. It is the invisible punch that makes every response of the spirited child immediate and strong. Managed well, intensity allows spirited children a depth and delight of emotion rarely experienced by others. Its potential to create as well as to wreak havoc, however, makes it one of the most challenging temperamental traits to learn to manage.

Spirited kids do not understand their own intensity. They don't know why they shriek so loudly that it makes our ears burn. They don't know why they still cry over the dog that died two years ago. They don't know why they lose it over things that seem minor to us. They just do. It is our task to help them understand and appreciate the power of their intensity, to teach them how to control it instead of letting it control them.

PICKING UP THE CUES

I have a love-hate relationship with my husband whenever we go shopping. I can walk into a store, pick out five outfits to try on and hate every one of them. He meanders around the store waiting for me. After my fifth failure, he'll point to one outfit and say, "Try that." Of course, it fits perfectly and is absolutely striking. I should be happy but it makes me furious. Furious because I can't do it myself. I never would have selected that particular sweater or pants/blouse combination. I have watched him for years and I still can't do it. Lately I've insisted that he tell me his secrets. "What do you look for? What do you feel? What do you smell that makes you *know* that's the right outfit for me?" I have demanded. It seems to be so natural for him and yet I'm beginning to learn that there are very specific cues he is picking up on. He sees elements of texture, color, and design that I have been missing. These are definite principles that I can learn myself.

I realized the same thing happens to us as parents. Our kids lose it and we wonder why. We watch other parents of spirited kids and they seem to know something we don't. Something that allows them to move in before their kids go over the edge. What I have learned is that there are subtle, nonverbal cues that you can learn to pick up. Cues that inform you that your child's level of intensity is building. No two children signal growing intensity levels in the same way, but they are sending out identifiable cues that they're on their way to the moon. Cues that you can hear, see, or sense. By learning to pick up the cues you can take preventive actions before your child becomes overwhelmed. What do the cues look like? Here's what other parents have told me.

"Damon starts prowling the house. Nothing satisfies him."

"Susie becomes very active and impatient."

"John's coordination goes downhill. He stops concentrating on what he is doing. Sometimes he even falls down."

"Five-month-old Susie stops smoothly cycling her arms and legs. Her movements become stiff and jerky."

"Paula starts hanging on me."

"Ryan is only eighteen months old. He starts to test limits. He 'forgets' the rules."

"Jenny gets louder. Suddenly I'm hearing the 'outside' voice in my kitchen."

"Tina cannot decide what to do and starts invading the other kids' space."

"Anna gets bossy when she is about to blow. She becomes directive to everyone around her. She doesn't listen to anyone, including me."

Whether it's revving up, getting louder, testing the rules, fussing over a decision, or becoming less coordinated or more grumpy, spirited kids will let you know when their intensity is building. It's very likely that you have felt your child's cues in your gut, but may have ignored them. Perhaps because you were too tired. Perhaps because you thought to respond to these cues meant that you were reinforcing your child's negative behavior. But reading the cues is like smelling smoke. If you follow up quickly you may be able to smother the fire before it engulfs you, saving you at least an hour of total turmoil.

Think about your child. What cues does he send you? How do his body movements change? What happens to the tone of her voice? What bugs her that doesn't when she is calm? Take note of these changes. Store them in your brain. Next time your child starts to act in that way, recognize it as a signal for you to move in and redirect him *before* he loses it.

TEACHING KIDS TO READ THE CUES

As you catch the cues tell the kids what you see. Ultimately we want them to catch their growing intensity themselves, to rely on their inner control rather than our control. By three and a half or four years of age, we can expect to be hearing things like: "Mom, I'm starting to bounce off the walls," "I can't make a decision. Help me," "Dad, I can't control my body," or "I'm really revved up."

Kathy, a mom in my class, shook her head in dismay, when she heard me make this suggestion. "To put it mildly," she said, "I don't find my nine-year-old really open to discussing her building level of intensity. I can't believe it works."

Kathy is right. You can't teach kids new words or to pick up their cues when they are reacting intensely. You have to wait until later, when they are calmer, to point out to them what you saw. Then, next time you can say to them, "Damon, when I see you prowling the house, I know it's time for you to find a quiet place," or "John, when you start falling down, it means you need to stop and read a book." Saying it once is not enough. You have to keep talking about it all of the time.

USING WORDS

Learning to express their potent reactions in words rather than in actions is critical for spirited kids. If they can tell us they're angry they don't have to kick us to get the message across. It's our labels that they turn to as they are building their vocabulary—the words we use to describe and explain intensity.

Three-year-old Al is a blond, tousled-haired mini tornado. "I've got 'gusto' " he informed me. "My dad says it's okay to do things with gusto—as long as you don't hurt anybody!"

"I'm 'full of it,' " a five-year-old shared, "just like my Grandpa Dick."

"My mom plays whisper games with me to help me practice my soft voice because usually I'm very dramatic," six-year-old Chrissa exclaimed.

"I have powerful reactions," eight-year-old Kerry told me.

These children, as young as three (and sometimes even two) understand their intensity and feel good about it. They haven't been told they were wild, aggressive, or mean. The words to describe their intensity have focused on the vim, vigor, and energy racing through their body in a positive way. It is those words that help them to feel comfortable with their intensity rather than embarrassed or frightened by it. As a result, they don't have to run wild, scream, hit, or throw things to express themselves—at least not most of the time. They can talk about it instead.

Language development is like an iceberg. A great deal lies hidden beneath the surface. Two-thirds of language development occurs inside of the brain, invisible to us. Months, sometimes years before children are communicating with their own words, they are understanding those of others. Parents of spirited kids who are learning to manage their intensity well are talking about intensity. They soothe the wailing baby by telling him that they understand it's frustrating to wait for the bottle to warm. They tell the toddler that they understand she is very angry. It's hard for her to stop playing outside and come in to the house. Soon, the children will be able to use these words themselves.. It won't happen overnight but it will happen.

Older kids who haven't heard the words need to hear them now. Words control the impulses; without them children have no protective devices to slow their reactions.

Frequently I am asked, "Aren't you just begging for a blowup when you talk about intensity with kids? Aren't you feeding them ideas or creating words for feelings that don't really exist?" My experience, observations, and interviews tell me that spirited children feel intensely whether anyone has talked to them about it or not. Ignoring it does not make it go away. Ask children what is happening inside of their bodies and they will tell you that they can feel their blood buzzing in their veins or hornets zipping through their body. If no one has informed them that other people experience these feelings, or if no one has helped them by giving names to them—like anxiety, frustration, excitement, and elation—they become frightened by them. Some worry that they are sick. Some feel odd; others, lost and overwhelmed. Talking verifies the sensations and emotions. It gives them legitimacy and allows the child to own them without being frightened. It also helps kids to know what to do with them, how to react and how to control their intensity.

Michael, a father of four, reported, "Talk, talk, talk—that's all we do. I'm always giving her a word for a feeling or pointing out the body movement that is a sure sign of trouble. I'm so tired of talking—but it works!"

Intense spirited kids need to hear phrases like:

You are enthusiastic.

You are expressive and lively.

You are easily frustrated.

You are very upset, but you are not dying.

Being intense does not mean being aggressive.

I think you are feeling anxious, angry, sad (or whatever the emotion might be).

When kids hear these messages over and over again, they are able to turn them into "I" messages.

An intense spirited kid can learn to tell himself:

I am getting upset.

I can be angry without hurting someone.

I am really excited.

I like being enthusiastic.

My blood is starting to boil. I can't stand it in here.

I'm feeling crabby.

The rubber bands inside of me are starting to stretch.

By giving them the words, we give them the tools to get their needs met—appropriately. With these words, your child may even be able to help you out like four-year-old Blake did for his mom.

"We had been shopping in the mall for several hours." she told the other parents in the class. "I hate shopping. Blake could see I was getting upset with a very slow clerk. 'It's hard to wait,' he said to me. I couldn't help smiling. How many times have I said that to him. He saved *me* from losing it!"

Take a few minutes and write down the words your child uses to describe her own intensity. Ask her what it feels like inside of her body when she is angry or upset. Give her positive words to use next time she feels this way. Let her know you'll listen carefully and help her diffuse it before she loses it.

SOOTHING/CALMING ACTIVITIES

Catching cues and talking about intensity is not enough. You have to know what to do with the intensity once you've grabbed it. Intense spirited kids can roll you right up in their intensity. Unknowingly we can add to the level of intensity rather than diffusing it because we are captured by their zest-fulness. We sense their energy and play wild music, plan a million activities, or encourage them to run up and down the hallway thinking that they need the stimulation or that we can tire them out. But spirited kids only wind tighter. What they actually need from us is soothing/calming activities that help them diffuse their intensity. When you pick up the cues that your child's intensity level is building or your child tells you she's getting that "feeling" again, divert her energies to one of these activities.

1. WATER   "When Bobbie starts to lose it, it's into the bathtub," Beth explained. "There are days the kid looks like a little raisin because he's been in there three times, but it snaps him right out of it. I've got two other kids. They don't need baths the way Bobbie does but if necessary I just put them in the tub with him. He needs it and they enjoy it."

"I started putting Nissa in the bathtub to soothe her when she was just a baby," Vicki said. Now at ten, she'll come home from a hard day at school and head straight for the tub. She'll lie in there for over an hour, reading, singing, talking to herself. It's a new kid that emerges."

"Water really works for Seth," Annette added. "When we're away from home, just placing a cool, wet washcloth on his forehead will soothe him."

"Jennifer doesn't like to get in the tub," Lana said, "but if I let her play in the sink while I'm making dinner it slows her down. She especially likes it if I let her scrub the potatoes and carrots for the meal."

Paul commented, "I let Brad paint with water. If it's nice outside I let him paint the driveway. Otherwise I set him up at the easel. I don't have to worry about paint spills and he loves it."

Warm or cool, water can be a very soothing entity to spirited children. By immersing their bodies in a warm comfortable bath, pouring it from one container to another, or merely letting it run through their fingers, they can diffuse their intense reactions.

The nice thing about water is that it is soothing for anyone no matter what his or her age. My friend Rachel has always used the "fun bath" to soothe her very spirited three-year-old daughter. She didn't realize how important these baths were for Jamie until a recent Mother's Day. Clutching a bottle of bath salts in her hand Jamie insisted that her mother have a fun bath. Jamie filled the tub with water and bubbles and ran to get her favorite books while Mom got in the tub. As Rachel lay there with the bubbles tickling her chin Jamie "read" her her favorite books. Then she jumped up and headed downstairs only to reappear with a plate of peanut butter crackers and a glass of milk. "Happy Mother's Day," Jamie exclaimed, delighted to treat her mother to a soothing/calming activity.

2. IMAGINATION   Most spirited kids have a wonderful sense of imagination. You can use it to help them moderate their intensity.

Grandma Leah's Dress Up is an imaginative game that calms a tense child anywhere and at anytime. Let your children pretend that they are going to an elegant ball or a costume party. Then "dress" them up for it. Have them stand in front of you or sit on your lap. First pretend to wash their hair, massaging their heads and running your fingers along their scalp lines like water spraying from a nozzle. You can tickle their ears with an imaginary diamond earring or a pirate's ring. If their fantasy includes makeup, run the lightest of fingertips along their cheeks, across their eyebrows, along the bridge of their noses and the outline of their lips. The gentle touch soothes and calms them. For boys you can pretend to shave them—brushing shaving cream on their cheeks; then stroking their faces like a razor; and, finally, trimming their mustaches, sideburns, and eyebrows. For good measure I always like to splash on a little after-shave. If the men in your family wear beards, you could gently trim their beards.

Slide a finger around their necks for a gold chain or a silk necktie. Run your finger down their backbones for a zipper or around their waists for a magic belt. Don't forget the long stockings that slide over each individual toe and up along the calves of their legs.

Rings and bracelets are the finishing touches. Place a ring on each finger, sliding down the finger to its base, adding first a ruby, then a diamond, then the gold pinky ring. Finally, end with a watch or gold bracelet, draped around the wrist. They're ready for the ball or party and in a much better mood.

Creative dramatics can work too. I once watched a music teacher working with a group of young children. She was trying to teach them the concepts of forte and piano. She asked the children to pretend that they were leaves. When she played the song forte the wind would blow and the "leaves" would dance in the air. As the music softened to piano, the wind would die down and the "leaves" would settle to the ground.

At the end of the lesson, one very spirited child was still dancing in the wind. "I think you have lots of wind blowing inside of your body," the teacher said to her. "Take a deep breath and blow that wind out of your body."

The child puffed her cheeks out and blew a steady burst of air, her chest visibly shrinking as the air diminished.

"There now," the teacher responded. "Do you feel the leaves all settling down inside you. They're in a pile, falling asleep."

The child nodded and quietly walked to the door. Her rich imagination had helped her to release her excitement and energy in a positive way.

3. SENSORY ACTIVITIES   Spirited kids are very sensual. They enjoy activities that allow them to touch, smell, taste, hear, or see things. Using their senses calms them. In a typical preschool program you will usually see one or two sensory activities. For the spirited child, we like to include as many as five. I encourage teachers to use plenty of sensory materials because the other kids like them and the spirited kids *need* them. It's important that you have them available at home because they are a great way to diffuse intense feelings.

Play-Doh and Silly Putty are favorite sensory activities for children of all ages. There isn't a right way to use them so a two-year-old can pull, roll, and stretch them, whereas an eight-year-old can create a log house, imaginary food, or whatever. Many parents of spirited kids just keep Play-Doh or Silly Putty in the cupboard, ready to pull out when needed. My favorite recipe for modeling compound (similar to Play-Doh) is the following:

2½ cups flour

½ cup salt

2 packages dry unsweetened Kool-Aid

2 cups boiling water

3 tablespoons oil.

Mix the dry ingredients together in a bowl. Mix the liquids together and pour into the dry ingredients. Stir until it forms a ball (at first it will appear as if it will never make a smooth mixture). As the mixture cools and becomes less sticky, take it out of the bowl and knead until it is smooth.

Your children can roll, pat, and pound any way they like. Add cookie cutters or little plastic animals to let loose their imaginations.

To make modeling clay (similar to Silly Putty), use the following recipe.

1 cup white school glue

¾ cup liquid starch

Pour the glue into a plastic container and then add the starch. Stir the ingredients and then knead the mixture with your hands. (If it sticks to your hands wipe a little starch on your palms.) To get the best results allow the mixture to set for a while. You may need to heat the ingredients in the microwave in order to get them to mix well. Store in a closed container in the refrigerator.

Modeling clay can be pulled, stretched, poked, and colored with magic markers. It's great fun and interesting for parents, too.

Every good preschool has a sensory table. Usually it's just a table frame with the middle cut out of the table so a large tub can be inserted. The tub is then filled with water, sand, oatmeal, cornmeal, snow, shredded paper, or whatever the teacher chooses. Spirited kids are always drawn to the one in our classroom. You can create your own sensory table. All you need is a plastic dishpan or tub. You don't need the table frame. Just put a vinyl tablecloth underneath the tub to keep spills off of your floor. Fill the tub with sudsy, warm water and make sure there are turkey basters and sponges for a fun tranquilizing activity. If the kids get tired of the sponges and basters, let them wash their dishes or favorite toys and dolls. If you don't want to use water, try sand, oatmeal, or cornmeal. Include cups, spoons, funnels, and a variety of other containers for hours of fun.

Finger painting the shower wall with shaving cream is another soothing exercise. Wash it down the drain when they're done.

Back scratches and numbers drawn with a finger on the back can also be a soothing, relaxed time that allows you and your child to focus on one another, enjoy healthy touch, and diffuse the intensity.

Any activities that use the senses are normally very inviting and soothing to spirited children. Infants who can't benefit from a sensory table may be soothed by a massage, a soft lullaby, or a walk in the sunshine. Sometimes dimming the lights in a bright room will work.

4. READING When you get stuck—there isn't any water available to you, sensory activities and your imagination have failed you—try reading. Many parents of spirited children have found the simple act of pulling out a book and inviting their child to sit on their lap or next to them on a comfortable couch or chair is all that is needed to diffuse an accelerating intensity level. Not only does your child learn the power of reading to manage her strong feelings but she is also exposed to the wonder of books. The research on reading states that children who have been read to by their parents grow up to be the best and most avid readers. Head to your local library or check out those garage sales for used books. Keep your child's favorite titles handy.

One of my favorites is *Screamy Mimi*, by Robert Krause. Mimi screams until her mom and dad send her to New York for voice lessons. In the end

Screamy Mimi learns to use her intensity as an opera star who performs at the Met!

5. HUMOR To fully appreciate this story you need to know that I am employed by the school district in which my children attend school. You also need to know a little bit about my husband. He's five foot, nine inches tall—if you stretch it—155 pounds, and very spirited. He loves movies where the little guy wins and is a sucker for every kid who comes to the door selling anything. There's another side to him, too. His father was raised on the Lake Superior docks and likes to regale us with tales of diving off the freighters after sandwiches thrown in the lake by the sailors. I believe him, although no one has ever been able to verify his facts. I'm afraid these macho activities have influenced how his son, my husband, sometimes expresses himself.

One day my son came home from school, threw open the door, and stormed into the kitchen, throwing his book bag on the floor and kicking at the refrigerator. "Cut it out," I commanded. "What happened to you?"

"That old witch on the playground accused me of fighting and I didn't do it," he roared.

"That must have been embarrassing," I said.

"It wasn't embarrassing," he corrected me.

"Well, it must have felt lousy then," I responded.

"Stupid aide," he bellowed. "She must be blind."

Losing patience, I tried moralizing. "Next time you might choose where to stand more carefully," I remarked. It only added to his fury.

He continued to rage until his father arrived home.

"What's wrong with him?" he asked, noting the steam rising in the kitchen. I quickly filled him in with the details, hopeful that he would know what to do. As he strode over to Josh I noticed a slight puff in his chest and I knew he was up to something.

"No problem," he announced. I held my breath.

Josh looked up in total shock. "What do you mean?" he stammered.

Joe continued, "Next time just say to the lady, 'Hey lady, was there blood on the ground?' " Then he jabbed himself in the chest and declared, " 'When I fight there's blood on the ground!' "

Josh's eyes bugged out. I almost fainted. Years of nonviolent training down the drain. I could just imagine this kid going back to school, sharing his father's words of wisdom and me losing my job.

"You can't say that!" I gasped.

By now they were both roaring, Josh fully realizing that his father was teasing. The intensity of the rage was diffused by humor. This time words and good listening had not been enough. Humor provided the catalyst to change the reaction. Later, when everyone was calm, we talked about more productive ways to handle fights on the playground.

Humor is a frequent visitor to the homes of spirited children who are learning to manage their intensity well—not sarcasm or ridicule but gut-busting, yuk-it-up good laughs and fun. Feel free to enjoy that sense of humor, use it to reduce the tension and bring you together. That's what Tom does.

"Sometimes I do something totally unexpected," he said, laughing. "Last night I heard Brett fighting with his sister. I was in a good mood, so I snuck around the corner on my hands and knees and growled at them like a dog. They were so surprised they started to giggle. They jumped on my back for a horse ride and the fight was over."

Vicki uses humor to back herself out of power struggles. "Tracie had really been helpful getting dinner ready. She had set the table, torn up the lettuce for the salad, and washed some of the preparation dishes. After dinner I asked her to take her plate to the sink. She started to balk. 'Oops, you've been good too long,' I remarked. She was stunned into silence for a second.

" 'Yeah,' she responded, smiling, and took her plate to the kitchen."

Humor—a delightful tool for reducing intensity.

6. TIME-OUT—NOT AS A PUNISHMENT   Taking a break is one of the most common calming activities for adults. Unfortunately for kids we've turned time-out into a punishment. Instead of being an invitation to our children to take a break and regain control, it has become a dreaded order. "Go to your room and don't come out until I tell you to!" or "You sit in that chair and don't move an inch!" No pain, no gain, we think, and feel better if they scream and holler to let us know that they are really miserable. But an opportunity to refresh is lost while we struggle to keep them in their room or chair, and they expend their energies kicking doors and throwing blocks against the wall. Time-out as a punishment makes everyone feel like a loser.

I like to recommend that parents of spirited kids think of time-out as a basketball coach does: an opportunity to take a break from the action, refresh the body, and pull the game plan back together. Watch a basketball team. The players are out on the court playing smoothly and coolly as the clock ticks away. One minute to go with the score tied. The ball goes up, spins on the rim and pops back out. Chaos erupts as elbows jab and hands grab air in the fight for the ball. "Time out!" screams the coach. The players trot to the sideline. The coach pulls them in tight pointing to the game board on his lap. Heads begin to nod, fists unclench, and even a few slight smiles appear. A break in the action, a minute to rest, a chance to pull the game plan back together—this is a time-out in sports.

It may appear that there is a flaw in comparing discipline time-outs with time-outs in sports. Most three-year-olds, even eight-year-olds, especially spirited ones, don't usually trot easily to the sideline when a time-out is called, nor do they listen intently while the game plan is revised. Instead, they may refuse to leave the floor and lie down, kick, scream, and hold their hands over their ears when you try to talk to them. So what is a parent to do?

You can start by reminding your children of the cues their bodies send to them: messages that say, "I'm tired," or "I'm getting overwhelmed." Help them recognize that their body tightening or the sensation of blood running through their veins is a signal that they need to call a time-out. If we have taught them that time-out is an opportunity to pull out of the action to rest and relax rather than a punishment to endure, they can feel comfortable taking a break. Taking a break means finding a quiet comfortable spot. It may be a bedroom, it may be a corner of the kitchen. At first we will have to gently help them find their spot. Speak softly to them, help them hear and feel the quiet, sense the anger or frustration draining from their bodies.

Children need to be taught what a relaxed body feels like inside. They need to understand that a time-out is not over until that sense of peacefulness fills their bodies. That's why you can't just send young children to their room alone. You have to go with them, talk softly, rub their back if they like it, and stay with them until that rosy, good feeling is inside of their bodies. Only then is it time to move back onto the "playing floor."

You might find yourself groaning right now, wondering what you are going to do with the baby who is crying to be fed or the toddler who is hanging on your leg or the phone that is ringing. Forget the phone, lay the baby in the crib for a few minutes, take the toddler with you, or place him in a safe place while you help your spirited child through a time-out. Soon he won't need you anymore, or certainly for shorter periods of time. In order to keep yourself calm, call the time-out *before* tempers flare.

What are you going to do for a punishment if time-out is supposed to be a chance to relax? First of all, remember that if kids learn to take a break before they blow up, there won't be any misbehavior to punish. If, however, you feel a need for a punishment, the basketball coach has got one of those for you too—bench them.

You'll notice on the court that the coach gives everyone a chance to relax and pull it back together again, but if a player goes back out to the court and doesn't do what she is supposed to do the coach pulls her and says "*You*—on the bench until I send you back out." There she stays until the coach lets her play again. This is a punishment, and there are times we need it for spirited kids. Time-out is not a punishment; being benched is.

Once children have learned to respond to the cues their bodies are sending them and understand time-out as a healthy opportunity to deal with their stress, they can call for one themselves. In fact, you may see your children slide out of the action and into their room for a quick break all by themselves. This is especially true if you have put a sign there that says, "I need a hug," or "I need your attention." The sign is there to hand to a parent when time-out alone isn't enough to pull the game plan back together. Even three-year-olds can begin to appreciate the power of words instead of using tantrums to get their needs met.

Learning to use time-out as a soothing/calming activity is critical for spirited children as they move toward the teen years. As hormones start to pump through their bodies the challenge to manage their intensity grows. At this point they are physically too big for you to force them into a time-out. They have to choose to do it themselves. If they are comfortable with time-outs, they will use them and will be successful managing their strong emotions.

A discipline time-out, just like a sports time-out, can mean the difference between a win or a loss, success or failure. Teach your children to use them and enjoy them. In the end, you'll all be winners.

When children understand their intensity, and recognize that they can control and channel it into athletic, creative, and other appropriate channels, they feel good about themselves. The number of full-blown outbursts diminishes drastically. This is preventive discipline. It teaches kids the "right" way to behave and stops the battles before they ever start.

WORKING TOGETHER

Children learn best from the adults they love. They watch carefully to see how you handle your intensity. Most of us, however, have not been taught to enjoy the richness intensity adds to our lives nor have we been instructed in the safety measures needed to use it appropriately. To help our children understand and manage their intensity, we have to feel comfortable with our own.

DEALING WITH YOUR OWN INTENSITY

The intensity of spirited kids sizzles and snaps. It can burn you to the core. You breathe deeply trying your best to block the blows. At first, like drops on a rainproof jacket they roll off. But the torrent grows heavier, the drops more penetrating, roaring in your ear, and piercing your composure until you may find yourself also screaming, threatening, and slamming doors.

"Keep your cool," I have freely counseled. "When your kids lose it you don't need to go with them. They'll be back to normal in minutes and you'll find yourself still hanging on the ceiling for hours, even days if you go with them." I can forgive myself for this insensitivity, because it was such easy advice for me to offer. I am not a spirited adult—spunky, but not spirited. It is humanly possible for me, at least some of the time, to stand back, watch my son erupt and not get caught in the frenzy.

I'm not sure if it was the despondent look in a parent's big brown eyes and the hopeless shake of her head or if it was listening to my husband the other morning screaming at the kids. "I promised myself I wasn't going to yell this week!" that made me realize that recommending that spirited parents keep their cool was a denial of their own intensity. Somehow, someway, spirited adults have to find an acceptable outlet for their own intense reactions before they can help their children handle theirs. It doesn't work to simply say, "I am supposed to be cool." The fact is you're not. The intensity sits like a rock in the pit of your stomach.

STUFFING IT DOESN'T WORK

I was sitting in a restaurant with Barb Kobe, self-esteem consultant who spends her days helping both adults and children understand their feelings. "What recommendations do you have for parents dealing with their own intensity?" I asked her.

She responded by asking, "Can I borrow your napkin?"

"Sure," I replied, wondering why she would want a used paper napkin.

"Here," she said, handing it back to me in one big wad. "This is your intense feelings. Today let's say it's anger. Now what are you going to do with it?"

I looked around the restaurant. Figuring out what to do with a dirty napkin or anger in the middle of a restaurant, I realized, posed similar challenges. I shrugged, not sure what to do.

"You could stuff it," she said, snatching the napkin from my hand and stuffing it down the neck of her shirt. She sat there with an obvious lump just below her chin. "There, now it's all taken care of, right?" she asked. "It doesn't affect me, I got rid of it. Stuffed it."

Then she started jamming more napkins in her shirt. The lumps grew, until she looked more like a warty toad than a human being. "That's what happens when we stuff our anger," she said. "We think we've gotten rid of it, but it's distorting everything about us."

Strong reactions and feelings are real. They're like the wadded paper napkin. They don't just go away. We have to deal with the rush of our own intensity before we can help our kids deal with theirs. I've asked the parents in my classes for their strategies and figured out a few myself. Here's what I've learned.

KEEP BREATHING

"I have to remember to keep breathing," Norm explained. "My doctor told me that when we're upset we hold our breath. We actually stop breathing, but our brain needs oxygen to function. If we're holding our breath, our brain isn't getting the oxygen it needs to think. If we can't think we can't figure out how to calm ourselves or our children. I have to remember to BREATHE!"

ASK FOR HELP

"My husband, Ben, and I have agreed that we'll work together—no matter what," Molly told the group. "This morning we got put to the test!

"I knew Joel was building up the minute he awoke," she told us. "He was tired. He had a loose tooth that hung by one corner of the root, making eating impossible and shooting sharp stabs of pain whenever anything touched it. I had listened to him moan and groan through breakfast and then watched as he crawled up the stairs to comb his hair. I knew there would be trouble. His spike had grown to the point where it was too long to stand up and too short to lie down. We had a haircut appointment scheduled for the next day but my gut said it was one day too late."

She paused for effect and then continued. "I listened to the brewing storm, waiting for the eruption I knew would come but didn't bother to stop because I wanted to eat my breakfast! [We all nodded in understanding.] Sure enough three bites in, it hit, 'Moooooooom!' he roared, 'my hair won't do anything.'

"I grabbed one more bite," she said, "and headed up the stairs. He was right, it was a mess. It resisted his efforts to plaster it to his head. I glanced over his arsenal of chemicals, hair spray, foam, and water. 'Have you tried gel?' I asked.

" 'There isn't any,' he complained.

"I searched through the shelves and came up with a half-full bottle. 'Try this,' I directed. Together we wiped gel all over his head. I thought it was going to work until little tufts of hair popped up around the crown of his head like little suction cups popping off a wall. He lost it, threw himself down on the bed and started screaming. I was out of ideas and definitely low on patience."

At this point she slouched down in her chair, shrugged, and threw her hands up in dismay. We waited for her to continue.

"I went looking for help." she explained. "I glared at my husband who was downstairs eating.

" 'I can't,' he said, 'I'm ready to scream, just listening to him.'

"That's when I gave him my 'look,' " she said, and proceeded to demonstrate for us by crossing her arms, puffing her cheeks, and squinting her eyes at us. Then went on.

"He got the message and went upstairs.

" 'I can't go to school,' Joel wailed.

"My husband glanced at our arsenal. 'My gosh what do you expect,' he quipped. 'You've created a toxic waste site on the top of your head.'

"I couldn't help it, I burst into laughter and so did my son. The outburst was over. Just like that. We got the hair plastered down the best we could and he went to school."

When you're in the middle and stuck, you need to know when to back out and call for help. If that person is someone you live with, set up your "signals," like Molly and her husband did. Use expressions or words that clearly signify I need your help *now*! It is imperative that parents of spirited children work together. It is not a sign of failure to let others assist you. It is a recognition and acceptance of your own intensity and limits. Blaming or ridiculing only fuels the intensity levels. Teamwork is essential. You have to talk about how you react when your child loses it. You have to decide how you can help and support each other. By working together you can take the sting out of your child's strong responses.

If you are a single parent you might think that you can't ask someone else for help. Single parents often say, "What if I call and interrupt their meal or family time" or "I don't want to bother anyone." But good friends don't mind being bothered. They appreciate the opportunity to help and the joy of giving. Look for someone you know who likes your child and won't be critical of him or of you. You have to be able to trust they'll support you, then feel free to call. As the parent of a spirited child, you have to know and use your resources well.

STEP AWAY FROM IT

Of course, there are times when your kids lose it, and you are all alone, with no one to help. Give yourself permission to step out of the fire. I know most of the discipline books will tell you to respond immediately, but if responding immediately means two bulls charging head to head into each other, it's much better to pull out of it and take a breather.

"I'm as intense as he is," Bob shared in class. "The things that get him set me off too. It's like two kids going to it instead of one. The only way we can both survive is if I pull out for a few seconds."

Let your child know you are too upset to deal with him now but you will be back in a few minutes. Then walk away, take ten deep breaths, and calm yourself down. Remind yourself that your child is losing it because she is intense and not because you are a bad parent. Gradually, with maturity and good instruction from you, the frequency and volume of the outbursts will diminish.

IF YOU NEED TO YELL, MAKE IT HEALTHY

People yell when they get angry or frustrated. Mind you I am not advocating yelling, but it is a reality. In some cultural groups it is very acceptable. In others it may not be as widely approved of but it remains a fact of life. All of us are aware of the traumas children experience when they lie in their beds listening to their parents screaming at each other, or stand there powerless victims as their parents rage at them. This is verbal abuse, which is as destructive—if not more so—as the physical assaults of punches and kicks. This kind of yelling is not acceptable. Fortunately there is another kind of yelling. I'd like to share it with you in case you are a yeller and have an overwhelming urge to let loose.

The healthy yellers I have met have gone to the treetops for their role model. Tarzan, king of the jungle, lets out a chest-pounding bellow that gets everyone's attention with nary a word expressed. No seething lashes like: "I hate you," "Why are you so stupid?" "I wish you'd drop dead," or "My life would be a lot easier without you." No statements that shame, blame, and abuse the psyche. A Tarzan yell is a wordless workout of the vocal cords that releases all of the frustration captured inside.

It's significant to note that Tarzan saved the big bellow for the real crisis. It wasn't overused, and he always explained to those involved the exact reasons for his outburst. So if you've got to yell think of Tarzan in the trees, open your mouth, and let loose as you pound your chest. No words, please, and no pounding on anyone else. Once you've got that worked out sit down and *talk* it through, maybe even add a laugh or two.

LOOK AT YOUR MESSAGE BOARD

The real issue in dealing with intensity is feeling comfortable with it. Recently I asked a group of parents, "What did your parents, teachers, and friends tell you about intensity when you were growing up?"

They looked at one another as if to say, "Does she really know what she's asking?" The silence stretched, then exploded as a defiant voice declared, "Calm down. Stop acting like a maniac." The voice belonged to Tim, a six-foot, four-inch professional athlete who was sprawled in his chair. There was a moment of surprise before the next parent jumped in.

"You need to relax. You're going to have a heart attack before you are thirty-five if you don't settle down," Patti offered.

"In our family," Joan explained, "we were always told children should be seen and not heard. I was constantly in trouble for laughing or squealing too loudly."

Her eyes bright with tears, her voice barely audible, Barb said, "You're the one who always spoils everything."

The messages of our own childhood can come back to haunt us as we work with our children's intensity: the messages that hurt us, that negated who we are if we're intense too. The ones that created a fear of intensity.

Review in your own mind the messages you carry about intensity. What are you telling yourself? What does intensity mean to you? If your thoughts are like Tim's, Patti's, Joan's, and Barb's, you will interpret intense reactions as bad and become angry at yourself and your child when they are experienced. Instead of working with your child's intensity or your own, you'll want to get rid of it. But intensity is a reality. Sometimes an exhausting reality, but a fact. It doesn't go away. We have to work with it.

The messages we carry around inside of ourselves about intensity are called self talk. In *The Winning Family,* Dr. Louise Hart says, "Self talk creates our feelings, which express themselves through our actions or behavior and become the basis of our self concept. With our self talk, we constantly lift ourselves up or put ourselves down. We are our own best friend or our own worst enemy. Only when we tune in and listen to it can we change it."

FEELING GOOD ABOUT INTENSITY

Changing your inner messages about intensity from negative ones to positive ones starts by using positive labels. You will feel less irritable toward your child's intensity when you can view it as vigor rather than venom. You will feel more in control when your child is expressive rather than explosive.

To redesign your labels you have to think about the ways intensity adds richness and depth to your life.

"My intensity allows me to perform," Tim responded as we continued our round of questions. "I can accomplish feats that others can't." His voice started to warm. "I'm enthusiastic about what I do. I can motivate people. At work they always give me the new recruits because they know I'll get them off the ground and build a team."

He paused, and Patti took over. "I see it in my husband. He is passionate and committed. His relationships are deep and meaningful. He is an active volunteer. Last year he headed a campaign that raised ten thousand dollars to buy equipment for an inner-city school."

"I am demonstrative," Barb added exuberantly.

Managed well, intensity adds flavor and excitement to our lives. It is the trait that allows our spirited child to be animated, vivacious, and zealous. It provides him with the drive needed to become the karate champ, the tumbling tiger, the enthusiastic creator, the lively entertainer, and the charismatic leader. If we can fill ourselves with positive messages about intensity, we can stand in front of a mirror and proudly tell ourselves, "Intensity adds value to my life," "I am comfortable with intensity," "I can accept my child's intensity," "I can help my child learn to manage her intensity," and *"I do not fear intensity."*

INTENSITY: A SUMMARY

Intensity is the driving force behind the strong reactions of the spirited child. It is the invisible punch that makes every response of the spirited child immediate and strong. Managed well, intensity allows spirited children a depth and delight of emotion rarely experienced by others. Its potential to create as well as to wreak havoc, however, makes it one of the most challenging temperamental traits to learn to manage.

Intense spirited kids need to hear:

You do everything with zest, vim, vigor, and gusto.

You are enthusiastic, expressive, and full of energy.

Your intensity can make you a great athlete, leader, performer, etc.

Things can frustrate you easily.

Being intense does not mean being aggressive.

Teaching tips:

Help your child to learn to notice her growing intensity before it overwhelms her.

Provide activities that soothe and calm, such as warm baths, stories, and quiet imaginative play.

Use humor to diffuse intense reactions.

Teach your child that time-out is a way to calm herself rather than a punishment.

If you are intense too:

Do not fear your child's intensity.

Diffuse your own intensity before you step in to help your child.

Take deep breaths, yell like Tarzan, step away from it, or ask for help to cope with your own intensity.

Review in your own mind the messages you were given about intensity. Dump those that negate the value of intensity.

7

PERSISTENCE: CHOOSING YOUR BATTLES

The difference between perseverance and obstinacy is that one comes from a strong will and the other from a strong won't.
—Howard Ward Beecher

JENNA WAS frustrated. Every time she tried to stop her thirteen-month-old daughter, Katlin, from doing what she wanted to do the child would throw herself back, scrunch her eyes shut, and let out a piercing yell as she flailed her arms and legs in the air.

Jenna called me, looking for help. I headed to her house, anxious to meet this little dynamo. Within five minutes of my arrival Katlin was throwing a fit. She wanted to climb the steps but her mom said no. There was no distracting her. Jenna offered her a bowl full of cereal hoping to pull her attention away from the steps. But it didn't work. Katlin pushed them away and continued to howl.

"Let's try something different," I suggested. "Sit at the bottom of the steps and let her go."

"Isn't that giving in?" Jenna questioned. "I know she'll stop crying, but won't she think she has won?"

"We're not giving in," I responded. "We're listening carefully and realizing this is much more important to her than either of us thought. I know you are worried about her safety, but let's allow her to try before we decide it isn't safe."

Jenna crouched at the bottom of the steps to catch Katlin if it was necessary and then let her climb. Katlin beamed. It was quickly apparent that she was very confident on the steps and didn't need any assistance. Within minutes Jenna and I were comfortably seated on the couch talking while Katlin happily climbed up and down the short flight of steps. Instead of fighting with us, all of her energy was focused on reaching her goal—climbing those steps.

Living with the "raw gem" of a persistent child is not easy. To tell these kids no, to thwart their efforts, is to risk their wrath. Even as infants they are incredibly determined and strong. They push where other kids don't push. They demand more than other kids demand. And they never give up. It is nearly impossible to ignore them or distract them. In every situation they meet us head on, ready to do battle.

Persistence is the temperamental trait that plays a major role in power struggles. Spirited kids need, want, and seek power. But like Jenna, we can learn to choose our battles wisely. We don't have to fight every day. At thirteen months Katlin was already demonstrating her drive and goal orientation. By recognizing it, we can teach her to channel her persistence appropriately—to use it as an asset rather than a weapon.

USING WORDS

Persistence is actually an admirable trait. Martin Luther King and the Wright brothers were very persistent individuals. Spirited kids need to hear from us that we appreciate and value their persistence.

"I used to go crazy," Leta told me during an interview. "Whenever I would tell my daughter to do something she would insist on doing it her way. It wasn't until I took a look at my own temperament that I realized I was persistent too. It's true there have been times my persistence has gotten me into trouble but for the most part it really has been an asset for me. Now when she says she wants something different at least I can listen without going nuts. I don't want to discourage her determination."

Look at your labels. The words you use to describe persistence. Do they help your child understand and feel good about it? Do they sound like these that I've collected from other parents?

You really stick to things that interest you.

You are committed and decisive.

You *know* what you want.

You're assertive.

Your friends will never talk you into trouble unless you want it.

You are independent and capable.

When spirited children are comfortable with their persistence, they are more willing to work with us. It is our task to encourage their persistence and at the same time teach them to respect us, others, and the world around them. For us it is a matter of learning to recognize when to say no clearly and when yes is a very acceptable and healthy answer.

GOOD PARENTS DO SAY YES

A key to stopping the battles with our spirited kids is to stop ourselves from automatically saying "No, you won't" to them instead of looking for ways to say "Yes, you may." Every time we say no, we can expect a battle. It may be a battle we don't need to fight.

LOOK FOR YES

When spirited kids get frustrated and angry, stuck on one issue or solution, we are frequently advised to ignore them or to try to distract them. These techniques often work with other kids but persistent kids won't let you ignore them. They'll just scream louder and longer until you can't stand it anymore. They also are not easily distracted. They know what they want and they're not about to give up on it until they've got it or found something better. What does work is letting them know you are listening, doing your best to understand what is important to them.

Next time your child starts to lose it, say to her, "I am listening. I am trying to understand what you need or want." This simple phrase, "I am listening," can help her to open herself to other alternatives. It can also help you to change an entrenched pattern of battle with your child because your willingness to communicate and work together is so evident.

It's important to listen for the purpose of *understanding*. Most of us have been taught to listen for weaknesses—the points where we can jump in and nail our adversary to the wall. Listening for understanding requires that we stop everything else that we're doing and think about what our children are saying. It does not mean looking for an opening for ourselves or thinking about what we will say next. When you are upset yourself, you may have to go back to the "keeping-our-cool" techniques explained in chapter 6, and say to your child, "Wait. I have to have a minute for myself before I can really listen to you." Then step back, take a breath, and cool yourself down.

Once you are calm, you can say to your child, "I am listening. I am trying to understand." The problem, of course, is how are you going to respond? Do you give in or do you hang tough? Fortunately, there is another way to respond—a method called negotiation.

NEGOTIATION

In *Getting to Yes, Negotiating Agreement without Giving In,* Roger Fisher and William Ury defined negotiation as "a back and forth communication designed to reach an agreement when you and the other side have some interests that are shared and others that are opposed."

An interesting concept but difficult to imagine working in a family. Most of us have had the experience of being told that back-and-forth communication meant talking back to our parents. A taboo behavior on our part. Reaching agreement was not an obvious goal. If Dad said do it, we were supposed to do it whether we agreed or not. The reason is that in the past we were aware of only two ways to negotiate: soft, you win, or hard, I win.

Fortunately, there is another way to negotiate. A method that doesn't lock us into power struggles designed to determine a winner and a loser. Fisher and Ury call it "principled negotiation." Principled negotiation focuses not on what each side says it will or won't do, but on finding common interests and solutions. It allows us to develop a relationship with our children that fosters a sense of teamwork: two individuals working together, respecting one another, and finding solutions that allow both a sense of dignity and personal power. This is the kind of relationship that can last us a lifetime.

Fisher and Ury don't tell us how to teach negotiation skills to spirited kids, so I've had to adapt their steps. My adaptation uses an acronym and is called "Looking for PIECE" (peace)!

POSITION

During a class on avoiding power struggles, I asked the parents to think back to the last time they argued with their kids. "What did you fight about?" I asked. It was an easy question. Their answers were immediate.

"Yesterday at lunch," Tom said, "I asked Ross if he wanted apple juice or milk. His answer was, 'I want pop.' "

"Lunch was our battleground too," Sherry added. "I told my six-year-old to sit down for lunch. She insisted she wasn't hungry and wanted to go to her friend's house."

When you ask your child if he wants apple juice or milk for lunch and he replies, "I want pop," each of you has taken a position—apple juice and milk versus pop. Positions can be anything—"I'm going to" versus "I won't let you," "I want to go visit a friend" versus "You'll sit here and have lunch." These are positions that slam us into corners every time. Like two boxers in the ring we can almost hear a gong ringing in our heads, marking the beginning of the fight. The question hangs in the air: Who will win and who will lose?

The challenge is to get out of our corners and find a solution that is acceptable to both of us. To focus on our common interests rather than on our positions.

INTERESTS

Every time you and your child lock into a position there is a reason: an interest or need you are trying to meet. To resolve our differences we have to clarify those interests.

Asking why can help you find the interests. In class I asked Tom why he thought Ross wanted pop for lunch.

"Maybe because I hid pop in my coffee cup." He laughed. The group chuckled with him—we'd all tried that a few times.

"What other reasons might he have had?" I asked the group, just to be sure we had explored all of the possible interests.

"Maybe he's sick of milk and apple juice," Mike suggested.

"My daughter likes ice cubes," Charlotte said. "She wants pop so she can get the ice cubes."

I asked a similar question of Sherry. "Why do you think your daughter wanted to skip lunch and go to a friend's house?"

"She'd been playing alone all morning," Sherry answered. "She's an extravert and I'm sure she was ready to recharge."

"What other reasons could there be?" I asked.

"Maybe she wasn't hungry," Charlotte offered.

Whatever the interest it's important to do our best to find it. Ask your child directly, why she wants to visit a friend or why he wants pop. If he's too young to answer you, you may have to guess by asking questions like: "Are you saying you want pop because Dad has pop?" and "Are you saying you want pop because you're sick of milk and apple juice?" Even a two-year-old will begin to realize that you are trying to listen and understand what it is that she wants. Her tension will diminish as you try.

It takes two to lock into positions and it takes two to unlock. Your interest is just as important as your child's. "Why did you want Ross to have milk or apple juice?" I asked Tom.

"Because that was the only thing left in the refrigerator," he responded.

"What other reasons might we have?" I asked the group.

"Good nutrition," Kathy offered.

"How about you, Sherry?" I asked. "Why did you want your daughter to eat lunch?"

"Because she goes crazy if she doesn't eat," she answered. "And anyway, I didn't want to be making lunch again at two o'clock."

Stating your interest helps you to clarify it for yourself. When you begin to look at why both of you are in your positions, you will realize there is a reason other than determining a winner or a loser. That awareness will help you move to an acceptable solution.

While finding interests isn't easy, especially when your kids are young and not able to explain themselves well, you are teaching a very important skill. You are helping your spirited children learn to express their needs and wants clearly with words rather than by pushing, shoving, screaming, and crying.

Once you have clarified your interests you can begin working toward a solution that is acceptable to you. But first you need to check if there are any expectations or rules that need to be considered.

EXPECTATIONS

"What rules or expectations need to be considered in these situations?" I asked the group.

"Lunch is eaten at noon," Sherry offered.

"Pop has no nutritional value," Tom said.

Before we can negotiate a solution with our kids we have to check the existing expectations and rules. Sometimes expectations like lunch is served at noon are somewhat arbitrary and could be negotiated. Others, however, such as no kids under seventeen allowed at an R-rated movie, are firmly set and must be considered. Review with your child the existing expectations and rules before you move on to finding a solution that is agreeable to both of you. Sometimes the answer will be provided by the rules and you won't have to look any further. That's what happened with this father and son.

"I'm going to do it and you can't stop me!" The words rang out as a battle cry, catching my attention as I walked out of church. Father and son stood poised. Son with a glint in his eye, shoulders squared and feet dancing. He was ready. Dad towered over him, blond hair glistening in the sunlight, a twist at the corner of his mouth gave away a slight smile.

"Why do you want to make this into a power struggle," he asked.

The son faltered for a moment, having expected a much different response.

"Because I want to watch *Roller Games,* and I'm going to," he demanded.

"What do you think is the most educational part of that show?" The dad inquired. "When they hit the ten-foot wall of death or leap the three-foot jump? Maybe it's the bikini-clad cheerleaders."

The son couldn't conceal the embarrassed smile creeping across his cheeks. His expression seemed to say, how the heck did his dad know what was in that show? He was off guard now, not sure how to come back. He was doing his best to pull his dad into the ring but Dad wouldn't come.

The son made several more feeble attempts, but the hassle fizzled, diffused by his father's humorous reminder of their family's expectations and rules: our family watches television shows with educational value. Their established family rules stopped the fight and offered the solution.

Before you begin exploring possible solutions with your child, check the existing rules or expectations. Do they provide the answer? If the rules and expectations don't provide the answer, you and your child will have to come up with your own. This isn't always easy with a persistent child who tends to lock in to his position

CONSENSUS

It takes time for spirited kids to unlock and move out of their positions. They need to hear from us, "You are very smart and creative. You can be a good problem solver. You can find another solution." Most power struggles happen when we're in a rush and we aren't allowing time to unlock. Whether we're in the middle of a store hassling over a grocery cart or in our front hallway fighting about mittens and boots, we have to stop when our kids lock into position, take a deep breath, and give them time to let go. Unlocking takes time.

You can also actively teach your child how to unlock by your own example. When you plan to go to the store and are stopped by a downpour, say out loud, "I wanted to go to the store right now, but it's raining too hard. I'll get soaked. I'll have to think of something else. That's hard for me to do. I really wanted to go right now." Whatever the situation, when you unlock show your child how you do it.

Brainstorming helps you to find "yes." When your child has had time to unlock, you're ready to look at other possible solutions. The rule for brainstorming is anything goes. At this point nothing is evaluated, put down, thrown out, or ridiculed. You can come up with any solution.

I divided my class into two small groups, one to help Tom and Ross find an acceptable solution and one for Sherry and her daughter.

Tom's group returned with these suggestions:

Have milk or juice for lunch and pop with popcorn for a snack.

Put ice cubes in the juice and pretend it's pop.

Tom can drink milk with his lunch too, and save his pop for later, when Ross is outside.

Sherry's group suggested:

Skip lunch.

Pack a bag lunch and let her take it to the friend's house.

Invite the friend to lunch.

Make lunch at two o'clock.

After reviewing the lists, I asked Tom and Sherry to pick the solution they thought would be most acceptable to their child and to them. Tom chose to put ice cubes in the juice, because that's what he thought Ross really wanted. Sherry selected inviting the friend to lunch or packing the bag lunch, whichever her daughter would prefer.

Brainstorming together with your child allows you to see that there are a multitude of solutions available to you. Solutions that will feel good to both of you. The younger the child the more you'll be developing the solutions. The older the child, the more you'll be stepping back and letting him use his creative powers to solve the problem.

As you look for solutions feel free to be imaginative. Spirited kids are incredibly creative. One parent told me she had stopped a preschooler's demands for McDonald's french fries, simply by handing the child a pretend packet and munching loudly. Another parent acted out driving in a car when his toddler wanted a car ride. Spirited kids can learn to use that wonderful imagination to help them be very good problem solvers.

EVALUATE

What if the solution you came up with doesn't work, or if after you try it you or your child decide that it isn't acceptable? Protect everyone's interest by agreeing to evaluate your solution at a later time. Obviously some solutions don't need evaluating—like ice cubes in a glass of apple juice—but perhaps you've agreed that one hour of television each day is acceptable. It isn't until later that your child realizes that the one-hour limit forces him to turn off the Notre Dame football game at half time, or you realize he is selecting a show to watch that is unacceptable to you. A scheduled evaluation time allows both of you to air your grievances and concerns and come up with a more acceptable solution. It also opens both of you to more creative solutions, because you know that you will have an opportunity to change your mind later if you need it.

It is not abdicating our parental authority to sometimes say yes and to allow our spirited children to try a new idea or come up with the solution to a problem. In fact, realizing that they are good problem solvers is a major breakthrough for persistent kids. It helps them to stop the struggles before they ever start.

Recently, Pat, a dad from one my classes, told me his seven-year-old daughter created a snowman in their front yard. She came running into the house to get a carrot for the nose only to find there weren't any carrots in the refrigerator.

"In the past," Pat told me, "this would have been a blowout. She would have wanted a carrot and insisted that I go to the store and get one, whether I wanted to or not. Yesterday, she just looked up from the refrigerator and said, 'I'll have to be a good problem solver.' Then she grabbed a stalk of celery and headed out the door. Teaching her how to problem solve has been a miracle!"

Think back to the fights you've had recently with your spirited child. Decide which ones could have been eliminated by looking for yes. Next time you run into a similar situation be ready to begin your child's lesson in negotiation.

WHEN YOUR CHILD DOESN'T TALK YET

Getting to yes takes communication skills that infants and toddlers don't have, but they still have very strong ideas of their own. Parenting the spirited toddler and infant is exhausting. The fewer times you have to get up and go after your avid explorer or stop your determined-to-try kid, the more energy you save and the fewer battles you wage. For this age group there is another way to say yes.

SAY YES WITH YOUR ENVIRONMENT

Walk into a good early childhood classroom and you'll find a *planned* "yes environment." There are chairs kids can get on and off by themselves. There are "toddler tables" where there are no chairs, the kids just sit on the floor or stand leaning against the table, learning how to use a table before they're expected to use a chair as well. There are shelves and hooks at heights children can reach without assistance. There are little cups that are easy to handle for their juice. Safe scissors, paper, crayons, and other supplies are out and available at all times. A trampoline, rocking boat, or jungle gym is ready for the wild leaps and jumps of the energetic kid. There are push and ride toys. Shatterproof mirrors hang horizontally an inch off the floor instead of vertically so even very young babies can raise their heads and watch themselves. Everything in the room says, "Show me what you can do, all by yourself," "Explore," "Learn," and "Feel self-sufficient and capable." This is a yes environment. The adults have *chosen* what materials and furniture to have available for the children, thus freeing up their time to talk with the kids, to teach them, rather than reprimanding or fighting with them.

We can't make our homes into early childhood classrooms and we wouldn't want to, but we can look around our home and plan for a yes environment that fosters peace. Is your home a good place for kids to live or is it a battlefield pitting parents against determined, energetic explorers? Are there cupboards available for little investigators? Or is it a struggle every time your toddler heads for the kitchen? Is there somewhere to jump, other than the couch? Where are the books? Are they easy to grab? Where is the television or stereo? Are they begging to have their knobs turned and wires pulled? Where are the coat hooks? Can a child get her sweater down without assistance? How big are the drinking glasses and where are they stored? Are they easy for a child to get to and handle without spills?

The more places in your home that are child-safe and manageable, the less you'll have to fight with your tenacious child about "getting out and staying out" of things and places. Yes, kids do need to learn to respect the things of others, but during the early years the need to explore is stronger than their ability to stop themselves. By saying yes with your environment you are working with your child's persistence instead of against it. You are appreciating and enjoying her inquisitiveness and her resolve and are avoiding a fight that doesn't need to happen. This isn't giving in. This is *planning for peace.*

WORKING TOGETHER

Looking for yes is a lot of work and takes time. Time you probably feel you don't have. It's also very unlikely that your parents ever looked for yes with you. As a result you may be wondering, why should you?

Marty, the father of two, was raised in a very strict, authoritarian family. "If Dad said jump, you jumped," he told me. "I've had my doubts about looking for yes," he said, staring at me sternly. "In fact, part of me gets angry just thinking about it. Last Saturday morning, my wife and I wanted to go downtown together and look for a bookcase. The kids had a fit. They didn't want to miss their cartoons. They hate shopping. They didn't want to go. I was furious. Why wouldn't they just obey and get in the car without a fight? I was losing it so my wife took over.

" 'Dad wants to go and you don't,' she said. 'What could we do?'

" 'How about calling the neighbors?' the older one piped in. 'You took care of their kids last week, maybe we can stay with them and you and Dad can have a date.'

" 'Yeah,' the younger one said, 'let's do it.'

"At first I was reluctant to bother the neighbors, and I'd been thinking that this would be a nice family time together. I relented, however, when I realized we *had* watched their kids and it obviously was not going to be a 'nice' time together. The kids called, the neighbors agreed, and my wife and I took off on our own.

"It was peaceful having just the two us during the drive, yet there was a part of me that was still frustrated. It was my wife that pointed out the fact that most of the time, they did come with us and actually with very little hassle. It was also she who said, 'We want to raise adults who can speak up for their own needs, solve problems, and sometimes question authority.'

"That wasn't how I was raised, of course, but I've been working years to try and speak up for what I need and have the guts to stand up for myself sometimes. It just isn't easy to parent this way when I wasn't raised that way.

"I calmed down a little, but then I thought of the twenty minutes it took to come up with this solution. I got mad all over again. It seemed like twenty minutes of wasted time. My weekends are precious to me. I don't want to spend them negotiating with the kids.

"I was still steamed when we got home, but the kids were in a great mood when we picked them up. We had to run the oldest to his basketball game and then decided to look a couple of more places for bookcases. They went along, no complaints. In fact they seemed to enjoy themselves. Even the next day it paid off. I had suggested a family walk.

"The oldest jumped in with, 'We never get to do what we want!'

" 'Wait a minute. What about yesterday!' I reminded him.

" 'Oh, well,' he stuttered, and put on his coat.

"It was a lovely family walk. That night I figured out that our twenty minutes spent finding yes had allowed the morning to pass peacefully. Everyone was happy. Everyone had been listened to and had gotten to do what he or she wanted. The goodwill it created carried into the afternoon with the basketball game and the shopping trip. There had been no hassle. Negotiation wasn't necessary. The next day it stopped a potential power struggle over a family walk. In fact that twenty minutes spent on Saturday morning had carried over for a good twenty-four hours of harmony. Twenty minutes out of twenty-four hours—I'd call that a very good investment!"

I can't guarantee that every search for yes will buy twenty-four hours of harmony, but it is a good investment. Looking for yes teaches our persistent spirited children to consider the needs of others, to solve problems amicably, and to make decisions that everyone can live with. It builds the foundation for a healthy relationship. A relationship that can survive adolescence and more.

WHEN YOU'RE PERSISTENT TOO

Like Marty, many of us find looking for yes very difficult. It may be because of the way we were raised, or it could be because we're persistent too. We lock in as strongly and as adamantly as our kids.

"Oh, yeah, am I persistent!" Claudia explained during our group discussion. "Sammy and I are like two bulls with horns locked. My hot button is when he tells me I'm wrong! That one *really* sets me off.

"Yesterday afternoon, Sammy was working on a letter. Sarah, our eight-year-old, was doing spelling words and needed my help. They were both driving me crazy. Sam demanded to know how to spell *neighbor*. '*N-e-i*,' I said.

" 'No, it's *n-a*,' he insisted.

"I said, 'it's *n-e-i*.'

" 'No, it's *n-a*,' he maintained.

"It made me angry. He'd asked me a question and now was telling me my answer was wrong. I was in no mood for this kind of treatment.

" 'If you don't want to know the right answer then don't ask me,' I snapped. He was so frustrated that he tore up the letter he'd been working so hard on. It wasn't until later that I realized that he had already written *n-a* on his sheet before he asked me the question. If the right answer was *n-e-i*, he had a mistake on his paper that couldn't be erased. I hadn't bothered to find out why he was disagreeing with me or why he was so frustrated with my answer. I didn't want to take the time. Anyway, I was busy with his sister who was moaning in my face.

"It so happened that we visited friends that night. I overheard the five-year-old tell his sister that a red block was black.

" 'It's red,' she responded.

" 'It's black,' he claimed.

"I couldn't help remembering a very similar conversation held just a few hours earlier. This one, however, had a less frustrating ending. The sister sighed, looked at him, and replied, 'You certainly have a creative way of looking at things.'

"I couldn't believe I had heard a seven-year-old respond in this way. She knew it was red and, quite frankly, so did he, but at that point in time he wanted it to be black. Her response said, 'You're creative,' not 'You're wrong.' Yet she knew that she was not wrong either. They both just walked away from it."

Persistent kids have persistent parents. Sometimes to avoid a power struggle with our kids, we are the ones who have to unlock. We must realize there doesn't have to be a battle. We don't have to be frustrated. There's just two strong, opinionated people with very different perceptions of the same situation. The world needs people of conviction.

GETTING OTHERS TO YES

The concept of looking for yes is a relatively new one. Most of us are much more familiar with the I-win/you-lose style of negotiating. It's a different world for which we are preparing our children. A world in which communication and problem-solving skills are critical to survival. Many people are unable to see the link between looking for yes with a persistent child and teaching important life skills. They don't realize that we are *intentionally* deciding when and how we will involve our children in the process. As a result, they criticize our efforts when we need their help and support the most.

When we look for yes with our children we need to let others know we are not abdicating our parental authority. We are recognizing our children's persistence and teaching them how to use it well.

In the grocery store, I overheard two grandmothers sharing grandchildren tales. One of them had a future star athlete, a spirited two-year-old who could climb anything. His father had let him climb a stepladder in the backyard. The grandmother said, "I almost died. He just let him do it. Stood right there and watched him go up, never said a word. He's going to kill himself and it's going to be at *my* house!"

It's very likely that the father of our future star athlete had *chosen* to say yes with his agile two-year-old. He had made the decision to let the child try, with his support. Grandma didn't understand. She thought the dad was being negligent because she knew most two-year-olds couldn't accomplish this feat safely. It frightened her and so she criticized the dad rather than encouraging his efforts. She needed the dad to tell her what he was doing, to share with her his delight in his son's determination and ability. To get her support he had to let her know that he was paying full attention as he stood there watching, encouraging his son's drive and building a healthy sense of self-esteem.

If your spirited child is a girl, teaching others what you are doing is even more important. Our culture is not as accepting of assertive, persevering little girls as it is of boys. We have to help others see the value and strengths of our spirited daughters.

FEELING GOOD ABOUT PERSISTENCE

Saying yes leads to a strong will. Whether it's buying a pint-size pitcher so your two-year-old can pour her own juice, allowing your three-year-old to choose his own outfit for nursery school, or spending twenty minutes with your five-year-old trying to figure out a mutually agreeable solution, you can win cooperation and avoid a power struggle by looking for ways to say yes.

If you're not sure if you should be looking for yes or saying no, ask yourself, "Is this a skill she'll need in life?" and "If I stay close and support her will she be safe?" If the answers are yes then let her try.

Kids can amaze you with their abilities and ingenuity. Don't be afraid to be flexible, to know when to say, "I didn't think you could do that, but I guess you can." Look for ways to encourage that strong will. Think carefully before you stop them from trying. Even if it takes longer, you have eliminated one fight in the day and fostered a sense of responsibility—an I-can-do attitude, which is so important in life.

GOOD PARENTS DO SAY NO

Saying yes is essential to living in harmony with our spirited children and teaching them good problem-solving skills, but just as important as our yes is our very clear no.

Spirited kids more than other children need confident parents—parents who are willing to be just as persistent and adamant as their strong-willed children when it comes to teaching the basic rules and values in our lives. They need parents who are willing to say, "I will not let you . . .," "I will stop you . . .," "The rule is . . .," and "I hear you, but . . ." Spirited kids need parents who are willing to go into battle when it is called for. It isn't easy.

CLARIFY YOUR RULES

Spirited kids are our future politicians, lawyers, salespeople, and agents of change. If we don't want to spend our time arguing with them every day, we have to be sure our basic ground rules are very clear.

Rules describe what behavior you expect. They usually tell us how to be safe, to treat ourselves and others respectfully and how to take care of the world around us. Author Robert Fulghum, in his book of the same name, says all he really needed to know, he learned in kindergarten.

Share everything.

Play fair.

Don't hit people.

Put things back where you found them.

Clean up your own mess.

Don't take things that aren't yours.

Say you're sorry when you hurt somebody.

Wash your hands before you eat.

Flush.

Warm cookies and cold milk are good for you.

Live a balanced life. . . .

Take a nap every afternoon.

When you go out into the world, watch out for traffic, hold hands, and stick together.

Be aware of wonder. . . .

Goldfish and hamsters and white mice and even the little seed in the Styrofoam cup—they all die. So do we.

. . . LOOK.

I suspect your family may be able to delete or add a few, but the most important point is there aren't too many. Spirited kids test every single rule. "Are you sure it's a rule?" they seem to question. "Is it true *every time*? Are you really going to insist I follow it? Do you follow it too?" Rules are your battle lines. The fights you are willing to face. The things that are so important to you that you are willing to dig your feet in and be as persistent as your spirited child.

When you are very clear about what your rules are and why you have them you will feel confident. When you insist that your three-year-old take a nap or at least have a rest period, you don't have to question yourself when he starts to put up a fuss. You know it's important for him and for you. So important that you are willing to take the time to lay down with him and show him how it's done! When you get in the car and strap your child's protesting little body into the car seat, you don't have to worry about wounding her spirit. You know it is the law. It protects her and you will wear your belt too. When you insist that your eight-year-old finish her homework before she watches television, you know it is critical to her education. You feel confident saying no and insisting that the rule is followed. It's worth the effort it will take.

Ada Alden, parent educator and mother of two adult daughters, is emphatic. "Limits are a must. Kids need reassurance that they are loved. If they don't have limits they don't feel loved and they'll look for it somewhere else. Self-reliance comes about after establishing a sense of personal security. Kids have to know these are the 'yeses' and these are the 'noes,' I can count on them. Spirited kids need it even more."

MAKE YOUR RULES CLEAR AND PRECISE

Spirited kids have the ability to always find the exception to the rule. That's why it is important that your rules are very clear and precise. If they aren't, you'll find yourself fighting all of the time, like Peggy.

"The rule in our house is that TV watching is limited. We were constantly fighting about it. I'd tell the kids to turn off the television and they'd fuss and fume that they had just started watching or they hadn't watched very much. It wasn't until we talked about it in class that I realized that our rule wasn't clear. What was too much television watching? How much could they watch? I went home and said, 'This is the rule: one hour of television watching a day, maximum. You can check the television guide and decide what you want to watch.' They had a fit and reminded me that if they watched a sports event or movie one hour wasn't enough, so I agreed that on Saturday and Sunday the limit could be two hours. They moaned, but the television set did go off. I'm sure it helped, too, that they were included in deciding on the final rule. Now when they are watching, I simply make it clear with them that this is their choice for the hour. If they say yes, they watch it, if they say no, they turn off the television themselves knowing they are using up their limit on trash. The fights have stopped. Even with Steven who never gives up!"

Write down your rules. Are they clear and precise? What time is bedtime? What toys are shared? What toys don't have to be shared? Where can your child ride her bike? Ask your kids what they think the rules are in your house. Look at them together and give them a precision tune-up if they need it.

BE CONSISTENT

Spirited kids go crazy if the rules keep changing or aren't enforced every time. You'll notice that Fulghum's rules fit whether you're two or ninety-two. They stay the same. It's true we have some rules that change as a child becomes more skilled, but it is critical that over time our rules are stable and are consistently enforced. What is a rule today must also be one tomorrow. If you're willing to go after them and stop them on Saturday, you must also be willing to do it on Monday.

Alden quips, "Consistency is like flossing your teeth. You have to do it every day. Flossing like crazy on weekends doesn't work."

When your rules are consistently enforced, even the most persistent of kids will learn that this is not a battle to fight. But they have to hear the message over and over again!

USE A FIRM VOICE

A firm voice is not harsh or loud. It is simply a voice of conviction—a voice that states clearly, "The rule is . . . . I will help you follow the rule." The tone communicates to your spirited child that you are committed and willing to get up and enforce this rule every time.

If you have had a hard time enforcing rules with your determined child, practice. Stand in front of a mirror. Throw back your shoulders, raise your head, look square into the reflection of your eyes, and in a sure voice say out loud, "I am a confident parent. I know what I am doing." If you keep saying it, pretty soon you'll start believing it and so will your child.

DON'T BE AFRAID TO STOP THEM

Spirited kids like to make very sure the limits stand firm. As a result, they test more than other kids. This is not a figment of our imagination. In a study conducted by Carolyn Lee of Indiana State University and John Bates of Indiana University, children rated by their mothers as temperamentally difficult (spirited) at twenty-four months were found to approach "mild trouble" more frequently than children perceived as temperamentally easy. We have to work harder to enforce our rules. It's tempting to just give up.

I'll never forget the day I was called on the carpet by a classroom teacher. She was livid. Seems one of the kids in her classroom had decided all the rules were for the other kids, not for him. When she called his parents, asking for suggestions of how to work with him, they responded, "He's spirited. He can't help it."

"They tell me, *you* told them he was spirited," she snapped, "so I'm calling you! What do you have to say?"

"Not guilty," I responded quickly. Being spirited is not a license to be a jerk. Understanding spirited children helps us to see their strengths and figure out how to work with them, and how to teach them to behave appropriately without destroying their spirit. But it is *not* an excuse for bad behavior. It is not an exemption from the rules. We can accept the active child, understand that he has a need to move, but still stop him from jumping over the baby's head.

When our kid is flooding the bathroom, throwing cereal around the kitchen, hitting his brother or sister, unrolling the toilet paper and stuffing it down the sink, or whatever he is doing that is breaking our rules, he has to be stopped. It's our job to do it even if we are tired, feeding the baby, or talking to a friend on the phone. To stop misbehavior we have to go after him, bend down, touch him, and say, "Stop," not harshly, not loudly, but firmly. *Stop* seems to be a more effective word than *no*. *No* begs for an argument from a persistent child. *Stop* says it all: quit, cease, stand still, halt, and cut it out! Then you can redirect him to an appropriate activity.

But what if they don't stop? What if they sputter and stomp, scream and wail? Spirited kids are intense and persistent. They don't like to be stopped. Our insistence that they stop has to be as strong as their protests. Our message has to be clear. "I do not fear your anger. I am your parent. I will help you stop. I am committed to this rule."

For a young child stopping her may mean picking her up and removing her. It may mean placing a hand across her arm to prevent her from hitting or throwing things. Toddlers and older kids may need us to give them a choice of other activities to do. If necessary, we may have to take them to another activity and get them started. It must be very clear to our spirited children that when they break the rules, our family's guidelines for appropriate behavior, we will stop them—*every time.*

CONSEQUENCES THAT WORK

When Lou Holtz, Notre Dame football coach, first arrived at Notre Dame, there was a very talented, young quarterback on the team. After reviewing the previous season's statistics, however, Holtz noted that the quarterback had thrown many interceptions. He called the young quarterback into his office. "You're a great athlete," he told him. "And you can expect to continue as the starting quarterback. However, you're not going to throw more than seven interceptions next year."

The young quarterback gave Holtz a puzzled look and asked, "How do you know that?"

"Because," Holtz drawled, "after your seventh, you'll be sitting on the bench next to me."

Holtz clarified his rules and expectations and established clear consequences if those standards weren't met. There are times when consequences are a critical tool for parents of spirited kids. A consequence is a logical repercussion that results from one's own behavior. Spirited kids need to know that if they don't stop, if they don't follow the rule, there will be a consequence.

What's an appropriate consequence? In *The Parent's Handbook: Systematic Training for Effective Parenting,* by Don Dinkmeyer and Gary D. McKay, good consequences are described as natural or logical. Natural consequences are innate. If you don't wear your mittens your hands get cold. This works for older kids who can understand the connection between cold hands and no mittens. It isn't effective with a locked-in two-year-old who doesn't have the faintest idea that the lack of mittens has something to do with the pain in his hands; however, natural consequences are a good place to start to make sure your consequence fits the crime.

Logical consequences are related to the crime. If you fight with your brother while cleaning your room, you'll clean it by yourself next time. If you don't come home on time you won't be allowed to play at the park next time. The consequence fits the crime.

Kids can help you come up with the consequences just as they can come up with the rules. Ask your child what should the consequence be if someone hits during a fight? What should the consequence be if someone doesn't stop when Mom and Dad ask them to? Together come up with consequences that are acceptable to everyone. To make sure your consequences don't backfire on you remember these three guidelines.

1. It is much easier to take something away from a child, such as the privilege of watching television, than it is to make them do something, such as vacuuming the living room.

2. Make sure it is the child who suffers from the consequence and not you. Take away a Big Wheel from the active child, and it's you that goes crazy with an energetic kid running around the house. Restrict her to the house for a day, and it's you that has to listen to her moan and groan. Trying to stop her only gets you into more hassles.

3. Set up the consequences when you are calm. Spirited kids can make us so mad that when we do slap on a spontaneous consequence it may be out of line much more than the misbehavior warrants or one that we really can't implement. If you do use a consequence make sure you follow through on it. If you realize you overdid it, back off and explain to your child that you lost your cool and are changing the consequence.

Frequently a simple reminder of consequences is enough to stop inappropriate behavior. You can say to your child, "Remember, if you don't stop fighting with your brother you will clean the room by yourself."

The problem with consequences is that punishment is the least effective means of getting good behavior. The most effective way is teaching appropriate skills and reinforcing your child when she uses them. In families that are working well with their spirited kids, consequences are employed as infrequently as once a month. Instead they're using all the preventive techniques. Lou Holtz's quarterback didn't sit on the bench that year. He threw only six interceptions. Why? Because the young man was willing to practice and Holtz was willing to provide the coaching support he needed to be successful.

It is very important that you establish the consequences for inappropriate behavior in your family so you know they are there when you need them. But don't rely on them as your only means of control. Instead look for ways to help your child be more successful in following the rules next time.

"Carl came home late again last night," Betty told the other parents in her group, "so today he had to play at home. But I sat down with him and said, 'Carl, when you're late I get worried. What can we do to help you remember to come home on time?'

"He looked at me and then said, 'How about if I wear the watch Grandma gave me. It has an alarm on it. If you teach me how to set it, I can use it to remind myself to come home.'

"Can you believe it? He thought of that all by himself!"

Consequences are an important tool for stopping the persistent spirited child. Use them as needed but then look for ways to help your child be more successful next time.

FINDING THE BALANCE

Spirited kids don't like it when we say no. The intensity and duration of their reaction can invade us, forcing us to question our own judgment. Finding a balance of control can be very difficult. We are forced to be confident when we may not feel confident, to walk a battle line that is not clearly marked. When we say no, we may wonder if we are wounding their spirit or misusing our parental authority. How do we know if we are over-controlling? Battling more than we should be? How do we know if we're undercontrolling? Letting our spirited child take control? Will we know when we have found balanced control?

I have learned from other parents that there are signs that will tell you when you have found that balance of control. You can look for them.

OVERCONTROL MAKES US FEEL LIKE A DRILL SERGEANT

Audrey's hands danced in front of her face as she talked to the group, adding rhythm and expression to her words. "I know I am overcontrolling," she said, "when I hear myself barking out reprimands to my son. Stop that! Watch out! Move over here. Get out of the way. Be careful. Don't touch that. It creates a tension that electrifies our home. As though each nerve ending were exposed. To protect himself, he goes 'mother deaf' and ignores everything I say, and if he doesn't ignore me, he fights with me."

Bob nodded as Audrey spoke. "I won't let him do anything," he added. "When I am overcontrolling I always think I can do it better. I won't take the time to let him zip his own coat. I do it because I can do it faster. The other day, I took a paintbrush out of his hand at the easel and said, 'Here, let me show you, I can do it better.' His eyes filled with tears, and he said, 'I don't want you to be part of our family any more.' "

"I know I need to back off when I realize I'm yelling at him for doing something that would be all right if I were feeling better," Paul explained. "It's the days when everything bothers me. Nothing feels good. I'm a lousy dad and he's a crummy kid."

"I know I'm not saying yes enough," Deb admitted, "when I realize I've said no without even really listening to him, or I interrupt him before he can finish his sentence."

If you are feeling like a drill sergeant or are filled with guilt because you are constantly dragged into battles and hassles with your persistent child, it may be a sign that you need to put more yeses into your relationship. Step back and ask yourself if you are allowing your child to practice making decisions or to complete tasks he is capable of doing. Are you encouraging him to say "I can do it," and "I've got a great idea." Are you letting him know you respect and value persistence?

UNDERCONTROL MAKES US FEEL RESENTFUL

"What does undercontrol feel like?" I asked the same group of parents. The answers were slow to come.

Everything about Sarah held back. She always slipped way back into her chair and hid her body behind crossed arms. When it came to setting clear limits and rules for her son David, she found herself feeling unsure.

"I don't want to stifle him," she said. "I thought, maybe this is what boys are like. Maybe this is good for him. My mother was ill when I was growing up and my father traveled all of the time. No one ever set limits for me. I don't know what limits feel like. I can walk right into a brick wall and never know it was there until I hit it. David knows it when I'm uncertain and he keeps pushing. I think he's trying to find the bottom line, but I don't know where to put it. Then I get angry because I feel like he's getting away with murder."

"I feel like I'm walking on eggshells all of the time, that I am constantly giving in," Ann replied softly. "When it feels like I'm doing everything, or everybody else in the family is always second to my spirited child, then I know he's out of control."

If you are feeling "invaded" by your child, helpless to stop him, it is very likely that you need to put more noes into your discipline. It's time to review your rules, make sure they are clear to you and your child. Then prepare yourself to enforce them, no matter how much your persistent child protests.

BALANCED CONTROL FEELS LIKE YOU'RE MAKING PROGRESS

Our real goal is to achieve a sense of balanced control, one in which both persistent spirited kids and their parents feel as if they were being listened to and respected. Where the yeses are healthy and the noes are clear.

What does balanced control feel like? This is what other parents say:

> It just feels like everyone is getting what they need without anyone coming out on the short end.

> Everyone seems happy and content.

> People are smiling, you can hear them laughing, they are working together.

It's a fine line we walk to balanced control, but if you listen carefully to your inner feelings you will know what side of the line you are on. If you are feeling like a drill sergeant, know that you need to say yes more often. If you are feeling resentful and out of control, stand in front of your mirror and remind yourself again that you can say no!

If you have experienced a family in which alcoholism, abuse, or a long-term illness has affected relationships, you will have to work harder to listen to your inner feelings. In these family situations, children experience uneven limits. As a result it is harder to find that inner sense of control that tells you what is appropriate and what is not. You can learn to recognize it if you listen very carefully to your feelings.

If you find yourself totally unable to tap into your feelings, it's likely that you have lost touch with them because of the abuse and neglect you have experienced. The feelings are there, but you will need the help and support of a competent professional to help you find them. Get the professional services you need. Both you and your spirited child will benefit.

PERSISTENCE: A SUMMARY

Living with the raw gem of a persistent child is not easy. To tell her no, to thwart her efforts, is to risk her wrath. Even as infants they are incredibly determined and strong. They push where other kids don't push. They demand more than other kids demand. And they never give up. It is nearly impossible to ignore them or distract them.

Persistent spirited children need to hear:

You really stick to things that interest you.

You are committed and decisive.

You are assertive.

You are independent and capable.

Teaching tips:

Teach your child how to find *yes,* to reach a compromise.

Help your child recognize when she is locked in and help her come up with a better or different solution.

Make sure your rules are clear.

Be consistent.

If you are persistent too:

Allow yourself time to unlock.

Recognize that good parents do say yes.

Know that good parents do say no.

Find a balance between overcontrol and undercontrol.

8

SENSITIVITY: UNDERSTANDING HOW THEY FEEL

*How do you deal with a child who can feel the "seams" in
tube socks and refuses to wear them?*
—Colleen, the mother of three

"MY DAUGHTER Nissa wasn't getting her work done at school," Kim told the group. Her brown curls bounced, emphasizing each word. "The teacher had told the kids at the beginning of the year that if they didn't finish their work they would have to stay in the Media Center instead of going out on the playground for recess. Nissa's work kept getting slower and slower. It wasn't long before she was spending every recess period in the Media Center. Finally in frustration I demanded to know why she wasn't finishing her work.

" 'Cause the noise on the playground drives me crazy,' she responded. 'The only way I can get some peace and quiet is to not finish my work!' "

Sensitive spirited kids feel emotions, see sights, hear sounds, and smell odors to a degree that most of us mortals will never know. They are not teasing when they tell us their socks are hurting their feet. They're dead serious when they refuse to eat lunch at school because the other kids make slurping sounds. If, on a Minnesotan November day, you catch them standing in their shirt sleeves at the bus stop it's actually true that they are *hot* rather than defiant. They truly know the difference between brands of applesauce and if you check it out, you'll find out it's a fact that the toilet paper in Perkins smells different from that in McDonald's, just like they told you.

Sensitivity allows the spirited child to form deep attachments and to nurture others. Mother Teresa and other noted humanitarians are blessed with the gift of sensitivity.

Problems occur for sensitive children when they are overwhelmed by the amount of stimulation and emotional stress around them. It can happen easily because within sensitive children emotions and sensations are collected and concentrated. They are soaked up rather than diffused. When this occurs a pressure can build that overpowers their control systems. It is our job to help sensitive children learn to monitor the concentration of stimulation in their bodies and to teach them how to manage their keen sensitivity in a positive and caring way.

CHECK STIMULATION LEVELS

I always tell the parents in my classes that if they ever feel like they are the only parent in the world with a sensitive spirited child, they should drop everything and head for the largest, noisiest, most congested store in their area. There they will find spirited kids dropping like little bombs. Two down in aisle one. Three in aisle four—the candy shelf—and six in aisle seven—the toy department. At first glance it will appear that the explosions are triggered by a denial to buy a candy bar, a desire to push the cart, or some other insignificant issue. The real trigger, however, is hidden in the fluorescent lights, piped-in music, flashing signs, colorful packages, and crush of people that create more stimulation than a sensitive child can endure, especially if his or her energy bank is low.

As the parent of a spirited child, you have to become aware of stimulation cues and recognize the breaking point for your child. The level of stimulation that pushes her beyond her ability to cope.

Sherry and Steve had never realized how sensitive their son Kip was until they started the spirited child classes. As they participated in the discussions they began to understand that too much stimulation was a major reason for his wild behavior. Behavior they could prevent simply by monitoring the level of stimulation to which he was exposed. In class Sherry proudly told us how they had stopped one flare-up before it ever started.

"On Saturday, we took the kids to a huge craft fair," she said. "Admission had cost us twelve dollars. I wasn't two steps in the door before I was struck by the sound of craftspeople yelling, hawking their wares. Splashes of red, orange, purple, and green assaulted my eyes. Dangling lights hung from the ceiling and swung in the air forming patterns on the floor. And the people—there wasn't room to turn around. They were pushing and bumping each other, rubbing up against my arm and back. It made my skin crawl and I'm not spirited. I looked at Kip and realized he would never make it through. The stimulation would drive him crazy. I was so disappointed and frustrated, too. I knew we couldn't get our money back. I took a very long, deep breath, then I pleaded with Steve, 'Please, give me thirty minutes. Can you help him last thirty minutes? I just need thirty minutes!"

Before learning about sensitivity Sherry and Steve had not been as aware of stimulation cues, but they were now. Sherry immediately recognized a potential catastrophe in the making. It was very likely that Kip would start to fuss and fume not because he was naughty but because the stimulation was so penetrating to him.

Monitoring the stimulation level around your child is critical to helping your child learn to manage his sensitivity well. When you are able to read the "cues" that tell you a sensitive child will feel bombarded in this situation, you will know how to respond and be able to avoid a fight. Be especially observant at shopping centers, fairs, parks, beaches, and parties. Anywhere there is a substantial amount of noise, smells, bright lights, and big crowds, your sensitive child is vulnerable.

USING WORDS

Because they had participated in class, Sherry and Steve knew they needed to help Kip understand the impact the crowd and commotion had on him. Kip didn't understand that the irritation and discomfort he felt were caused by the people, the bright lights, and noisy hawkers. He needed to know he wasn't sick. He wasn't weird. He was reacting to the stimulation.

"What did you tell Kip?" I asked them.

Steve responded, "I told him, 'It's pretty crowded in here. There's lots of noise and bright colors. You might start to get that weird feeling inside of you again. Like the one you got when we were at your cousin's birthday party.' I knew he would remember that because he had lost it at the party last week, and we had talked about the 'weird feeling.' Anyway, I told him that if he started to feel that way again, he should let me know and I would help him find a quiet spot where the noise couldn't bother him."

By pointing out the lights, colors, and people, Steve was teaching Kip to recognize the cues necessary to read the stimulation level. Someday, it won't be Sherry realizing that the craft fair may be overstimulating and uncomfortable for Kip. It will be Kip himself.

If your child has been using tears for years to express himself, he doesn't know that words can be more effective. You have to teach him the words that describe the sensations and emotions he experiences and demonstrate for him the power of these words to communicate.

Check your child's vocabulary. Does he know what *scratchy*, *bumpy*, *sticky*, *tight*, *stinky*, *noisy*, or *screechy* mean? Can he tell you when he is sad, lonesome, scared, hot, irritated, or happy? Sensitive kids need to possess in their vocabularies the words that can help them communicate the profound emotions and sensations that they experience.

REDUCE THE STIMULATION

"Sherry took off on her own," Steve continued, "and I strolled through the rows of crafts with Kip. I watched him really carefully, ready to catch the first hint that he was ready to explode. It only took about ten minutes before I noticed he was starting to forget the rules. He was picking up things roughly and jostling people back. I told him, 'I think you're getting the weird feeling,' then I took him by the hand and led him over to the snack bar. It was quiet there. He licked his way through an ice cream cone and settled down, but I didn't trust him to go back near the booths. I knew we'd pushed it as far as we could, so I took him out to the front of the building and just let him run up and down the ramps at the front of the building."

Steve had learned that when the stimulation levels are too high for a child, you need to reduce them if you can. Taking your child to a quiet room, suggesting a walk outside, getting the scratchy, irritating sweater off, using the soothing, calming activities described in chapter 6, or anything else you can do to reduce the stimulation your child is receiving will help.

If your child is three or older let him help you to figure out what he needs. Ask him, "Is it the noise that is bothering you? Then let's find a quiet place. Is it the jacket that is making you hot? Then let's take it off." Teach him how to reduce the stimulation level himself so he feels in control—capable of managing his own sensitivity.

KNOW WHEN TO QUIT

From experience, Sherry knew Kip could probably handle the commotion of the craft fair for about thirty minutes but after that they would be pushing their luck.

"It wasn't long," Steve told us, "before Sherry reappeared, with a lamp in hand ready to head home. It hadn't been the outing we had expected, but in its own way it had been successful. Kip had lasted thirty minutes. There hadn't been any fits—no embarrassing frenzies on the floor. We had worked together and that felt good. I know some day Kip will be able to tell us himself that he has had enough and needs to get out of there."

Mica had sat quietly listening to Sherry and Steve tell their story. As it ended she acknowledged, "You did a great job, but what do you do if you're at someone's house? You can't just leave."

"I've got a great technique for getting out of situations without hurting other people's feelings," Deanne exclaimed. "Whenever we go to a gathering I always let the host or hostess know we have another appointment and will probably have to leave early. I don't tell them the appointment is my tactful 'escape' for my daughter and me. I keep my eye on her. As long as she's doing well I let her play, but the minute I hear her start to get cranky or demanding, I know she's about to blow. That's when I say, 'Time for our appointment. We have to run.' I pick her up and get her out *fast.* She's only sixteen months so it works. I realize when she's older I'm going to have to fill her in to watch for the blowup herself. But for now it's just nice to have people say she's did a nice job and invite us back again. Before my 'mysterious appointments,' we weren't always welcomed back."

If you watch closely you too will realize how draining crowded, stimulating situations are for your sensitive child. It can be frustrating especially if you're having a good time or you're not ready to quit. But recognizing when to pull out is critical to your child's success and your own self-esteem. Leaving with a sour, cranky kid isn't fun. It feels lousy. It is much better to exit while everyone is still in good spirits. That way your child experiences success rather than failure.

Steve nodded in agreement. "On the way home from the craft fair," he said, "we decided that next year, if we wanted to stay longer, we would get a sitter and make it an adult-only event. But for now everyone was happy. We knew when to quit."

CONTROL TELEVISION VIEWING

Craft fairs, stores, and beaches aren't the only places sensitive kids can easily receive too much stimulation. One of the worst offenders is probably sitting in your own home—the television. Spirited kids tend to love watching television. I'm not sure if it is the bright colors, quick movement, or fast pace, but whatever it is they are entranced by it. It is very tempting to allow a spirited child to watch television for a few hours especially on Saturday mornings, because for that period of time he'll be quiet and won't demand anything from you. Beware! You'll pay for it later.

Spirited kids don't just watch Batman, they become Batman. You can almost see their personality changing before your eyes. Turn off the tube and you'll have a maniac tearing around the house. The amount of stimulation they receive overwhelms them and makes them wild and uncooperative. Limit the amount of television your spirited child watches to prevent overstimulation. Her behavior will improve dramatically.

CHECK YOUR EMOTIONAL BAROMETER

Spirited kids are the emotional barometer of any group. Not only do lights, noise, and other sensations lead to overstimulation for them but so does an overabundance of stress. If you are distressed or harried they will be the first to respond. You might not think they are picking up the fears or anxieties that you are coping with, but they do.

Paula, the mother of two, told the group about the stress her family was experiencing and how her spirited son responded.

"I wanted him to go to bed, needed him to go to bed," she said. "It was the night before our daughter's tonsillectomy. I hadn't packed our overnight bag. I was worried about the anesthesia. I needed a break from motherhood to deal with my own feelings. He wouldn't go to bed. Instead he started to cry. I wanted to scream at him, 'Leave me alone. Shut up and go to bed.' I suddenly realized though that I had prepared our daughter, I had made all of the plans for my son's care but I hadn't prepared him. My tenderhearted kid felt our stress. He needed to talk. I lay down on his bed and in the dark we cried together, scared, apprehensive needing to know we were there for each other. Five minutes of closeness and he was asleep."

The nice thing about living with an emotional barometer is that if you listen to your child carefully she will warn you when you are reaching your danger zone. She will let you know when it is time for you to slow down, get rid of some of the junk on your calendar and reach out to others for help. The sensitive child's emotional outbursts are fed by your stress. The only way to reduce the source of stimulation is to reduce your stress—an extra incentive to take care of yourself.

Some people are uncomfortable talking with kids about feelings, especially when the feelings are fear and anxiety. Spirited kids know these feelings and sense them in others. If we don't talk about those feelings, the spirited child may be frightened by them. Scared kids balk. They don't cooperate.

"But Krissa won't talk to me about feelings," Carol groaned. "She won't tell me why she's sad or mad. She just says she doesn't want to talk about it."

"Isn't Krissa an introvert?" I asked.

"Yes, she is," Carol replied.

"Remember introverts only like to share their feelings after they've had a chance to think about them," I said. "Let her know you're available when she is ready to talk, but give her the time and space to think through her emotions before you expect her to share them. If you push she'll only withdraw. Introverts need their space."

Even introverted spirited kids will open up to you, if you let them know you are willing to listen when they are ready to talk. If they need a little help try using books or puppets as a stimulus for conversation. Sometimes it's easier to talk about how "Mr. Pickles" feels than it is for a child to talk about how she feels.

"My problem isn't that Brett won't talk," Mya said. "It's that he is so sensitive. He is devastated when he loses a game. He'll cry for hours if a favorite toy gets broken or he loses a mitten. How do you deal with it when he has too much feeling?"

Sensitivity combines with intensity to make spirited kids very tender-hearted. They form deep and lasting relationships. They have a tremendous sense of justice. They are easily hurt. It is critical that they understand both their sensitivity and intensity, to realize that life may have dumped a bucket of water on their head but they aren't drowning. They will survive.

Talk about their feelings and direct them to soothing, calming activities. Help them to understand that although they cannot control the emotions they experience they can control their responses. It is all right to feel sad and to cry. It is all right to take a time-out. It is perfectly acceptable to go for a run or to read a good book.

DAILY TOUGH TIMES

Sensitivity is a major issue when we try to get spirited kids dressed and fed. It is their fine sense of taste that makes them very selective eaters and their incredible responsiveness to texture that makes dressing a major venture. These daily events, however, are also challenging because of the spirited child's adaptability, perceptiveness, and persistence. In chapters 15 and 16 I've described for you how to successfully negotiate your way through these daily tough times.

WORKING TOGETHER

Helping our children understand and manage their sensitivity means working with our own. "What happens if you're sensitive, too?" I asked the group of parents. They laughed. They moaned and they shuddered.

"Let me tell you it ain't easy!" Megan, said, joking. "The same things that drive Ben crazy bug me too. I can't stand noise and commotion either. I feel myself getting irritated and tingly and his crying only adds to the stimulation. It drives me nuts."

DEALING WITH YOUR OWN SENSITIVITY

If you, too, are sensitive it is very important that you constantly check the stimulation level around you and take note of the discomfort you are feeling. Be sure to fill your energy bank before going into a stimulating situation or immediately afterward because you will feel drained.

Over the years you might have learned to cope with your sensitivity and may not even be aware that you are being annoyed by the excitement around you. But if you listen carefully to your body, you will decipher those warning cues that tell you your own pressure valves are being tested. Focus on those cues. Teach yourself to either quit or lower the stimulation level, while you still have the stamina to not only take care of yourself but your child as well.

"I've learned so much about myself from watching Timmy," Brad remarked. "I never realized how sensitive I was. I just thought I was hyper and I didn't like it. Learning to pick up the stimulation cues for Timmy has really helped *me*! A few weeks ago we went to an ice show. My wife and daughter loved it, but Timmy and I were going crazy. I used to force myself to stay even though it was pure torture. Now, because Timmy needs to get out too, I have an excuse to leave. Boy do I appreciate him. My wife doesn't mind because she understands what's happening and appreciates our sensitivity in other ways."

LOOK AT YOUR MESSAGE BOARD

Sensitive spirited kids need to enjoy and be comfortable with their heightened responses and tender emotions.

"What words do you use to help your children understand their sensitivity?" I asked the group.

"You're tenderhearted," Ben remarked immediately. "I'm tenderhearted myself and I don't like to be called emotional."

"You're loving," Kathy responded. "Zach is so warm and affectionate. He really is a neat kid."

"You care," Bob added.

"You're sensitive," Pat said. "But Alex is more sensitive to light, textures, tastes, and colors than feelings."

"You're selective," John said. "Everything has to feel just right for Katie. You have to cut the tags out of her clothes. The cuffs can't be too tight. The potatoes can't be lumpy. She's going to make a great designer or chef some day."

Duane listened quietly to the group and then asked, "How can I tell my son I'm glad he's sensitive when it makes me flinch inside? I am embarrassed by my sensitivity and my son's too. When I grew up, boys didn't cry and I cried over everything. I have spent years trying to control my sensitivity."

Appreciating sensitivity in our children, especially our male children, sometimes requires throwing out old messages and replacing them with new ones that reflect the value of sensitive, caring individuals. We have to revisit the strengths of sensitivity and fill our minds and our vocabularies with the words that celebrate its worth. When that happens a special bond can develop between sensitive parents and their children. A bond that leads to personal growth for parent and child alike.

FEELING GOOD ABOUT SENSITIVITY

"Now that Timara is ten we have a special relationship," Joni offered. "I know what she is feeling and she knows what I am feeling. We just have to look at each other and we *KNOW*! We can help each other through situations.

"We're a great pair when we go to Target. We talk about it before we get there. How much we hate to shop because of the stimulation. When we get to the parking lot we sit in the car and count to three—one, two, three—we yell and then jump out, run into the store grab what we want and get out of there. We laugh about it. It's funny and it's neat to share it."

A special bond can exist, a nonverbal communication between parents and children who are both sensitive. In a unique and exciting way they can empathize and share with one another.

If you aren't as sensitive as your child, your biggest challenge may be understanding her. To you her reactions may seem to be *over*sensitive or *super*emotional. Be kind to your sensitive child. Understand that he may feel what you do not feel, that he may hear what you do not hear, that he may see what you do not see. Invite him to share with you his experiences and enhance your own sensitivity.

If it weren't for my sensitive son, I would never have noticed that when I am walking around a lake the wind feels cooler on my cheek facing the water. I would never have fully appreciated the aroma of pumpkin pies baking. I would have missed hundreds of sounds, smells, sights, and feelings that have enriched my life.

SENSITIVITY: A SUMMARY

Sensitive spirited kids feel emotions, see sights, hear sounds, and smell odors to a degree and depth that most of us mortals will never know. They are not teasing when they tell us their socks are hurting their feet. They truly know the difference between brands of applesauce and if you check it out, you'll find out it's a fact that the toilet paper in Perkins smells different from that in McDonald's just like they told you.

Problems occur for sensitive children when they are overwhelmed by the amount of stimulation or emotional stress around them. When this occurs a pressure builds which can overpower their control system.

Sensitive spirited kids need to hear:

You're tenderhearted.

Noise bothers you.

You're loving.

You are very sensitive to feelings and care about people.

You can feel other people's stress.

You are very selective.

You'll make a wonderful chef, artist, designer, etc.

Teaching tips:

Talk with your child about the rich array of sensations and emotions she experiences. Give her the words to describe them.

Be sensitive to how much stimulation your child is receiving. Noise, smells, bright lights, etc. bother her; protect her from overstimulation.

Limit the amount of television your child watches.

Teach your child to recognize when she is getting overstimulated and to ask for help stopping or reducing the stimulation.

If you are sensitive too:

Be aware that what stimulation bothers your child also irritates you.

Reduce stimulation while you still have the energy to help your child manage her sensitivity as well as your own.

Reduce your own stress so it doesn't overwhelm your sensitive child.

Refill your energy bank after being in a stimulating situation.

9

DISTRACTIBLE OR PERCEPTIVE: HELPING THEM HEAR OUR INSTRUCTIONS

We are able to process your call. We just don't feel like it.
—Ziggy

I WAS STANDING in a checkout at the discount store one day. A day-care provider with three preschoolers in tow was attempting to make a purchase.

"Tim, over here," she called. Tim stood in his tracks.

"Tim, I need you to come over here," she repeated sternly. No movement. Finally she went over to him, touched his shoulder and growled, "Tim, I asked you to come over here."

He looked up at her with his finger at his lips. "Shhhh, listen to the bell," he whispered.

I tensed, straining to hear a bell. At first I couldn't distinguish anything, then suddenly I realized he was talking about the bell rung by the Salvation Army person soliciting donations outside the store. The day-care provider was also puzzled. She darted a glance around the store, but seeing no bell she started to speak again. It was then that the faint tinkle of the bell reached her. "The Salvation Army bell?" she exclaimed, her brow wrinkled in exasperation. "You hate the Salvation Army bell?"

"It reminds me of morning," he soberly replied. "Every morning when the bell rings I have to get up!"

From outside appearances it looked like Tim wasn't listening. In fact he was. The problem arose because he heard every sound around him and didn't know which was the most important for him to tune in to and respond. He heard the day-care provider, but he did not react because he was attending to the bell outside.

USING WORDS

Spirited kids are perceptive. Their senses are keen, drawing in every aspect of the stimulation around them. They need us to tell them that they hear what others do not hear. They see what others do not observe. They feel when others are unaware. It is this ability to perceive that gives them an understanding and insight beyond their years. It is the basis of a sharp sense of humor and creative thought. To be perceptive is a special gift.

Problems occur for the perceptive child when he is barraged with information from his senses and is unable to sort it out. It is as though he were incapable of deciding which is the most important message or where his focus should be. When this occurs, he becomes distracted, confused, unable to concentrate on the task at hand or the instruction he has just been given by his parent or teacher. It appears as though he is not listening. It is our job to help kids like this understand their perceptiveness and to teach them techniques for distinguishing the most important messages in their lives.

MOTIVATING KIDS TO LISTEN

There's a Ziggy cartoon that reads, "We are able to process your call. We just don't feel like it." One of the first issues we have to deal with in helping our perceptive child to select our messages from others is to make sure that they *want* to hear what we have to say.

To motivate kids to listen we have to start thinking and acting like the marketing director from Coca-Cola. We need to make them believe that among the rush of messages they are receiving ours is the most important.

Coke—the fizzy, brown, sweet liquid—is almost indiscernible from its competitors. The marketing people have to convince us to buy it rather than the other brands. They tell us, "You can't beat it. You can't stop it. The feeling that you get with Coca-Cola Classic." In the world of advertising this is called an emotional extension. Suddenly we're not just buying a fizzy, brown, sweet liquid, we're also getting that "good feeling." The kind of feeling we won't get from the other brands. Coke's message stands out. We like it. We listen and respond.

We have to develop our own emotional extension with spirited kids. The one that lets them know we love them, we understand them, and we accept them. It feels good to be around us and to do the things we ask.

The other day I yelled at my kids. I told them I was tired of them not listening to me and doing what I asked them to do. "But, Mom," my son protested, "you're not listening to us. You're crabby. You're not giving us any choices. We ask you for help and you walk away. You even pick up our toys before we're done playing with them."

I was not pleased. I had not started this lecture as an opportunity to discuss *my* behavior. But drill sergeants who bark out commands do not garner a lot of popularity votes. Like Ziggy we may be able to process their message, but we won't feel like it.

"KRIS-S-S-S turn off the television and GET YOUR PAJAMAS ON NOW!" brings on a case of "parent deafness." "Kris, sit on my lap and I'll scratch your back before we get your pajamas on," brings her running. A hug, a thank you, a compliment all create a good feeling. The one that makes our spirited kids *want* to listen to our message rather than the other sounds around them.

You can display your "I love you," "You are special," "I like being your mom or dad," "You'll like to hear what I have to say" messages everywhere. For example, on a banner hanging across your garage that reads, "Honk, Tim is ten!" Or try a shiny red sports jacket that proclaims, "COOL KID"; a sign hung on the bathroom mirror that reads, "Gosh, I'm GOOD"; a plain brown lunch bag transformed into a piece of Magic Marker art proclaiming, "World's Greatest Speller"; or a key hung on the kitchen wall that reads, "The key to my heart. Good for one hug." The mugs, the button pictures, the family songs—all of these are ways to say to your child: "I love you," "You're special," and "You'll like listening to me."

Check your messages. Are they creating that good feeling? Are they motivating your child to heed your messages above the others?

USE MULTIPLE MEDIA TO GET YOUR MESSAGE ACROSS

Through extensive market research, Coca-Cola has learned that some people respond best when they hear a message, while others have to see it or feel it to remember it. They've also learned that if they want their customers to actually respond to their message one exposure isn't enough. So they inundate us utilizing every conceivable shape, form, and matter. They sing it to us on the radio, they picture it for us on the television. It's on the truck that just rolled down the street, the back of the magazine in the doctor's office, the highway billboard, my son's jacket, his coach's baseball cap, my daughter's sweatshirt, and the city bus. Daily, my senses are struck with the message: "You can't beat it. The feeling you get with Coca-Cola Classic."

Experiment with your child. Does she respond best when you verbally tell her to do something or when you write a note or a draw a picture for her? Does it help if you touch her first? What happens if you sing it to her? One of the most effective classroom techniques is the "clean-up song." The simple little tune that pleasantly reminds us, "It's time to put your work away so we can have a snack today." If you don't sing, try changing the tone of your voice. A robot voice or a whisper easily captures your child's attention. Vary the techniques that are most effective for you or use a couple of them together.

When you vary your techniques it's also easier to send your message more than once without feeling repetitive. Watch a classroom teacher and you'll see her step over to the light switch and blink the lights. A visual signal that says, "Stop, listen to me." Then she'll sing, "It's time to put your work away," an auditory message. To those who are not responding she will walk over, touch, and remind. A physical message. Finally, she may begin helping some of the children pick up the blocks or crayons they are playing with—a demonstration. In four different ways she has sent her message. In this way she is assured that everyone has heard it and knows this is where attention should be focused.

Touch seems to be a very important way of signaling a spirited child that this message is important. In our spirited child classes we make a general announcement of what is to come and then walk around the classroom, touching each child on the arm or shoulder and repeating the message. This touch is critical to helping them focus on the information we are giving them. Try catching your child's attention with a gentle touch.

Once you have learned which techniques are most effective with your child, teach him what you are doing. Let him learn to ask for directions in a written form, or to sit close to a teacher so it is easy for her to touch him and cue him in.

GET EYE CONTACT

To get potential customers to pay attention to their messages, advertisers have learned to catch their eye. Walk through the grocery store. If it's an adult product you will find it standing at adult eye level. If it's a kid's product it will be at a child's eye level. If it is for individuals using wheelchairs it will be at their eye level. Companies actually squabble over shelf space that will give them the most direct eye contact.

You can use the same technique. If you want your child to listen to you, avoid hollering at him from across the room. This technique lets off steam for you, but for spirited kids it is the least effective way of getting them to pay attention. Instead, walk over to them, bend down, and look them in the eye. If you don't want to bend down, pick them up and set them on a counter or table that brings them up to eye level with you. When you've got direct eye contact it is much easier for them to hear your message. This is especially important when your home is filled with relatives, music, food, and activities. Catch their attention and let them know *your* message is the most important.

What if they won't look at you? It does happen. Every time we ask our spirited child to do something we have to remember it is a transition. We ask them to stop watching television and come to dinner. Stop playing with the blocks and get in the car. Most spirited kids don't like transitions. To stop doing what they are doing and shift to something else is disgruntling to them. If your child turns away from you, making a deliberate move that seems to say, "If I can't see you, I can't hear you," stay calm. In the case of preschoolers they actually believe that if they can't see you, you can't see them. You know, however, that you have enough of their attention that they have to work hard not to hear you. Surprise them (this time it is all right). Tickle under the ear, or along the neck. They can't help glancing back to make sure this is for real. Keep your voice low and calmly tell them, "You're teasing me. I can see your ear, and I know you can hear me." At this point they might cover their ears with their hands. Repeat your direction: "The rule is . . .," "I need you . . .," "It's time for you . . .," or "You can choose . . .," Then take their hand and help them follow through.

Gradually your children will learn to look you in the eye, knowing that it helps them to understand your words better.

KEEP IT SIMPLE

You'll notice that Coke doesn't tell us you can't beat it because "It's really great stuff. It's got formula XYZ in it, just developed by HW and Co., and we think you're really going to like it." No way. Coca-Cola knows that in our busy lives they've only got a few seconds to catch our attention and get their message across. They keep it simple. "You can't beat it! The feeling that you get with Coca-Cola Classic."

With spirited kids who are taking in everything around them, we too can only expect to catch their attention for a few seconds. That means our messages need to be succinct and to the point: Stop! Bed. Shoes. Eat. Come. The reasons why we want them to stop or why we want them to get into bed are important, but we can save the reasons until we know we have their full attention. Our initial interaction with them is just the headline—the big words at the top of the page that grab their attention and pull them away from other distractions. When we know they are listening to our message then we can give them a full page of copy—the "why," or more complete directions. Sometimes we're running into trouble without even realizing it merely because our initial message is too complex.

Kim Ode, in an article titled "Learning to Be a Good Listener Means Taking an Active Role," wrote, "Sometimes the accusation of not being a good listener is less a question of style than of the speaker's expectations. When people complain that others aren't listening, it's really that they don't like the reaction they're getting: 'You don't understand what I said in the way that I meant it,' or 'You're not responding as I expect you to respond.' "

If you don't like how your child is responding to your direction, check out the clarity of your messages.

SAY WHAT YOU MEAN

Did you ever notice that Coca-Cola never says, "Please buy Coke," or "Buy Coke, okay?" They know that *please* and *okay* can get you into trouble because they change a clear directive into a question. For example, at eight o'clock at night, after a long, hot day, you want the kids to go to bed, right? Right! So you tell them, "Time for bed" and you mean it—no more stories, no more drinks of water, no more climbing out of bed. But without meaning to at all you may have sabotaged yourself by adding okay or please to your direction. Instead of clearly saying, "It's time for bed," you add, "It's time for bed, okay?" or "Go to bed, please?" It's easy to do. Spirited kids can muster such a fierce reaction to our directives that we add please and okay as a bit of a buffer. It is a tool on our part to diffuse the intense reaction we know we're going to get. But when please and okay are added, our spirited kids hear our directive as a question and immediately answer with a resounding no.

Choosing the right words is critical to winning your child's cooperation. If you want your child to do something and don't wish to debate it or give her a choice, be sure your message is a clear direction: "It's time for bed," "You may play in the yard," "It's time to leave," "Your Big Wheel can be ridden in the driveway," and "The rule is you must wear shoes in school." These are all straightforward directives. They clearly and simply tell the child exactly what he may do. Make sure you are not unintentionally blurring your direction by adding the words please or okay or even raising your voice at the end of your statement as though asking a question. Don't imply a choice if you don't intend to give one.

Clear directives are very important in a parent's repertoire of responses for the spirited child. When spirited kids are tired, hungry, near an "overload," or in a situation beyond their capabilities, it is essential that our messages communicate clearly: "I am in charge. You are safe and secure. This time I will choose to make the decision."

At the end of a class one evening, I watched as Jane used this technique to end her exit hassle. Every week she had struggled with her son Paul, who would refuse to put his boots on before going out the door. This time she simply said to him, "Paul, put on your boots."

He didn't comply. She looked up at me and smiled. "You know the old Jane would now be begging him to get these on," she said, "but today you see the new Jane."

She picked up the boots and strode to the door. Paul, seeing his mother head for the door, jumped up and followed her.

"My boots," he squealed, taking them from her hand and slipping them on. Jane gave me a "thumbs up" as she ambled out the door.

Today it worked. If Paul were younger or overtired, she may have had to pick both him and the boots up before walking out the door. In another situation, she may have had to stand at the door and wait a few minutes, giving him time to unlock. Today, the clear directive by itself was enough. The confidence in her voice and the clarity in her words caught Paul's attention and got the response she wanted.

TELL THEM WHAT THEY CAN DO

Notice that Coca-Cola doesn't tell us not to drink 7UP, they tell us very clearly to drink Coke! That's because people don't like to be told what they can't do. They want to hear what they *can* do. This is especially true for intense, persistent spirited kids. To get the response you want, focus your instructions on the things they can do.

In the airport, I watched a dad with a very spirited toddler, the kind of kid that makes the best of us want to scream, "STOP!" "Watch out!" or "Get out of the way!" The child was on the *move*.

The dad was very skilled. He followed him down the long hallways of the airport, never taking his eyes off him. When the toddler headed for trouble, the dad didn't waste his energy trying to stop this busy kid. Instead he redirected him. "Look. Let's try the walkway," he exclaimed pointing to the moving mat. The toddler stopped dead in his tracks and made a quick right turn, heading back toward his dad and the walkway. His dad beat him there and screeched to a halt at its edge, both feet planted firmly in place, hands glued to his sides, standing at attention. His whole body screamed STOP along with his words. The toddler stopped just like Dad, planting his feet and slapping his hands to his sides, a big smile flashing across his face.

They both laughed as the dad took his hand then raised his foot in an exaggerated step. The toddler did the same. "Step up," he directed. Together they did. "Stop!" the father commanded, his body jerking to attention again. The toddler did. Then with big, prancing motions they began moving along the walkway. As they neared the end, the father once again commanded stop and went into his military pose. The toddler followed suit. They raised their legs in unison and shouted together, "Step down!"

I watched them for ten minutes as they rode one way then the other on the walkway. The toddler was soon prancing ahead of Dad, but a firm *stop* from Dad brought him to attention. Soon it was unnecessary as the toddler brought himself to attention and waited for his dad to catch up at the end. "Step down and be careful," the toddler chirped.

This dad recognized that his persistent, active son needed and wanted to be on the move. He enjoyed his energy. He also knew that he had to teach him how to be safe on the walkway. To ensure that he was heard in the busy airport, the father gave his directions both verbally and physically. He not only said "Stop," he demonstrated it with his entire body. He didn't just say "Step up," he took a big, deliberate, oversize step. He emphasized his points. He limited their number and, most important, he told his son what he *could* do. As a result he received the response he wanted.

Listen to your directions. Are they telling your child what she can do? Do they say "Sit on your chair" rather than "Get off the table," "Drink your juice" rather than "Stop playing with it." When your messages inform your spirited child of what she can do, it's much more likely that you'll get the response that you had hoped for.

WORKING TOGETHER

Perceptive kids tend to have perceptive parents. Like your child, you may be working very hard to decide which information is the most important to you. The dad at the airport remained very focused on his young son, talking to him, teaching him how to use the walkway and following through. It isn't easy to do, especially if you are distractible yourself.

Marni called me at home one day, troubled with her three-year-old son. It was a typical question: "How do I get him dressed, fed, and out of the house in the morning without a fight?"

I asked her what she had been doing. She explained that she had set up a routine that they followed every morning. They would get up at seven, cuddle for a few minutes, then get dressed, eat, brush teeth and hair, and have a few minutes to play before it was time to put on coats and leave. "Sounds good," I responded. She told me it was working pretty well. They were fighting less, but she still felt rushed going out the door.

"We always seem to run out of time, no matter how early we get up," she lamented.

As she talked more about her morning routine, both of us began to realize that like her son, Marni was very perceptive and easily distracted. When she helped him get dressed, he would run to the window to watch a bird. She would go with him and watch it too. When she asked him to come and eat, he would say just a minute. She would give him the minute and start on a different task. Suddenly the minute had stretched to five. The cycle continued until the clock struck eight and they found themselves frustrated and rushed, flying out the door.

Becoming aware of our own distractibility helps us to communicate more clearly with our spirited children. It's important that we teach ourselves to be aware of interruptions and not let them pull us off in another direction unless we choose to do so. This is easier said than done when you're living in a house full of kids. Next time you are working with your spirited child and are interrupted by another child, the telephone, or a knock on the door, consciously ask yourself, "Do I wish to change my focus, deal with the phone, the other child, or the person at the door, or do I need to say I will get back to them later and continue with my spirited child?"

The decision will vary with each situation, but it is helpful to know that your child may not be responding as you had hoped because your message has been interrupted. You can choose how to deal with these interruptions, recognize them, and alter your communication accordingly.

Share with your child the techniques you use to keep your focus. When you are interrupted and feel pulled to do something else, tell your child. The phone is ringing. Part of me wants to talk to the caller, but I know I need to finish what I'm doing and call back later. He will learn quickly from your model.

When you know you and your child need to concentrate on a task look for a quiet place to work or play. It is amazing, however, that many very perceptive children are able to do their homework with a radio playing. These are kids who enjoy a certain level of stimulation but have learned to decipher which messages to give their attention to. If they are successful, you don't need to fight with them about turning off the radio.

AVOID INTERRUPTING

When you are distractible, it is very tempting to share with your spirited child the thoughts that come to your mind. You see him building with blocks and say, "Good job." The compliment is appreciated, but your words interrupt her work, breaking her concentration. You tell her to get dressed, then think to tell her to make her bed while she's in her room. She stops dressing and starts working on the bed. Five minutes later you're frustrated she isn't dressed.

Better to save your compliments or your next instructions until she has finished her project. Otherwise her concentration will be broken and she may fail to compete the task at hand.

IDENTIFY YOUR ATTENTION GETTERS

I talked earlier about getting your child's attention with multiple mediums, eye contact, touch, and short simple phrases. If you are distractible it may also be difficult for your child to get your attention. Think about the last twenty-four hours. What did your child have to do to get your attention, to get you to listen to him?

Your list may look like the one from a recent spirited child class.

He hit me.

She stands right in front of me and puts her face in my face.

He bites the baby.

She whines.

She hangs on me.

Or your story might sound like Dave's. "It was late and I was tired. As usual, my night stalker couldn't sleep. I soon felt his presence next to me on the couch, on the other side of my newspaper. I tried to ignore it. I'd already sat with him, tucked him in, and read him a story. Enough is enough, I thought. Suddenly my ear was assaulted by inorganic flatulent noises. Not the real thing mind you—this one created by the flapping of one's lips and the rolling of a tongue. It was grotesque. There isn't another word for it. The newspaper crumbled in my lap.

" 'What are you doing?' I demanded in my best authoritarian voice.

" 'Getting your attention,' he quipped, a big smile wiping his cheeks. 'You look at me when I make that noise.'

" 'You bet I look at you,' I thought. 'The better to eat you alive!' "

If you don't want to be hit, bitten, whined at, hung on, or disgusted you have to teach your child how to get your attention. Decide how you would like them to approach you and then show them. Do you want words? What words? "I want attention," "I need a hug," or "Please listen to me." Do you want actions, a tap on the shoulder or the shaking of your hand? Do you need eye contact? Do you want them to stand in front of you? Do you want them to pull you down to their level and talk to you?

There isn't one right way, but just as you have to learn how to get your child's attention, your child has to learn how to get yours. Next time he whines, say, "Stop. I think you are telling me you want attention. Say it with words." Or if she hits you, say, "Stop, hitting hurts. If you want my attention, take my hand." Then you have to be willing to garner your forces and give your attention to her.

Remaining focused takes a great deal of energy on your part if you are distractible. High stimulation situations like airports, family gatherings, shopping malls, and fairs are the most challenging. Teach yourself to think before entering one of those situations with your children. Do you have the energy to clearly direct them and help them to be successful or are you exhausted, needing all of your remaining energy for yourself?

Don't forget to give yourself and your child a break after you've been working hard to keep your focus.

FEELING GOOD ABOUT BEING PERCEPTIVE

In *Essays,* author E. B. White draws our attention to the white feathers in the swallow's nest that allow the bird to fly directly to its nest after swooping into a darkened barn from the bright sunlight outside. He describes the smells of the farm and the light playing on the pond. He is a perceptive individual who has used his talents to enrich our lives.

The world needs perceptive individuals. It is very possible to enjoy our children's keen awareness and still teach them to listen to our messages. It does take more energy, especially when you first begin. Spirited children do listen. They listen well. With your help they will also learn to identify the most important messages in their lives.

PERCEPTIVENESS: A SUMMARY

Spirited kids are perceptive. Their senses are keen, drawing in every aspect of the stimulation around them. They hear what others do not hear. They see what others do not observe. They feel when others are unaware. It is this ability to perceive that gives them an understanding and insight beyond their years.

Problems occur when they are barraged with information from their senses and are unable to sort it out. It is as though they were incapable of deciding which is the most important message or where their focus should be. When this occurs, they become distracted, confused, and unable to concentrate on the task at hand or the instruction that has just been given.

Perceptive spirited kids need to hear:

You notice everything that is going on around you.

Sometimes it is hard for you to hear instructions unless the person is talking directly to you.

You are very creative because you notice things other people miss.

You are perceptive.

You have a wonderful sense of humor.

Teaching Tips:

Motivate your child to listen, with words of support and love.

Send your message in many different ways including talking, writing, drawing, and demonstrating.

Touch your child lightly to help him attend to your instructions.

Make sure you have his attention by getting eye contact.

Keep your message simple.

Avoid asking a question if there really isn't a choice.

Tell him what he *can* do.

Limit the number of instructions you give at one time.

If you are perceptive too:

Be aware of your own distractibility. Don't let it stop you from following through with your spirited child.

Allow time to finish tasks uninterrupted.

Provide quiet places to work and play.

Refill your energy bank after working hard to stay focused.

10

ADAPTABILITY: MAKING TRANSITIONS EASIER

*Transitions are like a virus. They are the little things that
disrupt our days.*
—Lynn, mother of two

DARREN WAS elbow deep in the sandbox. His best friend Bobby was at
the other end building ditches with a bulldozer, and Kally, Bobby's sister,
was following behind him filling the newly formed ditches with water. "Time
for lunch," Darren's mother announced pleasantly. Bobby and his sister
looked up and smiled. Darren's face flashed red. "No!" he protested, and
threw a handful of sand at his mother. Darren's mother stopped in her
tracks, shocked then furious.

"There he goes again," she thought. "Why does he do this to me? All
I did was ask him to come to lunch."

Sometimes with spirited kids, like Darren, it's the little things that get
us. Transitions are one of those "little things" that can make or break a day.
A transition is a change or passage from one place, action, mood, topic, or
thing to another. It can be as simple as stopping play to come to eat, as
common as getting in and out of the bathtub, or as significant as moving
from one house to another. Spirited children adapt slowly to transitions—
any transition. To shift gears, to pass from one activity, place, or topic to
another requires a wrenching, grinding effort on their part. Transitions are
the virus that can destroy the system. If you can't even get the kids out the
door, in the door, to the table, from the table, or cleaned up without a major
hassle the good parts of the day lose their sparkle. The day feels rotten.
Listening to their vehement squeals of protest can make you feel like a
major overhaul is needed to correct the problem. Fortunately a mere
tune-up will do the job.

Smooth transitions are one of the most significant aspects of a good day. All kids benefit from smooth transitions. Spirited kids *need* clear, tranquil transitions. Temperamentally, most spirited kids are like Darren. They're not intentionally misbehaving. They are not trying to make their parents look bad in public. They truly find dealing with change extremely challenging. This is most apparent when they actually *want* lunch, or *like* going to school and yet find themselves in a tizzy, failing to cooperate and fighting every step of the way. Change is so hard for them that they'll get upset that the neighbors painted their house a different color, or the bank changed its sign. Transitions will never be easy for slow-to-adapt individuals but they can learn to make them more easily.

USING WORDS

To help spirited kids cope we have to help them recognize and understand transitions, then give them the words they need to express their feelings about them. To do so we have to look closely at our day and ask, "Where are the beginnings and the endings of activities and events?" and "How will today be different from our normal routine?"

The beginning or ending of anything—a visit, a television show, school, a meal—is treacherous ground for the slow-to-adapt child. By finding our transitions we can prepare for them and the discomfort they create. Spirited children need to hear:

> You feel grumpy the first day your stepsister comes to stay with us because it changes our routine.
>
> Change is difficult for you, but you can change and do all of the time. Remember last week when you . . .
>
> You like to be organized and know what to expect.
>
> I think you are upset because you were surprised.
>
> Take your time. I can wait for you to finish.
>
> You can be flexible.
>
> Our family works together. I will respect you but I also need you to work with me.

As you point out to your child the transitions in her life she will begin to look for them herself. Gradually her confidence and ability to cope will increase.

Introduce her to other people you know who are thoughtful and cautious during transitions. Let her know she isn't odd. She isn't different. There are many people who share her same feelings, people who make us aware of our traditions and history.

ESTABLISH A ROUTINE

Routines are the lifelines of spirited kids who are slow to adapt. They provide a sense of control. When spirited kids feel in control they can transition more quickly. It's surprises that really upset them. If they can expect a specific wake up time, snack time, and mealtime and special times for favorite activities, they can predict what is coming and begin making the change themselves. Routine reduces their anxiety and allows them to put their energy into other areas.

Look at your day. Does your child know when you normally get up? When you eat? When you go on outings? When she can invite a friend over or when she takes her nap? A spirited child needs to know these things. If she doesn't you can expect a fight.

"Every morning was a battle at our house," Deb explained during class one day. "Alex absolutely would not cooperate about getting dressed or eating. I tried feeding him first. Then I switched to dressing him first, but nothing seemed to work. I would be rushing around, trying to get myself and the baby ready and he would just be laying on the floor whining. By the time I dropped him off at day care we were both a wreck.

"It was tough on my day-care provider too because Alex's crying would upset the other kids. She suggested that we develop a chart with pictures on it of the things we had to do each morning and the order in which they should be accomplished. If Alex cooperated with me and did them, he earned a ticket. He could turn in the ticket at her house for a 'good morning prize.'

"At that point, I was willing to try anything. Together Alex and I cut pictures out of magazines and catalogs for getting dressed, brushing teeth, eating breakfast, etc. and wrote the words underneath. Each morning it was his job to check off the tasks and to pull a ticket out of the jar when he was finished. The response was immediate. Instead of arriving at day care in tears he was elated as he handed over his ticket for that 'good morning prize.'

"We used the chart for six months. After that we had the routine down and didn't really have any problems anymore. I can't tell you how grateful I am to that day-care provider."

Adaptability isn't an issue when your child knows what to expect. Sometimes by merely establishing a clear and consistent routine you can get the cooperation of the child who is uncomfortable with change. That doesn't mean that you will never have a spontaneous moment in your home again. Of course you will, but you'll limit them, knowing how challenging it is for your spirited child to respond quickly.

ALLOW TIME

"If I rush Charlie, we're sunk," Shannon said during an interview. "I can never throw him into a situation. The more time that I can give us the happier we both are. But it means I have to be one step ahead all of the time."

Time—spirited kids need time to make transitions. You might not feel like you have that much time, especially if you have other kids. Anna, the mother of four, felt overwhelmed by the needs of her spirited daughter.

"I don't have *more* time," she snapped during our class discussion. "Getting Tracie out the door is a full-time job as it is, and I've got three other kids. Our routine is clear and she still doesn't cooperate."

I tried to convince Anna to set her alarm fifteen minutes early by saying, "Now you're tired *and* rushed. Trust me. Set your alarm fifteen minutes earlier. You'll still be tired, but you won't be rushed. What do you have to lose?"

The following week she arrived at class *early*. "I've got good news," she reported as she breezed into the center. "You know how I balked at the idea of allowing more time? Well, after I thought about it, I decided to try it. I guess I'm slow to adapt too. Anyway, I set my alarm fifteen minutes earlier. I woke Tracie and let her lie in bed while I took a quick shower. When I was dressed, I woke the other kids and got Tracie out of bed. I didn't feel frantic because I was already showered and dressed. When she needed help with a shirt, I helped her instead of telling her I didn't have time (which I usually don't). When I was calmer, she was calmer, which allowed me more time for the other kids. I can't believe what a difference fifteen minutes made. You were right."

Then, just to make sure I didn't get a big head, she added, "I'm still *really* tired!"

Over the years I have learned that every five minutes spent in prevention saves you fifteen minutes of turmoil. If you would like more time in your day, allow more time for transitions with your spirited child. Slow-to-adapt kids are not wasting time. They are warming up, working into the change. This is especially true when the transition isn't part of your normal routine.

Other people can sabotage your efforts to allow your child time to warm up. Sometimes you have to be assertive. At the doctor's office you may have to ask the doctor to talk with your child and show him the stethoscope before she tries to touch your child. At Grandma's house you may have to assure Grandma and Grandpa that your child will sit on their laps in a few minutes. Until then, you're going to keep her on your lap.

Even at athletic events you might have to discourage the coach from judging your child's performance by her first game, knowing that after she has warmed up her performance will be much stronger.

It almost seems un-American, at times, to have kids who are slow to warm up. Other people tell us to push them—to force them to jump in—and they reprimand us for babying them. When your child adapts slowly, remind yourself that you will appreciate it when he is an adolescent. While all the other kids are running off on some ridiculous venture, yours will be thinking, moving slowly and cautiously. There are strengths to every temperamental characteristic.

FOREWARNING IS CRITICAL

Forewarning is the process of giving a visual picture of the future. Slow-to-adapt kids need to know what the future holds. Whether you will be eating lunch, going to the doctor, having company, changing nap time, going shopping, trying a new toothbrush, or washing a favorite blanket, spirited kids need to be apprised about what will happen. Make sure they know what they will be doing. How long it will take you to get there. What you will be taking along. What you will be leaving at home. Who will be there and anything else you know might happen.

The timing of forewarnings is important. Some kids need to be told hours, days, even weeks in advance what they will be doing. This gives them time to ask their questions, and mentally prepare. Others will mull it over and get wired if you tell them too far in advance. You'll have to decide what works best for your child. Here are a few forewarnings used by teachers and other parents:

In ten minutes you'll need to stop and come to . . .

In five minutes your time is up. Let me help you find a stopping point.

After *Sesame Street* we will . . .

When Dad comes home . . .

Today when I pick you up, we won't be going home, we will go to . . .

When the timer goes off, it's time to go . . .

You can play with Brad until his mom leaves for work at ten, then he has to go home.

Tomorrow when you wake up . . .

Three more jumps and then it is Mica's turn.

"We have to prepare Collin for everything that will happen," Janey told the group. "Like today," she said, "my friend came over to visit. I had to tell Collin who she was, why she was coming, and how long I expected her to be here. He needs to know the 'little' things. I can't take anything for granted with him. He does fine as long as he knows what to expect."

"Learning about transitions really made my husband feel better," Patrice explained. "Our two-year-old son, Brad, would scream whenever his dad came home. He would refuse to let him touch him and pushed him away. Thirty minutes later, however, he wanted to sit on Dad's lap.

"My husband started to take the 'greetings' personally and was really feeling badly. From our discussion in class I realized this was a transition. I started letting Brad know it was almost time for Dad to come home. When I heard the car, I would pick him up and hold him as my husband came in the door and tell him he could let Dad know when he was ready for a hug. He started reaching out right away. I think it was the forewarning that helped."

Stella, the mother of thirteen-month-old Leah, said, "I've felt silly telling Leah what to expect because she is so little, but it's worked. She really understands now, even though she is just a tiny toddler."

It isn't uncommon to give a toddler a "one more time" warning only to have him start crying because you've given the warning. Tell him you know it's hard for him to stop but keep giving warnings. Gradually it will get easier for both of you.

Remember that the younger the child, the less he understands about time. Tell a two-year-old that in five minutes he'll need to stop, and you may still be picking up a screaming child five minutes later. Kids this age don't understand the concept of time unless you make it concrete. A paper chain with a loop for each day helps a child count down the days until a holiday or birthday party. A picture calendar allows a child to keep track of the number of days until Grandma comes to visit. Directions such as, "You can throw the ball five more times," "When the music box stops," "When the sand settles in the bottom of the hourglass," "At the next commercial," and "When the tape is done" all make time something real and easy to understand.

Forewarnings are also a magic key to prompt obedience. If you want your kids to impress the relatives and *jump* when you say jump, make sure you whisper in their ear that in five minutes they'll need to jump. Without that warning you're looking at trouble. Spirited kids do not respond well to abrupt transitions. A simple warning can help you achieve your goal.

If it seems like extra work to clue your child in on what will be happening and when, take note of how many times a day you look at the clock and think "in ten minutes" or check your calendar and make your plans. Little kids can't do that, they need us to help them. All you need to do is share your thoughts and actions with them. As kids get older you can put more responsibility on them. For example you might say, "Mom goes to work tomorrow. What do you need to do to be ready?" Eventually they'll prepare themselves for transitions.

ALLOW TIME FOR CLOSURE

Spirited kids like to finish what they're doing. Before moving to a new activity we have to help them put closure on the existing one. You can acknowledge their feelings by saying something like "It's hard to stop doing this. You can go back to it later" or "You can take your time. You don't need to hurry. I'm just letting you know ahead of time that we will be leaving in twenty minutes."

Once you have forewarned them, give them the space and time they need to finish up what they are doing. If you're short on time you may need to help them bring closure by closing the paints, putting away toys, or storing all of the crayons they're using except for the one in their hand. Invite them to put their project in a safe place so they can return to it later. Sometimes to bring closure and move spirited kids to the next activity you will need to allow them a "transitional" object. Let them take a block with them in the car or bring the ball to the table, asking them to lay it next to their chair.

If they don't want to quit, let them know you are waiting. If you ask your child to put something away and she refuses, sit down and say, "I'm waiting. I'll wait until you decide to put your things away." Once she realizes that you're just going to sit there, she'll frequently put it away or stop what she is doing. If she doesn't cooperate you might need to say, "You can do it now or I will help you." Then do it.

At the same time you are helping your child bring closure to her present activity remember that you'll need to remind her of what is to come. Be sure you have provided forewarning, otherwise you might "surprise" her and she'll fall apart.

Finally, understand that a sense of closure is as important to your child as it is to you. Imagine if you were watching your favorite television show and someone came in, turned off the set in the middle of the show and said, "Go to bed now." You would probably be upset and not all that cooperative. What kids are doing is important to them. They need an opportunity to find a stopping point.

USE IMAGINATION

Spirited kids have a wonderful imagination. You can use it to move them from one activity to another. My colleague Beth finds moving the spirited child group from the classroom to the lobby is a major transition for them. Her solution is to take a "moon walk" with them. She tells them they are all astronauts about to walk on the moon. The lobby is the moon, but before they get there she asks them, "What will we need to do before we're ready to visit the moon?"

"Put on our space suits," one will yell. Each pretends to slide a space-suit over their heads and clamp on the helmet. They slide on gloves and boots. Someone else always remembers the tether rope, which has to be clamped on. They talk about gravity and how it will affect the way they'll walk. All this discussion quiets them down and helps them to move smoothly and quietly from one place to another.

I've watched parents get their kids to wash their hands by pretending they were a dump truck opening and shutting their hands under the faucet "dumping" water. I've seen kids act like caterpillars and spin a cocoon as they put on their jackets, or float like a butterfly to the car. I've watched as kids headed for a pretend picnic in France, and I've seen toddlers so engrossed in galloping like a pony that they didn't even realize they were in transition. All of these little imaginative journeys won cooperation.

This isn't playing games. It's being smart.

LIMIT THE NUMBER OF TRANSITIONS

It had been a hectic day for two-and-a-half-year-old Michele and her mom. A rushed breakfast, a trip to the doctor where they waited and waited, a stop in the lab, a hurried lunch at McDonald's and finally a last-minute dash to class. Michele missed the greeting in the lobby, the parent and child activities, the books to read, and the tunnel to climb through. When she walked into the children's classroom all of the children and their parents were in a circle, singing, clapping, and jumping together. Suddenly the teacher said, "Give your mom and dad a big hug and say good-bye." Michele lost it. She grabbed onto her mother's leg and wouldn't let go.

Mom looked almost as stricken as Michele, although I wasn't quite sure if it was pain, anger, or embarrassment. "This is an overload," I remarked. "Think about her day. She had to change quickly and frequently this morn-ing. How many times has she had to move from one activity or one place to another? There have been too many transitions too fast. Some kids might have made it through, but for Michele, who is more uncomfortable with transitions and has also missed her nap, the strain of one more transition is just too much."

Spirited kids can only take so many transitions each day, especially if they are major transitions like Michele was experiencing. Overdo it and you will lose them. Look carefully at your day. Think about the number of transitions you have included. If you are planning an outing count the number of times you'll be in and out of the car—the number of changes from your normal routine that will occur. Know that for your child to be successful you will have to *limit* the number of transitions.

Next time Michele's mom may choose to get a sitter when she has to go to the doctor and spare Michele those stops. If that isn't possible she might pack a picnic lunch of familiar foods and bring it to the lobby of the center, eliminating the entry and exit from the restaurant. She may also choose to skip her class, deciding instead to take Michele home for her nap and give both of them a break. Transitions are more difficult when kids and parents are hungry and tired. Be especially watchful at those times.

Limiting the number of transitions gets tougher when the relatives get involved. At family gatherings you'll need to advocate for your child. Advocating means helping your child be successful. Sometimes that requires knowing when to say no or insisting that you drive your own car so you're not dependent on others. While a quick stop at the store may mean nothing to your father, it could be the trigger for your spirited child who has reached his limit of transitions for the day.

Limiting the number of transitions requires creativity and forethought, but it *does* alleviate the problems. The older spirited kids are, the more transitions they can handle. The younger they are, the more difficult transitions can be. Spirited toddlers are especially prone to problems caused by quick transitions. When you recognize your child's limits and know when to quit, your child will be more successful and your days will run more smoothly.

Lynn, the parent of six-year-old John, found knowing when to stop brought harmony to her family. "I had told John the night before what our day would include. I'd given him time to finish what he was doing and had even thanked him for his cooperation, but when I wanted to run one more errand he resisted.

" 'I want to stay home,' he demanded.

"I started to push him and realized he had had enough. We'd been to school, out for lunch, and had stopped at the park. He was tired and adamant that he wouldn't go. It really wasn't a power struggle—he simply couldn't do any more. I used to resent it when he'd do this but I didn't this time. I stopped. We had a very pleasant evening and he went to bed early.

My husband and I even got some time alone together. It was well worth it."

If you listen carefully, your spirited child will tell you when he is at his limit. Pay close attention, and look for a way to readjust your schedule or accomplish what you need to in a different way, rather than pushing or shoving until someone goes over the edge. There is always a solution, a way to respect your child's needs and your own. Look for it.

HELP THEM DEAL WITH DISAPPOINTMENT

Disappointment hits spirited kids hard. That's because disappointment is actually a transition—a change in plans, an unexpected surprise. Spirited kids need to understand that disappointment is very difficult for them. They experience a rush of emotions that easily overwhelms them. If they don't understand this they may turn on you.

You can help take the sting out of disappointments by playing "what if" with them. When you are about to go somewhere talk through the things that could possibly happen. For example, if you are going to a movie, ask your child, "What if we got there and all of the tickets were sold out? How would you feel? What would we do?" or "What if you went to a birthday party and they served fruit salad instead of birthday cake? What would you feel? What would you do?" or "What if you went to swimming lessons and they called everyone's name but yours?"

"What if" teaches kids to be good problems solvers and sets them up for success. If the "what if" actually happens, they're already prepared. They know how they feel, they have words for it, and they *know* what to do. Even if you haven't quite guessed the "what if" situation correctly you've probably come close enough to make comparisons.

"Doesn't this raise anxieties?" parents ask me. Potentially it could, but the emphasis of "what if" is not on what terrible disappointment or calamity could happen. The emphasis is on our confidence in their ability to solve the problem. What *can* they do. This is a supportive, comforting message. Kids don't become anxious when they feel in control.

Spirited kids are deep feelers. They can learn to handle their disappointment without letting it drown them, but it still is real and needs an outlet.

I remember a New Year's Eve celebration in which we had planned to go out to dinner with neighbors and then to see *Three Men and a Baby*. We finished dinner earlier than we had expected and found ourselves at the theater forty-five minutes before show time. My neighbor glanced at the advertisements for other movies. "How about if we go to this one instead?" he said, pointing to *Dirty Rotten Scoundrels*. The other kids cheered. I darted a quick glance at my son wondering if he would survive this "surprise." I saw tears welling in his eyes and pulled him aside.

"Can you handle this?" I asked. "I know you didn't expect it and it's hard for you to change like that."

"You promised we'd go to *Three Men and a Baby,*" he stammered.

"I know," I said, "but you have also talked about *Dirty Rotten Scoundrels.* Think about it for a minute and then we can decide."

Amazingly my son survived the switch in movies. At five he wouldn't have but at eight he did. I was pleased, but afterward I could tell he was still upset. The neighbors had invited us to their house for treats after the movie. I was pretty certain he wouldn't make this transition without some kind of "refueling."

"I need to check on our puppy," I said, excusing myself. "Josh, would you like to help me?" I didn't really need to check on the puppy but I knew I needed to give my son a chance to let it out. He did too—walked in the house and started screaming.

"You said we could see *Three Men and a Baby.* You promised. That movie was *awful* [he was right]. Why did we have to change?"

I let him blow, and then said, "That's it buddy, time's up. Change is always hard for you but that's enough for now. You did a great job at the theater. Maybe later this week we can see *Three Men and a Baby.* We've got to go back to the neighbors' now." I handed him a tissue and waited while he blew his nose. Together we walked out the door. He had survived and so had I. Disappointment doesn't simply seep away. Someway you and your spirited child need to find a respectful release.

WORKING TOGETHER

Let your children know how proud you are that they have made the transition well. Appreciate how they stopped riding their Big Wheel after three rounds and came in for lunch. Cheer when they get in the car without a fight—not sarcastically but triumphantly because they are growing and learning to adapt. Remark about the preparations they have made themselves to get ready for school or going to a friend's house. Thank them for their flexibility. In these little ways you reinforce their cooperation. Celebrate their successes, always remembering that one success leads to another.

If you are slow to adapt, too, recognize that you are working harder to cope during transitions. Recognize your own limits and be sure to dip into your energy bank so you have the energy you need to help your child as well as yourself.

FEELING GOOD ABOUT ADAPTABILITY

Even if you're not slow to adapt yourself you may find that being aware of transitions and planning for them is actually a very pleasant experience. That's what Nancy found out.

"Transitions are tough in our family for everyone but myself," she said. "I can whip through them so fast that I often lose the people around me as I hop from one topic to another, one activity to the next. I don't need help making transitions but my family does. I have learned to always give fore-warnings. I am always saying things like, 'We will be stopping at the library,' and 'In five minutes it will be time to leave.' At times it has felt like a hassle and of little personal benefit to me."

I didn't realize how much I too appreciated planned transitions until a group of us from work piled into a van and headed seventy miles southwest of town to our colleague's wedding. We arrived early and decided to use our extra time enjoying a cup of coffee and a doughnut at the local bakery.

I sat there engrossed in conversation, not aware of the passing time. Suddenly I realized everyone—but me—was headed out the door or already seated in the van. I was still in the bakery, without a coat on and desperately needing to use the rest room before I hopped back into the van. No one had prepared me for the transition!

It was a quick and rather embarrassing trip to the rest room while everyone waited for me. I may not *need* planned transitions, but since that day I realized that I *like* planned transitions.

The investment of time it takes to plan transitions is well worth it: A spirited child who feels competent and more flexible, and a confident parent because there are fewer hassles and more successes.

ADAPTABILITY: A SUMMARY

Spirited children adapt slowly to transition—any transition. To shift gears, to pass from one activity, place, or topic to another, requires a wrenching, grinding effort on their part. Smooth transitions are one of the most significant aspects for a good day. Transitions will never be easy for slow-to-adapt individuals but they can learn to make them more easily.

Slow-to-adapt spirited kids need to hear:

Change is difficult for you.

You like to be organized.

You need to know what to expect.

You can be flexible.

Teaching tips:

Establish a routine and explain the plans for the day to your slow-to-adapt child. Avoid surprises.

Allow time for slow transitions from one activity to another.

Forewarn your child of what is to come.

Allow time for closure.

When planning activities limit the number of transitions that will be required.

If you are slow to adapt too:

Allow yourself time to transition.

Recognize that if your day has been filled with transitions you will need to dip into your energy bank before moving on.

11

REGULARITY, ENERGY, FIRST REACTION, AND MOOD: UNDERSTANDING THE "BONUS" TRAITS

He's got them all. No wonder I'm tired!
—Martha, the mother of three

WAIT A MINUTE!" Bill exclaimed, as he scanned the class outline. "There isn't a discussion scheduled for energy. Isn't high energy an issue for spirited kids?"

"It isn't for mine," Carol answered.

"What about first reaction? No matter what we suggest, she says no," Martha grumbled.

"I wish it was just a first reaction," Mark added. "Tara wakes up in a bad mood. Don't we get to talk about mood? We used to refer to this kid as 'grump' baby. Of course," he added quickly, a twinkle in his eye, "that was before we learned about labels."

The conversation scattered around the room, with small groups spinning off. Our cohesive group was experiencing dissension among the ranks. They looked to me to explain it, because one of the best things about the group was finding other people who understood what it was like to have a spirited child. "You're talking about the bonus traits," I remarked. "They include regularity, energy, first reaction, and mood. As you can tell, some kids score high on the temperamental scale in these categories and some don't. That's why I call them the bonus traits. Unlike the first five temperamental traits (intensity, persistence, perceptiveness, sensitivity, and slow adaptability), which are common to almost all spirited kids, the bonus traits run about a fifty-fifty chance of appearing in the 'five column' for your child. Because they aren't common to every spirited child I thought we'd cover them when we discussed bedtime, eating, dressing, holidays, and other typical tough times." I paused, waiting for a reaction to my suggestion—one glance around the room told me—it was a bomb! We needed to talk more about the bonus traits—now!

REGULARITY

"I can hang in there all day, knowing I just have to make it until eight o'clock," Colleen stated. "I put him to bed at eight and he sleeps until eight the next morning."

Kathy turned to her in dismay. "Twelve hours," she practically choked. "I can't even remember the last time I got eight hours of uninterrupted sleep. John is sixteen months old and I'm still waiting for him to sleep through the night."

Some spirited kids are quite regular and their parents can count on a good night's sleep after a hectic day. It is their saving grace. Others however, are unpredictable. Their bodies do not seem to fall into natural rhythms. They're never hungry at the same time, can go days without having a bowel movement, and it's anyone's guess as to when they will be tired.

It is important to remember that if your child is irregular, he is not intentionally trying to wear you out or drive you to tears. He has a body rhythm that moves to its own drummer. He doesn't know why he lies awake at night unable to fall asleep. It is a mystery to him, why he isn't hungry when everyone else is, and all this fuss about regular bowel movements is rather confusing. He isn't trying to be contrary and you aren't doing something wrong. You simply have a child whose body works differently. He needs you to help him adapt to social schedules and learn the skills he needs to survive as an irregular person in a very scheduled world.

USING WORDS

Irregular kids are often the odd man out. Because their body rhythms frequently don't match with those of others they may think there is something wrong with them. It's important that they hear from you words that help them understand their irregularity and feel good about it.

"What can you say to your irregular child?" I asked the group. Blank stares met me.

"You drive me crazy, probably doesn't count, right?" Tom, our resident humorist, joked.

I laughed, noting that a sense of humor is essential to the survival of a parent with an irregular child, but encouraged him to try again.

"You really are very flexible," Patti offered, and the others followed.

"I don't have to worry about having dinner ready right at six o'clock. If you're not hungry we can eat later."

"You are full of surprises."

"You can be a disc jockey like your dad and work the swing shift."

Our brainstorming ended as Tom quipped, "You're going to love college life." Then dropping his voice, he whispered, "I'm not going to tell him that I am going to send him very far away so I can get some rest!"

Sometimes when your brain is fogged from lack of sleep it is difficult to think of positive messages to give your irregular child, but he needs to know that you understand his style and that other people—even grownups—experience irregular body rhythms too.

CREATING CUES

Lack of sleep, the disruption of routines, digression from "social schedules," and the inability to plan are major issues facing the parent of an irregular child. In order for you to survive, you have to help your irregular child adapt enough to be able to function within a school and family schedule. It isn't easy. Their natural body cues may be so erratic that you don't know where to start. In fact, mealtime and bedtime are such frequent issues for spirited kids that I have included a chapter on each. In chapters 14 and 15 you will find information that will help you to develop a routine that includes external cues—predictable signals—that help your irregular child adapt to your family's schedule.

Remember as you face the challenge of moving an irregular child toward some semblance of a schedule that it will take time. You are dealing with Mother Nature—the child's innate temperament. Remind yourself that your neighbors are not better parents because their child promptly falls asleep at eight o'clock every evening, nor have they discovered some magical way to lay him down. Their child simply experiences regular body rhythms. Your child is irregular. He arrived that way.

TEACH SELF-HELP SKILLS

Although irregular kids can gradually adapt to routines, it's very unlikely that they will ever become regular. Even when you get them to the table along with everyone else, they still need extra snacks. And although you may be able to get them into bed with relatively little hassle, they may still lie there for thirty to sixty minutes before falling asleep. To ensure that you can count on a decent night's sleep and avoid a career as a short-order cook, it is very important that as soon as possible you teach the irregular child to make his own snacks and dress himself. How to teach these self-help and other skills is addressed in chapters 14, 15, and 16.

WORKING TOGETHER

"I hate routines myself," Becky noted. "They are booooring. Kristin's irregularity isn't an issue for me. If she wants to stay up, I stay up. If she wants to sleep I sleep. When I was working, I never drove home the same way twice. I can't imagine anything more mundane."

If you are irregular too, your child's irregularity may not pose a problem for you. Be aware, however, that irregular parents may find it difficult to provide enough consistency in their child's life. Although it's unlikely that you will ever develop the kind of routine a regular parent may (or want to for that matter) you do need to be sure that there is enough predictability in your home for your child to get the rest and nutritional food she needs and to be able to function in a school schedule.

If you are a regular parent understand that your irregular child is not intentionally trying to torment you. His body just doesn't work like yours. Gradually he will be able to accept a schedule and may even like it, but his body rhythms will always be his own.

Feeling Good about Regularity

Take heart as you work with your irregular children. We need them. They grow up to be the nurses and doctors we find in the emergency room at two A.M. and the firefighters, police officers, pilots, disc jockeys, chefs, and other professionals who work crazy hours while the rest of us sleep. It isn't easy to live with an irregular two-year-old, but sooner than we might think, they'll move away and let us sleep and eat in peace!

ENERGY

"So what about energy," Bill demanded. "The kid sleeps but he never stops moving all day long. I'm worn out from chasing him. Is there anything I can do to settle him down?"

I thought for a moment before replying, then said, "Imagine for a moment that you are trapped, here in this room. It will be at least five hours until you are released. Take note—there is no rest room. A quick mental check on your bladder should let you know how comfortable the next five hours will be for you. You might be in big trouble. Inside your abdominal cavity, you may note a growing pressure. Your bladder may be announcing to you a grave need for release. Your brain might be telling you to tough it out, ignore the mounting tension within you, but if Mother Nature provided you with a small-capacity bladder, no matter how tough your brain might tell you to be, this may not be a case of mind over matter. If you don't get out of here you're going to be embarrassed. The sense of urgency increases. You feel strained, stretched to capacity. Your body practically screams for release."

Out of the corner of my eye, I noted that Bill was squirming in his chair and a few others had crossed their legs. I stopped. I didn't want to lose the whole group to the rest room! But it's important to remember that sense of pressure because just as your bladder signals a need for you and creates a pressure when that need goes unanswered, a child who is temperamentally active has a body that not only likes to move but *needs* to move. Your high-energy child isn't leaping off of the furniture in order to scare you to death. He isn't falling off of his chair at dinner to annoy you. He isn't trying to wear you out or distract you with his constant motion. He's on the move because he was born with a high energy level and he needs you to help him direct it in positive and fun ways.

USING WORDS

High-energy kids need to hear from us that we appreciate and value their energy, especially energetic girls. Although women's athletics have grown tremendously in recent years, an active little girl may still find herself chastised for rough-and-tumble play.

Look at the messages you give to your child about her energy. Do they help her to understand and feel good about it? If they do, they might sound like these our group came up with:

Your body is full of energy.

I wish I had your energy.

You need to wiggle and be on the move.

You'll make a great athlete and parent.

You are an energetic worker.

You like to learn by using your body.

Your whole body tells me that you are happy.

These messages and others like them help a high-energy child to understand the urge to move that lies within her body. They let her know that her energy is a valuable trait.

EXPECT ENERGY

It isn't your imagination that your high-energy kid is on the move more than other children. Recently I observed two eighteen-month-old children in our early childhood classroom. During the fifteen minutes that I watched, one child sat quietly at a table and played with a button game for ten of the fifteen minutes. His parents had rated him a two for energy level on the temperamental chart. During that same fifteen minutes the other toddler climbed into the rocking boat, climbed out of the rocking boat, climbed into the boat again, leapt out of it, grabbed a telephone off of the shelf, ran to show it to his teacher, and threw the phone into the rocking boat before climbing in after it. In the time that I watched, his body hardly stopped moving for more than a few moments. Even when he sat down to "read" a book he alternated between standing and sitting. His parents had ranked him five plus for energy.

All toddlers are on the move, pushing, shoving, dumping, climbing, and taking things apart. Toddlers learn with their bodies, however the high-energy toddler is the epitome of energy—an energy that follows her into adulthood.

If your child is a high-energy kid, expect it, don't fight it. Plan for it. "After we completed the temperament chart," Kathy said, "I realized that Brent has a high energy level. Before, when he wouldn't sit, I thought I was doing something wrong. I just couldn't figure out how to get him to sit. He was out of control sometimes. Then I wasn't in control of my child and it felt awful. When I realized that he has a high energy level, I started planning active play times into our day. If we take care of his need to move, everything else seems to go more smoothly."

"What kinds of things can you do?" I asked the group.

"I enrolled him in karate," Alice said. "I went to different schools and found the one with the shortest lines. I knew if the classes were big and he had to wait for his turn too long, he'd get in trouble for turning somersaults in line. He loves it. I was worried he'd use it on the playground and get into more trouble, but the karate instructors teach the kids to be very disciplined. It's been great."

"I let him jump on the couch," Patti responded. "We don't have room for a trampoline or something like that. I've told him he can't jump on other people's couches, but it's okay on our old navy blue one."

"We only go to fast-food restaurants," Bill said. "If we have to wait for a table, I know he'll be in the fish tank. He's only two, so I'm hoping someday soon, we'll be able to go other places."

"We let her be the errand runner at dinner," Martha added. "We send her for another carton of milk, the napkins, or whatever. That way it isn't as noticeable when she's constantly getting in and out of her chair."

Mike leaned forward, anxious to offer his advice. "I went to school and looked for the most active second-grade teacher. The guy was on the floor with the kids, walking around the room, talking with his hands—obviously a real high-energy guy. I said, 'Put my daughter in that classroom,' and they did. She's doing really well."

"I'll have to remember that," Kathy remarked as she continued with her suggestion. "We stop every hour and a half when we're traveling. I think my husband needs it the most, but it keeps the kids happy too."

No matter what the situation, you need to plan for your high-energy child's need to move. Expect it. Don't set him up for failure. Select athletic activities where lines are short and the action is fast, such as soccer, basketball, and karate, rather than baseball, where there may be a great deal of down time. Tour your home from an active child's point of view. Recognize that high-energy kids need more space. When you plan a trip, include stops for energy releases. By recognizing your child's innate need to move and planning for it, you help him to direct his energy in a positive way.

RECOGNIZE HOW ENERGY IS TIED TO OTHER TRAITS

When your kitchen sink overflows, water running across the floor may be the first indication that you have a problem. But unless you find the faucet and turn off the water—the real source of the problem—mopping the floor won't do you any good.

The same is true when your high-energy child "revs up." While it may be a wild leap off of the couch that catches your attention, the real issue may not be "wild" behavior but the underlying emotion that he is expressing—an emotion tied to one of the other temperamental traits. Stopping him or slowing him down may not solve the problem unless you discover what he is really trying to say and teach him more appropriate ways to express himself.

Think about the last time your child got revved up and out of control. Was there another temperamental trait involved?

"Company was arriving," Mark offered, when I asked the group this question. "The first person arrived at the door and Emily took off racing around the room. It's embarrassing trying to greet people while your child is pinging around the room. I thought she was just being a jerk, but when you think about it, it was a transition. She really is slow to adapt, maybe she was expressing her discomfort."

"Last Christmas I thought someone had put drugs in my son's food,"

Laurie added. "He was in overdrive. I wasn't prepared for that, I guess it could have been from too much stimulation. He really is sensitive."

"We had company last night," Mari responded. "He was up moving around, taking things apart until eleven o'clock even though the company had left at nine-thirty. I think Laurie is right, the stimulation was more than he could handle. He was pretty good while they were there, but he had to work it out afterward."

"I think the issue for Brandon is intensity," Tom added. "He's intense about everything and when he's playing, he doesn't just grab one ball, he grabs four and then throws them all at the same time."

"Persistence is the problem for Jamie. I took him to play at the gym. They let the kids play on all of the equipment and then have parents and kids sit in a circle to sing songs. The other kids run to find a spot on the circle, but he won't get off the trampoline. He absolutely locks in."

High-energy kids express themselves with their whole bodies. That means that if a child is energetic and intense he may tackle his friend because he is excited to see him. If he is energetic and slow to adapt he may feel uncomfortable with the transition when grandparents arrive and run wildly around the room. And if he is energetic and sensitive, when overwhelmed by stimulation his activity may turn into a frenzy.

If you have a high-energy child, watch carefully for "rev up." When you start to sense that the activity is getting out of control, move in and check closely. Is your child just being active or is he acting out another temperamental trait? If it is another temperamental trait, you will have to help him deal with that particular need. For example, if he is intense and excited about seeing his friend, talk with him about the appropriate way to greet the friend and how to diffuse his energy and intensity by inviting the friend to play ball. If a transition is the issue, you may need to hold him and talk him through it. If the real issue is overstimulation, you may need to direct him to a soothing, calming activity like playing in warm water or reading a book.

If your child is expressing another temperamental trait rather than just being energetic, more climbing or jumping will not wear him out or slow him down. High-energy kids don't wear out. In order to channel his energy well and to teach him to express his needs appropriately find the real reason for his wild behavior. Don't let the movement mask the true issue—another temperamental need.

EXPECT TO DIRECT HIM WITH GENTLE TOUCH

High-energy kids are usually very kinesthetic learners. They solve problems by using their bodies. That's why they are always taking things apart or climbing across the table to get a toy rather than asking for it. They think with their whole body. As a result it is very difficult if not impossible to direct the high-energy child with words alone. When the temperamental traits of high energy and perceptiveness are linked together, the only way to let this child know that your message is the most important is to touch him with it.

Your touch needs to be gentle. A sensitive and intense child will react negatively to a harsh or rough touch. Grabbing him will only result in a struggle, but you do need to get eye contact and gently touch his arm or shoulder when giving him directions. Then he will know that this is the message to which he needs to listen.

WORKING TOGETHER

High-energy kids demand a great deal of attention from their parents. Safety is a constant issue. You are always on guard, monitoring their whereabouts and activities and getting up to direct them. If they are ex-traverted, their energy may come out of their mouths, as a continuous chatter from morning to night. Each word from them demands your full attention, and every toy they pick up may be brought to you for your appraisal. If you are a high-energy person yourself, you may be doing well keeping up with your energetic child. If, however, your energy level is lower than your child's by the end of the day, you may feel as if a Mack truck has hit you.

Of course, the obvious answer is to get a sitter to allow yourself a break, but as Bill reminded me in class one night, this may be easier said than done.

"Who," he asked, "are you supposed to leave him with? He wears out an older person and a younger sitter may not be able to keep him safe."

True, this is a problem, especially with a young toddler, but you need to get a break. Talk with teachers at your local high school or check with youth leaders at your church or temple to find a responsible teen you can train to watch your child. Then invite her to your home and work with her and your child until you feel comfortable leaving them alone together. If you still don't feel comfortable wait until your child falls asleep and then go out, leaving the sitter to watch him. If you take this tack, be sure your child is familiar with the sitter and knows she's coming; otherwise, he may be very upset if he awakens while you're gone.

If you are a high-energy person, realize that when you have to sit still for long periods of time at a desk, or are confined in the house with small children, the pressure to move builds up within you too. You can't cope as well when you're trying to manage your own surging need to move. Exercise is a very important outlet for you. Plan it into your day.

As high-activity kids grow and learn to channel their energy into appropriate channels the drain on you will be reduced. In fact if you are a high-energy person also you may enjoy biking, playing ball, and exercising together. If you're not, the opportunity to sit on the bench and watch while your child runs around a soccer field may be a wonderful break.

Enjoy Energy

Bo Jackson is a high-energy individual who has honed his skills and maximized the opportunities available to him. As a professional baseball and football player he provided hours of entertainment for millions of people. Although not all high-energy people become professional athletes, in our fast-paced society, adults with a high energy level are generally esteemed. They can keep up with a household of kids, the demands of the workplace, and still find the energy to volunteer in the community. Being energetic is an asset.

FIRST REACTION

"What's the difference between encouragement and pushing?" I asked the group.

"Encouragement makes me feel confident," Alice replied. "Pushing makes me feel out of control."

Understanding the difference between pushing and encouragement is critical when your child's first reaction to new situations, people, or things is to reject them or to approach them very cautiously. Spirited kids who experience a negative first reaction need our encouragement—not our push.

Studies of temperamental contributions to social behavior conducted by Dr. Jerome Kagan at Harvard University have demonstrated that about 15 percent of all children are born with a tendency to become upset in new and unfamiliar situations. Their blood pressure rises, pupils dilate, and vocal cords tense.

It's hard to imagine that your child isn't deliberately attempting to embarrass you when he refuses to get in the pool at his first swimming lesson. It is extremely frustrating when you take your child shopping and she rejects everything in the shop or when you prepare a new dish and she pushes it away. It is draining when your child cries all day because you got rid of the old couch and bought a new one. But for the child whose first reaction is to withdraw or reject anything new her behavior is not a ploy to get your attention. According to Kagan, "These kids inherit a neurochemistry that makes them very excitable."

For these children their first and most natural reaction to every new food, stranger, place, and even smell is to push it away. They need our help to calm their strong reactions and our assistance in learning how to feel comfortable and in control in unfamiliar situations.

LESSONS IN ENCOURAGEMENT

I first thought about the lessons in encouragement one day when I was waiting for my kids to finish swimming lessons. On that particular day there was a four-year-old sobbing at poolside. His eyes red and swollen, he shook his head in dismay, refusing to respond to the instructor's words. She jumped out of the pool to bring him closer, but his spindly wrist slipped through her grasp as he backed away from the edge. He stood tense, wanting to run yet hating to give up. He looked imploringly at his mother who was sitting next to me. I wondered what she would do and as I watched she clearly taught me a lesson in the steps to encouragement.

Without any hesitation she walked confidently toward her son and warmly gave him a hug. She didn't let his reluctance or tears embarrass her. She recognized that he was afraid. Her actions said, "I am here for you. I understand. I am not angry. I will help you." *The first lesson in encouragement: I will support you.*

I heard her ask him what he was feeling inside. Did his stomach feel pinched? Could he feel his heart pounding? He nodded. "That's fear," she explained. "You haven't had swimming lessons before and your body is telling you to be careful. It is all right to be afraid. I feel fear sometimes too." *Lesson number two: Encouragement helps us understand our feelings and know that others have felt that way too.*

The mother continued talking. "What helps me when I am afraid," she said, "is to sit back and watch for a while. I like to see how the other people get the water out of their eyes, how they kick their feet, and move their arms. Then I plan what I will do." *Lesson number three: Encouragement allows us time to think and an opportunity to observe so that we feel in control.*

Together mother and son moved back to the bench along the wall and sat there watching the other swimmers. She reminded him how he used to hate having his hair washed when he was a toddler and now he never cried and could almost wash it all by himself. "Maybe," she said, with a smile, "You know more about swimming than you think." *Lesson number four: Encouragement builds bridges from our past successes to the present situations.*

The mom and son sat silently for a while, his body resting against her arm. His breathing visibly slowed as he relaxed, realizing he wasn't alone in this venture. The teacher came back to poolside and invited him to dangle his feet in the water. She promised not to pull him in. He looked at his mom. She nodded. "You can do it. Remember, it's just like the bath-tub."

He sat down gingerly, first dangling a toe in the water, and then letting his feet sink to his ankles. Soon he was kicking with both feet, and squealing with delight when the water splashed up on his legs and then on his face. The teacher clapped. "Great kicks," she exclaimed. "Maybe tomorrow you'll be ready to hang on to the edge and slide into the pool." *Lesson number five: Encouragement helps us to see the parts of a task so we don't feel overwhelmed and allows us to choose when we are ready.*

I saw the boy and his mother leave. His head held high, a smile on his face. He hadn't entered the pool on his own, but I could tell he was feeling good. He didn't feel like a failure. He didn't feel pushed. He felt encour-aged, capable, and hopeful for success. Who knows, maybe tomorrow he'll be ready to say, "I can do it." *Lesson number six: Encouragement takes time.*

You cannot convince a cautious child with facts that she shouldn't be afraid. The fact is she is. Her heart is pounding, her mouth is dry, and her blood pressure is rising. She can't be rushed. If your child will be forced to participate in an activity immediately, do your best to arrive early at the school, the pool, or whatever the new situation is so that she will have had an opportunity to watch, listen, think, and calm herself before she is ex-pected to participate. If you can't visit ahead of time, talk about what to expect. Show her pictures if you can or anything else that will help her feel more comfortable.

Kathy had been listening intently to my story, and as I finished she nodded in agreement. "Sarah is so active. We wanted her to play basket-ball, but she absolutely refused. She wasn't going to try it. I knew that she would love it, if only I could get her on the court. I told her, 'Sarah I know you haven't done this before and you're feeling that you won't like it, but I think it will be fun—think about it.'

"Our neighbor Tonya was playing on the eighth-grade team. We went to a game. Sarah watched intently. She asked a lot of questions, but I couldn't tell if she liked it or not. I kept my mouth shut. The next morning she handed me the registration form and said, 'Fill this out, will you? I want to play like Tonya.' "

It's important not to let a negative first reaction trap your child in a corner. By giving her a chance to think, to observe, to gather information, Kathy allowed Sarah the opportunity to let go of her first reaction and choose to participate. It's important to give spirited kids this second chance—to let them know it is all right to change their minds. This isn't coddling them. It's recognizing their temperament and working with it.

Our encouragement is very important for children who experience a strong first reaction, without it they may miss out on many opportunities, not realizing that with time, thought, and practice they'll truly enjoy themselves. Practice is important. Children who experience a strong first reaction need practice to develop their skills and build their confidence that they can handle and even learn to enjoy new experiences.

WORKING TOGETHER

When kids demonstrate an immediate resistance, it tends to bring out a similar reaction in us, especially if our first reaction is rejection too.

"My kids have learned never to ask me for an immediate answer," Kim joked. "I didn't realize how strong my first reaction was until I heard my fourteen-year-old warn the other kids, 'Don't ask Mom a yes-or-no question. Just say think about this. If you ask her for a quick answer she always says no.' "

Whether it's your first reaction, or your child's, recognize that you need time to think before making a final decision. Your first reaction may not be your final one. And like your child, you may also be feeling afraid. Self-talk can help get you through. Tell yourself, "I'm not feeling comfortable, but I really think I will like this [or, it will be all right]." If you are with your child, talk out loud. That way she will learn to talk herself through new situations too.

Enjoy First Reaction

Although helping your child work through her first reaction may take time, it is a trait that most parents come to appreciate as they begin to realize that their child thinks before she acts. During adolescence the value of this trait will be even greater.

If you experience a strong first reaction, reread this book! You may find helpful information that you passed by with the first reading.

MOOD

It was a beautiful sunny August morning. My eleven-year-old son was on his way to basketball camp. "Have a good day," I called as he opened the door to leave.

He stopped dead in his tracks. "Have a good day," he exclaimed incredulously. "How can I have a good day? The president has sent troops to Saudi Arabia, Iraq is rumored to be using poisonous gas in Kuwait, oil prices are skyrocketing, and the stock market fell ninety-three points. How can I possibly have a good day?"

"Do the best that you can, honey," I remarked, and gave him a quick kiss on the cheek.

Studies show that the secret to a child's disposition may lie in a specific pattern of brain activity. In the 1980s, in a study of how frontal brain asymmetry predicts infants' responses to maternal separation, researchers at the University of Oregon and the State University of New York at Purchase observed that some individuals are more upset by distressing events and less cheered by amusing things than individuals with a less serious disposition.

"It's true," Bill remarked. "I never see the positive first. I always think about what's not working and because I'm an extravert my emotions flow right out. Everyone knows when I don't like something."

For the children who are serious and analytical, their mood has nothing to do with a good night's sleep. It is directly linked to their brain patterns. They need your help understanding their disposition and to learn to be positive and tactful as well as cognizant of the things that need to be fixed.

USING WORDS

Serious and analytical kids aren't trying to be mean or to put a damper on the day's activities, they simply see the world from a very serious perspective. They need us to give them the words to express those serious thoughts without offending others or creating a sense of hopelessness. There's a children's book called *Puppy Too Small,* by Cyndy Szekeres, that provides a delightful lesson for analytical kids. In the book Little Puppy wails, "I'm too small! I can't reach the doorknob."

"But you can reach the cookies on the table," Mouse replies. "Please share one with me."

And Puppy does. "I'm too small!" wails Puppy, on the next page. "I can't pull my toy box."

"But you can pull my wagon full of dear ones," Mrs. Bunny replies. "Would you?"

And Puppy does.

Analytical kids go through life like Little Puppy. They need our help recognizing what's working as well as what's not. We can say to them, "Tell me what you enjoyed today and then tell me what you didn't like." Or ask them, "If you can't do that, what can you do?" Let them know that you appreciate their analytical point of view by saying things like, "You're a good analyst," "You notice the things that need to be fixed," or "You think deeply. You will make a great judge or newscaster." Teach them to break things into parts so that they can clearly see the pieces they enjoyed as well as those that need to be reviewed or revised.

When you watch the world news, point out to your analytical child the anchor's serious presentation of the information. If there are other people in your family who share this perspective let your child know that others see the world from an analytical point of view too.

TEACH GOOD MANNERS

Small children are egocentric. If they feel it, they say it, believing that everyone must feel as they do. Help your serious and analytical child stay on good terms with the relatives and neighbors by teaching her good manners. This is especially true when it comes to receiving gifts or enjoying a holiday meal. In chapter 18, I'll talk about this more.

WORK TOGETHER

If you are a serious and analytical parent it is easy to go right past what went well to what you want to be better. Remind yourself to pat yourself on the back for your accomplishments and celebrate each success, no matter how small it might be. Don't let one problem rob you of the joy of the good moments.

Remember, too, that your first inclination is to see the flaws. Allow yourself to look for strengths as well as weakness in your spirited child, in the people you work and live with, and in the situations you face daily. Hold a vision that maximizes their potential.

If you are not an analytical individual understand that your serious child is seeing the world from his own perspective. When he points out to you the things he doesn't like or those that didn't come out quite right, he isn't necessarily unhappy—to him it is just a fact. Listen to his concerns, address those that are significant, and let go of those that are simply an expression of his view.

Enjoy Your Child's Mood

Serious and analytical kids can come in handy, especially when you are making a major purchase. In class, Richard told us how his twelve-year-old son helped them make a very important decision.

"We were looking at a new house," he said. "My wife and I really liked it and we were just bringing the kids through to get their reaction. Todd is a real estate agent's nightmare. As we went through the house he kept pointing to different things saying. 'Our furniture would never fit in this room. Why would you want this? Look at this carpeting, what a dreadful color! The garage is too small. Look at the hill in the yard. You don't expect me to mow that, do you?' His critical eye took in everything. My wife and I really hadn't noticed those things—and you know—he was right."

The world needs people with a critical eye. They grow up to be evaluators making sure our programs are well run. They aren't afraid to make the tough decisions—and they can save you money . . . just ask Richard.

REGULARITY: A SUMMARY

Unpredictable describes many, but not all spirited kids. Their bodies do not seem to fall into natural rhythms. They're never hungry at the same time and it's a good guess as to when they will be tired.

Irregular spirited kids need to hear:

You are really flexible.

You are full of surprises.

You'll make a great emergency room doctor, disc jockey, pilot, police officer, or other professional that works crazy hours.

You're going to love college life.

Teaching tips:

Provide a routine and a schedule that is consistent so your child can gradually adapt to it.

Expect your irregular child to take longer to adapt to a routine, but with patience and consistency he can.

Teach your child self-help skills as soon as you can.

If you are irregular too:

Be aware that you may be inconsistent with mealtimes and bedtimes because you are irregular. Your child may need more consistency than you are providing.

ENERGY: A SUMMARY

Many, but not all, spirited kids are energetic. The need for them to move is real and inside. They like to climb, jump, run, and in general be on the move. The challenge for their parents is to keep them safe and to teach them to use their energy in positive and fun ways.

Energetic spirited kids need to hear:

Your body is full of energy.

I wish I had your energy.

You need to wiggle and move.

You like to learn by using your body.

You'll make a great athlete and parent.

You are an energetic worker.

Teaching tips:

Plan for your child's energy. Provide many opportunities to run, jump, and climb, but monitor stimulation levels closely to prevent rev up.

Avoid activities that require sitting for a long period of time.

After your child has been sitting still for a long time or has been confined to a small space expect to allow him time and space to move.

Recognize that wild activity is often related to the other temperamental traits such as overstimulation or too many transitions.

If you are energetic too:

Plan exercise in your day.

Know that it is difficult for you to cope when you are forced to sit for a long period of time.

Enjoy athletic activities with your child.

FIRST REACTION: A SUMMARY

Studies conducted by Dr. Kagan at Harvard University have demonstrated that about 15 percent of all children are born with a tendency to become upset in new and unfamiliar situations. Their blood pressure rises, pupils dilate, and vocal cords tense. Spirited kids who experience a strong first reaction need our encouragement—not our push.

Spirited kids who experience a strong first reaction need to hear:

I will support you.

It is all right to watch before participating.

You like to check things out before you jump right in.

You can think about it and then decide.

New things and situations are difficult for you but remember last time
. . . when you were successful.

It's all right to change your mind.

Teaching tips:

Encourage your child. Don't push him.

Warn your child about new things that will be happening. Talk about what to expect.

Arrive early or visit a new place ahead of time, before your child is expected to participate.

Allow your child time to observe.

Provide lots of opportunities to practice.

Remind your child of similar situations that she rejected at first but enjoys now.

Allow your child a second chance.

If your first reaction is negative too:

Reread this book! There may be information you rejected the first time you read it, but with a second reading may prove to be useful.

Recognize that your first reaction may not be your final one.

Allow yourself to think before you respond to your child's questions.

MOOD: A SUMMARY

Studies show that the secret to a child's disposition may lie in a specific pattern of brain activity. For the child who is serious and analytical, her mood has nothing to do with a good night's sleep. It is directly linked to her brain patterns. She needs your help understanding her disposition and learning to be positive and tactful as well as analytical.

Serious and analytical kids need to hear:

I appreciate your suggestions.

You are a good evaluator.

You think deeply. You will make a great judge, newscaster, etc.

You are a serious person. That doesn't mean you are unhappy.

Tell me what you enjoyed. Then tell me what you would like to see done differently.

Teaching tips:

Help your child see the positives. If she can't do something, help her to see what she can do.

Teach your child good manners.

Ask specific questions that require her to think about the parts of an issue or time rather than making one general analytical statement about the entire thing.

If you are serious and analytical too:

Practice looking for the positive aspects of people and situations as you analyze them.

Celebrate the little successes. Don't let one problem rob you of the joy of the good moments.

12

TANTRUMS: SPOTTING THE TRIGGERS

My grandmother told me I used to go out on the porch and let loose. She referred to me as the "emotional hurricane."
—Naomi Judd, of The Judds singing duo

Y OU'VE GOT to help me *now!*" blurted the voice on the other end of my telephone line. A plea for assistance from a friend across the country. Seems her four-year-old son Michael had spent the day doing everything he could to get her goat—swearing, punching his sisters, talking back, and refusing to do anything he was told. He had just been sent to his room to rot for the rest of his life. He saw it as an opportunity to tear the sheets and blankets off of his bed, dump the table, and even tip over the lamp. My friend had stormed into the room, demanding that he clean it up before he showed his face again. Needless to say he threw himself onto the bed in a hysterical heap and was still there when she called.

Sometimes, despite your best efforts to work with spirit, the words haven't come, the soothing activities haven't been effective, there have been too many transitions, too much stimulation, or too much stress. Your child is on a rampage. The force is penetrating. You feel bruised and maybe even powerless to respond.

All kids throw tantrums, but spirited children do it with much more pizzazz, finesse, and frequency. My friend who has raised five kids, now all grown, says, "If I put on one chart all the tantrums of the four younger ones, the total wouldn't even come close to what the oldest one pulled all by herself. Today I can tell you she's an absolutely sparkling adult, but it's a miracle we're both still alive to see it."

SPIRITED KIDS EXPERIENCE SPILL-OVER TANTRUMS

Michael's tantrum looked like a classic manipulative temper tantrum. It sounded like one too, but it wasn't. As I talked with my friend, I realized that Michael's tantrum had nothing to do with power or wanting control. It wasn't even meant as a personal attack on his mother or sisters. His tantrum had been building for hours even days. For the last three weeks his father had been locked in negotiation meetings from six in the morning until well past midnight. Alone at home with three preschoolers, Mom was exhausted and short on patience. Michael is spirited. Michael is temperamentally sensitive. He absorbed the stress and strains his family was experiencing until he reached his limit. Then he blew, taking the contents of his room with him. This is a spill-over tantrum.

Dr. Stella Chess and Alexander Thomas, authors of *Know Your Child,* define a spill-over tantrum as "an outpouring of emotion in a disorganized way." The steamy reactions of spirited kids make them much more vulnerable to spill-over tantrums—a flood of emotions that overwhelms them and pushes them beyond their temperamental ability to cope. *In my experience, most of the tantrums experienced by spirited children are actually spill-over tantrums.* They are not premeditated. They are not intended to manipulate.

That's why the typical advice for handling temper tantrums doesn't work with spirited children. A spill-over tantrum can't be stopped by ignoring it because your child is dealing with a temperamental issue. Your child needs you to help him discover the source of the emotional flood and *stop* it. He needs your direction to help him calm himself and regain self-control. Without that direction he can rage for hours because his inner restraints have busted, letting loose all his wild emotions.

As one five-year-old explained to his dad, after losing it in the car during rush-hour traffic in New York City, "I wanted to stop, Daddy, but you see, it's like people who can't stop smoking. I really couldn't stop."

SPILL-OVER TANTRUMS APPEAR DURING INFANCY

Spill-over tantrums are different from manipulative tantrums in when they appear. Most manipulative tantrums begin around the age of two when children are first learning to be independent. Spill-over tantrums, because they are tied to temperament, are apparent even during infancy.

"Travis was only a week old the first time he flooded," Pat offered during a discussion of temper tantrums. "Company was arriving just at his nap time. Strangers were holding him and talking to him. The noise level in the room was very high. His dad and I were trying to entertain, pouring coffee and getting food for everyone. We weren't focusing on him. Travis had been listening and watching everyone very intently, but because he is sensitive and slow to adapt, he couldn't take it. Abruptly his face flushed red and he started to scream. The sobs came from deep inside him, totally overwhelming him."

Spill-over tantrums during infancy are often one of the first signs of spirit for many families. For those like Travis the flood results in sobs that emerge from the soul. Their movements are jerky and their faces red. But not all spill-over tantrums look the same, especially as children grow and develop.

Tammie, whose son Steven has the gleam of spirit in his eyes, explained, "Steven doesn't cry, he goes into a frenzy of activity. Last Sunday we invited friends over for dinner. He was so excited that within minutes of their arrival his intensity was out of control. He was a flying saucer whirling around the room in every direction. It was impossible to stop him."

Kathy's son Collin doesn't scream or act out. His intensity turns inward. "Last week Collin couldn't tie his shoe," she told the group, "I could tell he was getting really frustrated, but he didn't holler, instead he fell face first on the floor, his body sagging like a cardboard box left out in the rain. 'I can't do it,' he moaned, then started to weep."

Whatever your child's spill-over tantrums look like, it is critical to recognize that it is a spirited child swamped by his own emotions, pushed beyond his temperamental ability to cope, not a child out to get you. A child who doesn't know what happened to him, what to do about it, how to stop it, or if he should even try. You have to teach him all of these things.

DEALING WITH YOUR OWN TANTRUM

The problem, of course, is that people talk about temper tantrums as though the kids go out on an island and stand there and scream. Nobody talks about what it *feels* like to be the parent of the kid who can back up an entire checkout line while she gyrates on the floor and lets loose with bloodcurdling wails. Magazine articles never discuss how to make excuses for being late because your child wouldn't get in the car seat. And holiday stories fail to include the reality of watching in horror as your eight-year-old bursts into tears because Grandma didn't cut the cranberry gel into turkey shapes as she has for the last eight years. Temper tantrums—it isn't only the kids that are experiencing a major reaction. It's you, me, and any other parent that has to survive the penetrating intensity of spirited children.

It's much easier to keep your cool when you can quickly identify the reason for the spill-over tantrum. There are times, however, when it isn't easy to be analytical, especially when your toddler is pulling at your leg, the telephone is ringing, and the baby is fussing. At that point it's pretty difficult to calmly stop and ask, "Why are you really doing this?" You may just want to scream right along with her.

If you find yourself unable to think because you are so upset, go back to chapter 6 and review the methods for diffusing your own intense reaction. In this situation you have to keep your cool in order to help your child.

LOOK FOR THE TRIGGER

Think about the last time you screamed, swore, or hit the kitchen cupboards. This is an adult tantrum—an outpouring of emotion in a disorganized way. It may have started because you are temperamentally active but all day you were forced to sit through an incredibly boring meeting and you desperately need some exercise. It could have been because you are slow to adapt and your day at work was full of surprises. You have worked hard to cope, but despite your best efforts your strong emotions overwhelmed you and you blew up. The same thing happens to your kids.

Next time your child starts to fuss and fume, run a mental checklist of his temperamental traits. One or more of them are the source of the "flood," the force that is pushing him beyond his ability to cope. The temperamental triggers vary with each individual, but whatever it is, there is a pattern. Watch for it. Find it. Every time your child has a tantrum, write down when and where it happens, and at what time of day. When a sensitive child is overstimulated, a persistent child isn't successful, a slow-to-adapt child is surprised, or an energetic child isn't allowed to move, he is vulnerable to a spill-over tantrum.

Teach yourself to think about what is upsetting your child. Avoid the trap of discounting him, by telling yourself, "There he goes again." He is flooded, unable to stop the forces surging within him. He experiences a tantrum not to embarrass you but because he has been pushed beyond his temperamental ability to cope.

PEAK TIMES

Spill-over tantrums can occur at any time of the day or week but there appear to be certain peak times when you really need to be prepared. I once asked a group of parents when their children experienced the most spill-over tantrums. They told me, between four and six P.M. I didn't hear their response correctly and thought they had said, "When their parents wanted to have sex," which could be true too. The time of day when your child loses it may vary with every child, but merely understanding that there are peak periods for spill-over tantrums can help you to be more patient with your child.

Late afternoons: If you keep a log of your child's spill-over tantrums it's very likely that the greatest number will occur during the late afternoon. That's because it is easier to flood when everyone is tired and hungry, when you've had the whole day to collect sensations, or when the transitions have piled up. Think carefully about your plans for late afternoon, and avoid situations that require your children to work hard at managing their behavior. They just don't have the energy to do it at this time of the day and flood more easily. It's very likely that you have less energy to help them as well.

Developmental surges: Kids go through developmental surges. You can mark it on your calendar. Somewhere around their birthday and their half birthday, you can expect trouble. They'll get cranky and uncooperative. They might be incapable of doing what they were able to do just a few weeks before. Nothing seems right. They're easily frustrated. Every time you turn around they're crying about something else. They won't cooperate. They want to be held and then push you away when you hold them. They're angry—angry at you, at the world, and at themselves. They are *more* easily upset by *anything*!

The developmental theorists tell us that this is a time of disintegration. A time when children are moving from one stage of development to another. Their inner systems are restructuring, creating a new, more complex way of understanding the world.

Think of five building blocks. Stack them one on top of the other until you have a tower of five blocks. This is your five-year-old, his inner structure that controls how he sees the world and responds to it. It works well for him but as he nears his sixth birthday, changes begin to occur. A new block will be added to the structure, but it won't just be added to the top of the stack. Instead, the tower will come crashing down—it will disintegrate and a new structure with six blocks will be formed. This time it may be in the shape of a pyramid, with three blocks on the bottom, two in the middle and the sixth resting on top. It will be a totally different structure. During this construction time, which can take four to six weeks, everything that was working well for your child doesn't seem to be working anymore. He becomes overwhelmed easily and is more vulnerable to spill-over tantrums.

It happens to all kids, but as is always true for spirited children, their reactions are much stronger. Mark your calendar and be ready for the surges.

Empty energy banks: Empty energy banks can also lead to spill-over tantrums. If your child is an introvert and hasn't had any time alone to recharge you can predict that she may flood. If your child is an extravert and hasn't had an opportunity to play with other children or with you, expect her to lose it. When coping levels are low, there's nothing to stop the flood of emotions.

WHAT TO DO WITH TANTRUMS

When spirited kids experience spill-over tantrums they are incapable of stopping themselves. They need us to help them calm down and regain control. Because each spirited child is unique, what works for one child may not work with another, but here are a few techniques that have been effective for others. Use those that work for you.

Stop the flood: In *The Difficult Child*, authors Stanley Turecki and Leslie Tonner suggest, "If you can, stop whatever triggered your child."

If she is overstimulated, take her to a quiet place. If you have been shopping and there have been too many transitions for her to adapt to, forget about going to one more store. If she has been still too long, find a place to let her run. Whatever is flooding her, pushing her beyond her ability to cope, has to be stopped before she can regain control.

"Isn't this giving in?" many parents will ask me.

Recognizing that this tantrum is a spill-over tantrum is not giving in. It is being respectful of your child's temperament and acknowledging her limits. With your guidance, she will become more capable and better able to cope, but that takes time. Until then you have to be sensitive to her limits and help her to be successful.

Stay with or near your child: Your presence is essential to helping your child calm down. I was observing at a day-care center one morning when a mom dropped off her preschooler. The little girl started to scream and kick the minute Mom started out the door. I recognized a slow-to-adapt child who was having trouble with a transition, but her teachers and her mom weren't familiar with temperament and didn't understand what was happening. They thought it was a manipulative tantrum and sent her to the corner to cry it out on her own, while they went on with their business. I moved close to her. She didn't know me and didn't want me to touch her, but I kept my body relaxed and nonverbally invited her to come closer. Gradually she moved nearer until her head rested on my lap. Only then did she stop crying.

To be left alone with such strong emotions can be very frightening to small children. They need your physical presence to let them know you care and that you are available if they need you. If your child is older and wants to be left alone, respect that wish, but be sure she is comfortable with it before you leave her to handle it on her own. Let her know you are near and will help her stop if she wants your support. With your words and your actions invite her to come closer.

If you find you are getting upset too, you may need to walk away for a few minutes but then come back. Tell your child you are stepping away, but assure her that you will be back.

Touch her: Many times a hug, a back scratch, or any other warm, gentle touch is just what your child needs to close the floodgates. Think about your child. What kind of touch soothes her?

"Stroking Robbie's eyebrows will quiet him," Duane responded to this question when I asked it in a class.

"Carl needs me to wrap my arms around him and hold him tight. Sort of like going back into the womb," Ann replied.

Touch—soft, gentle touch—can help our children regain control. Often when kids tantrum we don't feel very gentle, but if we can regain control of our own emotions and reach out lightly rather than harshly, our mere touch may stop the flood.

Give him space: Space seems to be very important to many spirited children, especially those who are introverts. "The worst thing I can do is try to pick Brett up. He needs to be near me, but he doesn't want to be held," Kim told me.

For some children, moving into their space may add to the stimulation level. If this is true for your child, respect his boundaries and move away slightly, but do not leave him alone.

Tell her to stop: After ten to fifteen minutes, if your child has not pulled herself out of the flood, gently but firmly say, "Stop. You are flooded. It is time to stop now." It's as though she were incapable of stopping herself. She needs you to call it quits for her. Show her how to take deep, relaxing breaths. The ones that pull from your diaphragm and are let out slowly. Ninety percent of the time, she will come out of it, if you are firm, gentle, and focused on her. The other 10 percent of the time you may need to give her more time, or call in another adult to take over for you if you feel yourself being sucked into the tantrum.

Talk about what's flooding her: Even while your child is still cry-ing, you can try talking with her. It may work or it may have to wait until later but it is worth a try. Let the first surge of intensity pass. Then explain to her what has happened. "This is a flood. You are being overwhelmed by your emotions."

Kids don't know what is happening to them. They only know that they are out of control and it doesn't feel good. If you know why they are being inundated, tell them. If the trigger is adaptability you might say something like "You've done a super job today, but there were too many transitions" or "Finding company here after your nap was really shocking to you."

If the trigger is sensitivity, your message could be "The amusement park was fun but you've had enough stimulation" or "I miss Daddy too. You always let us know when we need time together again."

If the trigger is energy that hasn't been released, you might say, "You've sat quietly for a long time, but now your body is telling you it's time to run and play."

Whatever the trigger, by telling your children what is flooding them, you help them to understand what is happening to them. This in itself is soothing. It also gives them words to use the next time they experience a similar rush of emotions or sensations.

Spirited babies flood too, especially from overstimulation, too many transitions, and new situations. Talk to them as you would an older child. You won't get the same kind of response but some day, sooner than you might imagine, you will.

Use a soft, but firm voice: Getting your child to listen to you during a tantrum can be tough. For Tom success is tied to the tone of his voice.

"I bend down and look her right in the eye," he said. "Then I tell her I can see she's frustrated. I talk in a very soft, controlled voice. The soft voice seems to be the key."

The last thing a flooding child needs is for you to add your intensity to hers. Make an effort to keep your voice soft but firm.

Make sure your rules are clear: Rules for appropriate behavior during a flood of emotion are critical. They provide the boundaries, the guidance your child needs to control his intensity appropriately. Setting the rules for tantrums can't be done in the middle of one. You've got to set them up at another time. If you don't have them set up yet it's time to do it now.

Ask your kids if they know what the rules are in your house for tantrums. If they don't know sit down and talk about them, but choose your discussion time wisely. Select a time when everyone is well rested, cool, calm, and relaxed. Then you can actually have fun with it. Kids as young as three can help develop the rules. Go ahead, ask them. It is fascinating what they'll have to say. If your spirited child is an infant or toddler, know what your rules are and say them out loud so your child will begin to learn them.

At our house the rules for tantrums look like this. It's all right to cry and throw yourself on the bed. You can stomp your feet, yell like Tarzan, and ask to be held. You can use scuzzy words that aren't swearing or won't hurt someone's feelings. (Personally, I can't think of any, but it makes my kids happy if I agree to the general concept. I don't know yet if I've been taken.) It's not all right to hit, kick, pinch, scream in someone's ear, throw things around the room, blame others, spit, scratch, or swear.

Your rules may be similar or very different. It doesn't matter. What does matter is that the rules fit your family and everyone knows them.

Clarify the consequences: Clear rules are usually honored but sometimes the passion of the moment is just too overwhelming. It's important to have your consequences in place so you can remind your child of them if necessary. Consequences are the penalties that are meted out when rules are broken or the screaming doesn't stop after a reasonable amount of time.

During a tantrum a simple reminder of the rules and consequences is often enough to stop the inappropriate behavior. If they do start to kick or break the rules, say to them, "Are you choosing to do the dishes? Remember the consequence for kicking, spitting (or whatever) is doing dishes."

Usually a reminder is enough to bring them back within the boundaries. If it isn't enough or if they are very young, you may have to firmly but gently place an arm across their legs or arms and say, "Stop. The rule is no hitting or kicking. I will not allow you to hurt yourself or others. I will help you stop!"

If your children are older and don't stop, enforce the consequences. Spirited kids are notorious for blaming their parents for their troubles. Make it clear that you will not accept this responsibility. When they get upset with you for "forgetting" to put a juice box in their lunch or not washing their favorite shirt, remind them that making lunches and getting clothes down to the washer is their responsibility, then step away or enforce the consequences. Do not allow them to harass you. This is where you remind yourself, "I do not fear your intensity!"

If you are unsure of how to develop consequences go back to chapter 7.

When you are in public, talk out loud: There's nothing like a kid losing it in a shopping center, restaurant, church, or at the family reunion. Alice Honig, professor at New York University in Syracuse, says, "Forget about the strangers. You'll never see them again anyway." Take care of yourself and your child. If you're with friends or family ask for help. If you're not comfortable doing that then focus on what you need to do to calm yourself then your child. Know that you'll deal with the relatives later.

As you calm your child, raise your voice enough for the others around you to hear what you are saying. It will make you feel better that they know you are handling the situation effectively. It also keeps them from offering unwanted advice.

"We had just finished eating at a restaurant," Deb explained during a class on tantrums. "Paul didn't want to leave. He was coloring the placemat and wanted to finish. I couldn't wait for him because I needed to pick my daughter up at school. 'Time to go,' I told him.

"He started to squirm and protest. I *knew* I wasn't going to get him out of here easily. Everyone was looking at us. I started talking out loud, 'I know it's hard for you to leave. You haven't had a chance to finish your picture. We have to pick up your sister, you can finish it at home.' I don't know if it helped him, but it kept me under control."

Don't second-guess those around you. If they're strangers, who cares what they think. If they're friends, they'll support you, and if they don't, they're probably not really friends anyway. If they're relatives, listen to them and then decide what you want to do with their advice. It may be helpful and it may be worthless. You can decide.

Spanking doesn't work: In fact, it only intensifies the reaction and sends the child over the edge because it adds to the flood of emotions. My advice, my plea, is do *not* spank the spirited child. Behind the tough-cookie demeanor of a spirited child is a very soft center. And because of the penetrating intensity of a spirited child it is very easy for the spanking to get out of control.

THERE ISN'T ONE RIGHT WAY

There isn't one right way to calm your child and stop the tantrum. Finding the technique that feels good to you and your child is what is important. Take a few minutes to think of your most effective techniques. Keep them in mind so the next time your child experiences a spill-over tantrum, you can be ready with your plan for action.

PREVENTING TANTRUMS

During tantrums we do our best to work through them, but our real goal is to prevent the majority of tantrums from occurring at all. There will always be some with a spirited child—progress, not perfection, is our goal. But most can be prevented by working with spirit rather than against it. That's why follow up is critical. It helps prevent future floods.

Tell your child what she did well: We help our spirited children manage their strong feelings best by focusing on what they did right. After a tantrum tell her, "You were very upset, but you remembered not to hit me" or "I'm glad that you didn't throw your toys. You're really growing up. Six months ago you had difficulty remembering that rule."

Focus on whatever she did that is appropriate: The things you want to see repeated in the future. Look for it. There is always *something* that she did right. Find it.

Teach him responsibility: If your child has hit the walls, torn apart his room, or made a mess, help him to clean it up. Remind him that he is responsible for his actions, even when he is flooded. Repeat your rules. It is all right to cry or yell but you cannot throw things at the wall. Let him know that you expect him to learn to manage his intense feelings. Assure him that you know he can.

Bring closure to the tantrum: When the intense feelings have been diffused, bring closure to your child's tantrum. Give her a hug and promise each other that you can start over again.

Prepare for next time: Make sure your child understands what flooded him. Review the temperamental traits with him. Help him to understand that there were too many transitions, too much stimulation, or too much of whatever it was that flooded him and pushed him beyond his ability to cope. Help him to understand that if he works with his temperament—uses words to express it and employs the techniques that allow him to manage it, he won't be pushed into a spill-over tantrum. If you're not sure what to say, go back and reread each of the chapters on temperamental traits. Ultimately he must be able to catch and diffuse his strong feelings before they overwhelm him. Life with a spirited child or adult will always be intense, but it doesn't have to be a chain of nuclear reactions.

Take care of yourself: Tantrums are exhausting for everyone. At the end of a long, emotional day, call a sitter and plan a night out or hop into a hot bath. Handling tantrums drains moms and dads. Take care of yourself. Then you can be loyal to your child.

WHEN THE TANTRUMS DON'T STOP

There are times when, despite our best efforts to understand our children's intensity and teach them effective ways to diffuse and use it the tantrums continue. If you find yourself angry, resenting your child, unable to see his potential or dreading another day with him, it is time to enlist professional help. The idea of involving a counselor in your family may feel uncomfortable to you but seeking help is actually a sign of a healthy family. In her book *Traits of a Healthy Family,* Dolores Curran wrote, "It isn't that healthy families don't have problems, they do, but they know when to get help."

Make that appointment, take care of your relationship. Children are not replaceable. Now is the time to build your relationship for a lifetime. It is worth the time, effort, and money.

TANTRUMS: A SUMMARY

The steamy reactions of spirited kids make them much more vulnerable to spill-over tantrums—a flood of emotions that overwhelms them and pushes them beyond their ability to cope. A spill-over tantrum can't be stopped by ignoring it because your child is dealing with a temperamental issue.

Spirited kids experiencing a spill-over tantrum need to hear:
This is a flood.

You are being overwhelmed by your emotions.

I am here. I will help you.

Stop. It is time to stop now.

It is all right to cry, but you may not kick or bite.

If we can, we will stop what is flooding you.

Teaching tips:

Stay with, or near, your child. To be left alone with such strong emotions can be very frightening to your child.

Run through a mental checklist of your child's temperament in order to identify the trigger—the source of the flood (too many transitions, an overload of stimulation, etc.). Stop it if you can.

Reduce the demands on your child during peak tantrum times, especially late afternoons, during developmental surges, and when energy banks are low.

Touch your child gently. Many times a hug, a back scratch, or any other warm touch will close the floodgates.

Do not spank your child. Spanking can too easily get out of hand when everyone is upset.

Make sure your rules and consequences are clear.

After the tantrum, talk with your child about what happened and develop strategies for preventing it in the future.

Dealing with your own strong feelings:

Recognize that your child is overwhelmed. She is not intentionally trying to embarrass you.

After a day of handling tantrums, take a walk, a long, hot bath, or call a sitter. Take care of yourself so you will have the energy to help your child.

If, despite your best efforts, the tantrums continue, know that healthy families know when to enlist the help of professionals.

PART THREE

LIVING WITH SPIRIT

13

PLANNING FOR SUCCESS: PREDICTING AND PREVENTING THE TROUBLE SPOTS

I never thought about planning for success. I just worried about surviving.
—Kate, the mother of one

WHEN MY KIDS were little, grocery shopping was a family outing—with two grocery carts. One for my husband and the children to meander around the store with and one for me actually to get the food we needed. You might see this as a luxury. In our case it was a basic survival technique and cheaper than divorce court. (Neither one of us was willing to pack two weeks' worth of groceries alone.) It had to be early Saturday morning before the crowds hit, or a Saturday night family date. Not what I imagined for excitement when I was sixteen, but what the heck.

The kids *always* chose to go with their dad. There were times I felt a few pangs of guilt. They loved him better than me, I worried. Fortunately my insanity was short lived, and if I were honest, I would have chosen to go with Dad too. Instead of wrestling with them to stay in the cart, he loaded them up firefighter's style. The one who got the seat was the driver, the one hanging on the outside was the tillerman. It didn't really matter because everybody got in and out of the cart a dozen times anyway.

They started at the dairy case. That was where everyone first jumped off the cart and started perusing the yogurt shelves, checking out the little containers and the big containers, deciding what looked the best. The next stop was determined by how they *felt*. Sometimes they went back to the front of the store for a doughnut. It just *felt* like they should have a doughnut so they got one. Then it was down the aisles in random order, ten then five then two then six. In the end they hit all of them but the cart rolled with the whim of the moment.

Forty-five minutes later I met them at the checkout counter. I had a basket bulging with fruit, meat, and canned goods. The dog food was hanging off the bottom shelf and the bread was teetering on the top. They had five half-gallons of milk, two flavors of ice cream, five boxes of cereal, an empty doughnut sack, three empty juice containers, and big smiles.

It hadn't always been this way. With a spirited son *and* husband, one spunky daughter, and a very persistent and focused Mom, grocery shopping was ripe for turmoil in our household—until we figured out how to *plan for success.*

What we learned is that grocery shopping is repetitive, just like 75 percent of the activities in life. When something is repetitive you can *predict* how you and your child will respond, because it has happened before. If you can predict everyone's typical reaction you can plan for success. You don't have to wait for the blowups. You can prevent them from ever occurring.

Think about it. In the last twenty-four hours what have you been butting heads about? If you're like the parents in my classes it's very likely that you've spent thirty minutes with either you or your child in tears over getting dressed. Someone has left the table in disgust. Either the kitchen is still a mess or you have picked it up yourself. Homework was a bust again and there was at least one hassle over going somewhere.

You *know* these things will happen because they happen all of the time. As the parent of a spirited child you can use that awareness to *plan for your child's success!* You can put into use your knowledge of temperament, the words that you have learned to use, and the techniques that work for managing spirit to prevent daily hassles. I've designed four simple steps that you can follow. They are

1. P redict the reactions
2. O rganize the setting
3. W ork together
4. E njoy the R ewards

Just remember POWER. (Yes, I can count. I cheated, but I'm close!)

PREDICT THE REACTIONS

Predicting the reactions means beginning each day thinking about how you can help your spirited child be successful. An interesting thought isn't it—not focusing on how to make him behave, or how to survive but how to be successful.

In the morning mentally run through the day. What will your child be doing? What typical tough times will you both encounter? Will his routine be normal or disrupted for some reason? Who will your child be talking with or meeting for the first time? Where will he be going? Will he be exposed to any new experiences? Will he have to wear clothing that is unfamiliar to him or less comfortable? Will he have to be quieter than usual? Will there be lots of stimulation?

If you answered yes to any of these questions, think about what type of reaction you could expect from your child in these situations. If you always fight about getting dressed, expect to fight today. If you are going to start gymnastic lessons and your child hates new things expect a reaction.

In class, I asked the parents to predict some typical tough times. Their list looked like this:

getting dressed

coming home from day care

taking medication

leaving dance class

going to bed

"Now," I said to the group, "review the temperamental traits—all of them, including the bonus points. Which ones might explain your child's reaction?"

Jim looked at his list and answered, "Dressing is a hassle because she is persistent. She always wants to do it herself. She is sensitive, so the textures bother her and she is slow to adapt so changing clothes is difficult."

"You've got it!" I exclaimed.

We quickly ran through the others. The reaction to coming home from day care is an issue of adaptability. Taking medication is difficult because of persistence, sensitivity, and intensity. Leaving dance class is challenging because of adaptability and sensitivity—there has been a lot of stimulation. Going to bed is a major effort because of persistence, adaptability, sensitivity, intensity, and if you throw in the bonus traits of regularity and energy for good measure it can be really tough!

By using the temperament charts, you can predict your child's reactions to typical situations. If you can predict these stressful times, you can use the management techniques you have learned to diffuse them or prevent them. Remember your child can't change her temperament, but she can learn how to express it in an acceptable and positive manner. As your child grows older include her in predicting her reactions. Help her to identify situations that may be stressful for her. The older she is the more you can expect her to take over this responsibility herself. Eight-year-old Alise can do it.

"I wanted to run to the grocery store before supper last Friday night," Alise's mother explained. "Alise was watching television. She seemed pretty wiped out, but I didn't want to wait until Saturday when the crowds are the worst. I forewarned her, 'Alise, at the next commercial we're going to the grocery store and you have to come with me.'

"She groaned. I braced myself. 'Mom, I just can't do it. I can't take all of the people and noise and the lights in the store today. Can't you wait until dad comes home? Then you can go all by yourself and I can stay home.'

"I didn't know what to do. Part of me said that I should make her go, because not going would be giving in. Part of me said that I should listen to her. She's not trying to control you. She's telling you she can't be successful in the store today. It won't kill you to wait thirty minutes. But I'm persistent and this was tough on me.

"I called my husband to find out what time he would be coming home and to talk through my decision with him. I am an extravert and I need to hear myself think. He's a good sounding board and helps me unlock. His perspective is helpful because he is a lot more like Alise and understands her better than I do.

" 'I can empathize,' he said. 'It's been a hard week. We were out on both Tuesday and Thursday nights. I'm exhausted too. I couldn't face going to the grocery store tonight.'

"I folded another load of laundry and waited until he got home to go to the store. I wasn't sure whether to be happy she had used words and hadn't thrown a fit or to be angry that I had to wait. I still wasn't certain if this was giving in. But I did it. I have to say it was a lot easier to shop without her and when I came home they had supper ready. That was nice. I guess in the end we both got what we wanted."

Alise had predicted her reaction and a potential trouble spot. Her mother had respected her prediction. Together they avoided a blowup in the store. Respecting temperament means thinking about it and trying to set up situations so that everyone wins.

For infants and toddlers you will have to do all of the predicting but make a habit of telling them what you are thinking. They will learn from listening to you, and they will begin doing it themselves when they are ready.

Preschoolers can begin making some predictions for themselves. You can help them by asking questions such as, "We're going to the store today, how do you think you might feel in the store?" or "Tomorrow is a nursery school day. What do you need to be ready in the morning?"

Be careful not to fall into a rut. Your predictions will change as your child grows and develops and becomes more competent in managing her temperament. Although a spirited two-year-old may not be successful at a birthday party for twelve kids at McDonald's, a spirited six-year-old may be. The reactions change and so must our predictions.

After thinking through your day, expand to your week and even to the month. You can predict that the shift to daylight savings time will cause problems at bedtime and morning time for your slow-to-adapt child and be ready for it. Changing seasons means switching from shorts to jeans. Expect a problem for the sensitive kid. Your mother schedules Thanksgiving dinner for two-thirty P.M.—smack in the middle of your two-year-old's nap time—and she expects him at the table. A slow-to-adjust child will not be happy.

As you make your predictions, think about your own reactions as well. Is the switch to daylight savings time difficult for you too? Does the stimulation level in a store drive you crazy? By predicting both your reaction and your child's, you can create a plan for success.

ORGANIZE THE SETTING

In theater production there is a stage designer—the person who takes the script and creates the environment in which the action can happen. Along with a lighting director he also creates the cues for the changing of scenes or the passing of time.

Once the stage is set and the cues established, a stage manager makes sure the actors always have the objects they need to go forward—the clothes in the closet, the chair to sit on, or the water to drink. And it is the stage manager who ensures that the cues for the transitions from one setting to another occur smoothly and consistently at every performance.

As the parent of a spirited child you have to think like a stage designer and act like a stage manager. Knowing that your child is spirited, you have to create the environment that will help her behave appropriately. You have to decide what cues she will need to help her perform. And you have to consistently provide her with the props and cues she will need to be successful. Ultimately she'll take over these tasks herself.

We actually have many choices for altering our environment in a way that promotes our child's success. The more we can organize the setting to fit with our child's temperament, the happier everyone will be. Ron found this to be very true.

"Whenever we get together with my family, they insist on going out to eat," Ron told the group. "It's a two-hour drive to their house. My son Matt is very active. The last thing he needs is to sit in a chair again for another hour. I know it won't work but my father is insistent. I don't want to get in a fight with Dad, so I force Matt to go and try to make him sit. Of course, he won't and I get snarled at for not controlling him. I can't win. If I take him he's a brat and if I refuse to go because he can't handle it, they say I'm spoiling him.

"Last weekend I decided to try planning for success. Knowing that Matt wouldn't be successful in a restaurant but that my dad would want to eat, we planned a picnic. We called ahead and had them meet us at the park—just like old times, I said. He bought it. It was the best visit we've had in years. My dad was actually boasting about Matt, pointing out to other people that his grandson was only four years old and could hang by one knee on the monkey bars!"

Ron had predicted that Matt could not be successful in a restaurant after traveling two hours in a car, instead he planned a picnic. He selected a location where he knew Matt could be successful. He organized the setting for success.

Sometimes, without thinking, we put our kids in situations where it is impossible for them to be successful, like taking the spirited toddler to a formal wedding reception or planning a gourmet dinner for twelve and expecting our six-year-old to just hang around quietly. But carefully creating and selecting a setting can help your spirited child to be more successful.

Consider stimulation levels, amount of space for movement and/or touchables versus breakables as you make your selection. Don't be afraid to remove tempting nontouchable items. Avoid objects like toy guns that promote aggressive play. Choose a familiar site over an unfamiliar one if your child will also be changing his schedule or meeting new people. Create a setting that helps your child be successful.

PLAN APPROPRIATE ACTIVITIES

The set manager knows that if he wants the actors to eat, there has to be food. If he wants them to put on a hat there has to be a hat. The right props have to be available for the proper behavior to occur.

As the parent of a spirited child, you have to make sure that the right props are available for your child—the objects that encourage the kind of behavior you want. If you know your child will have to sit quietly, make sure she has books to read and paper and markers to use. Remember, intense kids need soothing, calming activities. Sensitive kids like things they can touch, taste, and smell. Energetic kids like to move. By bringing along or including activities and objects that your spirited child will enjoy, you prevent him from getting into trouble. If he doesn't have the appropriate things to do, you will find him touching things that shouldn't be touched, or jumping on things that shouldn't be jumped on.

"I always take along our survival kit," Christie offered. "It includes Handi Wipes, juice boxes, crackers, a notepad, crayons, a Nerf ball, and a blanket. Lately, Carrie, who is only three, has even started packing her own backpack. She brings it everywhere. But if I don't want her to take it in, she is willing to leave it in the car."

Activities, objects, and props allow the actors to do what they are supposed to do. The same holds true for kids.

CREATE A SPACE FOR INTROVERTS

Introverts need a quiet, out of the way space to recharge. Many settings, however, even classrooms especially designed for kids, don't include a hideaway for introverts to refuel. As you organize the setting be sure that you have created a space for your introverted child. He'll need it to keep his energy level high.

Let your child know what you are doing as you organize your setting. Let him help plan the activities or collect the objects he will need to be successful. Gradually he will take over this job himself.

WORK TOGETHER

We can't plan for success all by ourselves. We also have to get cooperation from our spirited kids. Working together is *not* playing games. It is respecting temperament.

In theater it is the director who creates the vision of what should occur. It is the director who adapts the script to the particular situation and actors and it is the director who works with the actors to help them understand the script and their parts in it. In planning for success you are the director and it is you who holds the vision of your child's success. It is you who adapts the expectations to fit the situation and your particular child. It is you who helps your child to understand what is expected of her and to perform to the very best of her ability. In the previous chapters you have learned many techniques that allow you to work together with your child to bring out her best. Use this new awareness as you plan for success.

Consider energy levels: To ensure your child's maximum performance, consider energy levels when you schedule appointments, classes, parties, or outings. Energy levels are usually highest at the beginning of the day and lowest late afternoons or evenings. By carefully selecting the best time of day for your child, you are helping her to be successful.

"I used to schedule Ellen's gymnastic classes in the evenings, because I liked to keep my weekends free," Judy said. "But it was always a fight getting her there and getting her out again, even though she loved gymnastics. Once we missed a sign-up date and were forced to take a Saturday morning class. What a difference. Her energy level is so much higher. She's up and ready to go. Even getting her out is less of a hassle, and I find myself more patient too. We may never take an evening class again."

The more you can schedule activities and events during your spirited child's peak energy times, the better her performance. Look for the schedules and times that will fit your child best. You will be expending energy in a positive and preventive way, rather than in a struggle.

Of course, not everything can be scheduled around your child's peak performance times, but if the majority of events fit, those that don't will be easier to handle. If you know you can't change the schedule then do your best to help your child refill her energy bank before the activity begins.

Share your vision of success: What is success? If you don't tell your child she won't know. Make sure your child knows what *being successful* means as you work together.

a. If your child is intense. Remind him of his cues and let him know what soothing/calming activities are available if he needs them.

b. If your child is persistent. Look for yes with him. "I take away the mystique," Leon told the group. "I let him do something to participate. If I say no, it's too hard or too dangerous, he'll be right there in the way. But if I give him a job to do, like pick up the log and carry it to the garage, he'll work and work. You have to expect it will slow you down and it won't be a perfect job, but he sure feels good about himself."

And remember to clarify the rules and expectations with your persistent child. "Breanna is five. We sit down together and talk about what the rules will be. It's easier for her to follow them if we review them before we go or if she helps make them up."

c. If your child is sensitive. Talk about feelings and remind him of his cues for overstimulation.

d. If your child is perceptive. Talk about how you will get his attention. Write down directions or schedules if you need to.

e. If your child is slow to adapt. Let him know the agenda. Tom wins his son Mark's cooperation by making sure he knows the specific details.

Tom explained, "I'll say things like, We're going in the car. We will drive down Cedar, past City Hall and Burger King until we get to Perkins. We will have dinner there. You can pick out a prize from the treasure chest. You can order a hamburger, a hot dog, or a grilled cheese sandwich. Think about which one you would like."

Letting Mark know the agenda gives him the time he needs to make a decision and to make a transition easily.

Know when to quit: Spirited kids can be successful in restaurants, amusement fairs, traveling in the car, and just about anywhere, as long as we realistically consider the length of the time we expect them to behave well. One of the most popular outings offered through my family education program is a trip to the Minneapolis Institute of Art. The families take a thirty-minute ride on a school bus to the institute, then have forty-five minutes to view the art before returning on the bus. Recently a disgruntled parent complained that forty-five minutes was not long enough to tour the museum. I encouraged her to try it and decide after the tour.

We met up at the door. "Did you have enough time?" I asked her.

"I didn't," she remarked. "But my child did."

A good director knows that selecting the appropriate length for a performance is key to its success. Our family field trips are planned with the kids in mind. Sometimes they are much shorter than the adults would like them to be, but we have learned that overall, everyone has a better time if the kids are still smiling at the end of the trip.

Remember to limit the length of events so that at the end your child is still smiling too. For spirited kids who are sensitive, intense, and sometimes energetic this may be a shorter period of time than for other children their age.

ENJOY THE REWARDS

At the end of a great performance the actors are rewarded with applause and cheers from the audience. When you and your child have been successful you too deserve recognition for a job well done. Capture those moments of success and celebrate them.

Recognize your child's achievements: It is very easy with a spirited child to focus on what she has done wrong instead of what she has done right. Let your child know how proud you are of her good behavior. Say it with smiles, hugs, and words. If you have not been taught to celebrate strengths you may find this difficult to do.

Tim was afraid of creating an egomaniac. "I never told Daniel how proud I was of him when he behaved well. I thought he should just do it. I was worried that if I praised him, he would get conceited or would expect it all of the time. My wife pointed out to me how good I felt when my boss told me I had done a great job on a project. 'Don't you think Daniel would like to hear he did well too?' she said.

"I couldn't disagree. Daniel really seems to be responding. The other day he said to me, 'Dad, you did a good job keeping your cool with that nasty sales clerk.'

"How's that? My kid giving me pats on the back!"

Feel free to be creative with your approach: "I thank him," Joanne, the mother of seven-year-old Brett, said. "I make sure he knows exactly what I am thanking him for, like, 'Thanks for sitting so quietly in the movie theater. We'll have to do that again because you did such a good job.' "

You don't have to restrict your good words just to your child. Hearing you tell other people how well she picked up her room or how easily she handled swimming lessons can be a great incentive to spirited kids to repeat that super behavior.

Appreciate yourself: As the parent of a spirited child you have to remember to pat yourself on the back for the little successes, to celebrate your moments of greatness. When you have predicted a difficult situation and prevented it, tell a friend, write it down in a journal, or stand in front of the mirror and tell yourself, "I'm Good!" Treasure the moments of success, don't let them slip away without the recognition they deserve. Remember, directors and stage designers win awards too.

PLANNING FOR SUCCESS CAN BE USED ANYTIME

Planning for success—learning to Predict your child's reactions, Organize the setting for success, Work together, and Enjoy the Rewards—gives you POWER to face those typical tough times head on.

For several weeks Kathy had been struggling to make it work. Finally, bubbling with excitement and waving her fists in the air, like Rocky in the ring, she cheered for herself, "I've got it! I made it work! Chris's tantrums were so loud and terrible," she said, "that I would start screaming too. I couldn't figure out what was wrong until we talked about predicting. Then I began to recognize that he started screaming every time there was a change or a 'surprise.' Putting on his coat to come home from day care, changing the dinner menu, or getting in the car to go to church could make him crazy. I checked the temperament chart. Intense certainly fit, but that wasn't the trigger. Then I saw adaptability. Ah ha—I realized each of these situations was a transition. He is slow to adapt. I couldn't believe it. He wasn't just being bad—the trigger was transitions. I could work with that! I didn't need to feel like the world's worst mother.

"I told his day-care provider and she agreed to help prepare Chris by shutting down some of the learning centers and getting his coat out so that when I arrived, the setting was geared toward going home.

"Chris and I worked together too. I started planning ahead, allowing myself enough time to call him before I left the office to say I was on my way. I stopped rushing him once I got there and I always told him ahead of time what to expect for dinner. I also taught him the words to describe what I thought he was feeling so he could say it instead of *screaming*.

"I won't say it is a miracle cure, but it certainly is better. I just keep reinforcing his success. I tell him I know I'll always be able to trust him not to jump into anything. I am enjoying the rewards!"

I was so proud of Kathy I would have hugged her if she hadn't been sitting across the table from me. "That's it!" I exclaimed. "You are *planning for success*."

In my excitement I burst into a monologue. "By planning for success you can:

"avoid daily battles,

"prevent tantrums,

"help your child handle frustration, anger and other intense feelings,

"reduce the whining—"

Nods of agreement from Kathy and several other parents in the group kept me rolling.

"—minimize the morning battles over dressing and eating,

"avoid bedtime hassles and sleepless nights,

"plan birthday parties and family gatherings that are fun for everyone,

"travel comfortably with your spirited child, and

"reduce the fighting between brothers and sisters."

I was breathless as I finished my list and glanced at the faces of the people sitting in front of me. Many were smiling, and nodding in agreement, but a few of the others sat quietly in their chairs, averting their eyes.

I reigned in my excitement and asked them, "What are you feeling right now?"

"Overwhelmed," Joan confessed. "I feel distraught. It seems like there are sixty things to remember. I don't think I can do it because I don't have that kind of time."

The others listened intently. Peter remarked, "I feel angry. Why should I have to plan for success for Scott? I don't have to do it for the other kids, why should I have to do it for him?"

Laura sagged in her chair. "I don't know if I have the confidence to pull if off." She groaned. "To do this you have to know you're a good parent. You have to feel capable. I'm not sure I do."

Feeling like Joan, Peter, or Laura is not unusual. Planning for success does take effort, especially in the beginning. Changing parenting styles isn't easy, but with practice, planning for success becomes almost automatic. You don't even have to think about it anymore. You just do it and soon your child will take it over herself.

It's true your other children may not need your help planning for success, but they will benefit from it too. They will appreciate the peace and extra time you have for them, because planning for success can save so much time. When you aren't caught up in battles or seething with frustration, you have energy and time for other endeavors. There will always be something that surprises us, but by planning for success we can go back to the many things that are working right. Each year our planning gets better, the surprises fewer, and the successes more frequent. The result is a sense of confidence for both parents and kids.

It isn't possible for me to address all of the daily tough times with spirited kids, which range from bedtime to brushing teeth, washing hair, getting in the car, and more. But planning for success with the POWER approach is your key to addressing most of the problems you may encounter. In the chapters that follow I'll show you how the process works with some of the most common daily tough times.

PLANNING FOR SUCCESS: THE POWER APPROACH—A SUMMARY

As the parent of a spirited child you can plan for your child's success. You can put into use your knowledge of temperament, the words that you have learned to use, and the techniques that work for managing spirit to prevent daily hassles.

Predict:

a. Describe your child's reaction to a typical tough time.
b. List the temperamental traits that may affect how your child reacts to this situation.

Organize the setting:

a. Can your child be successful in this setting or location?
b. What activities or objects can you bring along that will help your child be successful?
c. Have you created a hideaway for introverts?

Work together:

a. How will you help your child manage her intensity?
b. Is there a way to say yes to your child? Does he know the rules?
c. How might your child expect to feel?
d. How will you get his attention?
e. Does he know the agenda and what is expected to happen?

Enjoy the Rewards:

a. What has your child done well?
b. What have you done well?

14

BEDTIME AND NIGHT WAKING

*The kids are supposed to be in bed by nine . . . you'd better
start about six.*
—"Crankshaft"

WHEN I was twenty I wanted to travel to Europe. My parents insisted
that if I went abroad it had to be with a bona fide student study group. I
found one—destination West Africa. A mere detail, I figured—to me,
abroad was abroad. And so, late one very dark night I found myself starkly
alone with my suitcase in hand, dumped at a Yoruba compound, a walled
fortress of homes. Goats and chickens roamed freely around open gutters,
the water ran one hour a day, and electricity flowed sporadically. I cried,
but that is another story. For two months my mission in life was to study
Yoruba child-rearing practices.

I quickly discovered there weren't any cribs in this compound. In fact,
there weren't any cradles, bassinets, infant seats, walkers, or backpacks.
Babies (any child under three) were either being carried on their mother's
back, playing at her feet, or sleeping with her on a mat. My questions
concerning bedtime and night feedings were met with confusion. Babies
slept when they were tired and were rolled from their mother's back to her
breast when they were hungry. Mothers hardly stirred in their sleep while
babies fed. There weren't any issues about bedtime and night feeding.

They were amazed when I explained that in our country babies were
placed in cribs or cradles to sleep. When I clarified that the apparatus was
frequently set in another room, away from the mother, they were horrified.
They couldn't imagine banishing a baby to another room, away from its
mother. I share this story with you not as an advocate of the family bed but
as an example of cultural preferences. My life with the Yoruba taught me
that many of our most firm child-rearing rules are based on cultural pref-

erences rather than fact. Who is to say whether babies should sleep alone in cribs or on mats with their mothers? Will children in one culture grow up with healthier attitudes or stronger bodies?

What's most significant about this to me is that my discovery of cultural preferences has given me a license. Permission to question all of the child-rearing rules, norms, and techniques that are not working with my child. It has made me realize that there are many different methods of addressing the same issue. I do not have to accept without question the traditional "shoulds."

This is a critical discovery for parents of a spirited child, because one of the most frustrating issues we face is the fact that what works for other kids is ineffective with ours. What *everyone* tells us is the *right* way to respond may be *wrong* for our kids. We are caught in a trap—meeting our child's needs or meeting societal expectations. It feels like a no-win situation, at least it did for Kari when she called me at my office.

"My twenty-one-month-old son has lots of trouble sleeping," she said. "He has always had difficulty sleeping. When he was a baby, I found that if I lay down with him he would go to sleep. Now that he's almost two he still wants me to lie down with him and rub his back. I honestly don't mind, but my parents keep pressuring me to leave him alone and let him cry himself to sleep. I have tried. I've left him alone but he becomes frantic. I've tried going back in every five minutes to tell him I was there, but he's really persistent. He just keeps crying. I can't stand to let him cry for hours and that is what he would do. So I guess I give in. I lie down with him and five minutes later he goes to sleep."

Kari had discovered an effective technique for helping her son unwind and fall asleep and lying down with him was not an imposition to her. She was comfortable with it—until her parents told her she *should* be responding in a different way.

"Watch the shoulds," I advised. "You and your husband are the ones who have to decide what's right for your family. There isn't really one correct way to handle bedtime. You've recognized that your son needs help unwinding. You know he is persistent and intense. If he starts to cry he'll only wind tighter. You're recognizing his needs without compromising your own."

A few days later a letter arrived from Kari. "In our discussion I heard you say that to help Mark, I must truly listen to what he is telling me and trust that message. Then to trust myself to advocate for him, regardless of shoulds and societal expectations. I'm sure that will be one of the lessons I will always be learning as a parent."

Listen to your child, trust the messages that he sends you, and advocate for him. These words of advice are not frequently heard by parents and yet they describe the core ingredients of a healthy, strong relationship with our children. To prevent those daily battles with spirited kids we've got to be creative, willing to recognize their individuality, and strong enough sometimes to buck the crowd. The pay off is harmony.

BEDTIME—GOING TO SLEEP AND STAYING ASLEEP

Kari is not alone in her struggle at bedtime. In fact it is one of the most frequent and frustrating issues for parents of spirited kids. At bedtime everybody is tired and short on patience. Worst of all, no matter what you do you *cannot* make a child sleep. You can, however, recognize why it is difficult for spirited children to call it a day, create a routine that encourages sleep, and do your best to work together.

PREDICT

Take a look at the temperamental traits. Knowing your child, predict which ones make it challenging for her to simmer down and fall asleep. Is she sensitive and easily over stimulated? Is she persistent and hates to take a break? Is she irregular, needs little sleep, and doesn't fall into a schedule? Are transitions difficult for her—is making the move to bedtime stressful? Is she active and always on the move? Are her protests powerful because she is intense? Each of these traits makes relaxing and falling asleep more difficult to accomplish.

There may be one particular temperamental trait that makes bedtime especially challenging for your child or perhaps it's a combination of several. By detecting the real culprits you can have a better understanding of what you are dealing with and can quiet the inner voices that try to tell you that your child is intentionally trying to aggravate you.

Getting spirited kids to bed is only part of the problem. The other and perhaps more disturbing issue is waking in the middle of the night. In her book *Crying Baby, Sleepless Nights*, Sandy Jones wrote, "Waking up once, twice or three times during the night is very common. Between one third and one fourth of all babies continue to wake up during the night even after one year of age." Sensitive, irregular, spirited kids make up the majority of that wakeful group, a group that continues to exist long after their first birthday.

"At eighteen months Christopher just doesn't seem to need much sleep," his mother, Paula, lamented during one of our classes. "It's a real strain when you haven't had a full night's sleep in a year and a half and have three other kids."

Sitting next to Paula was Terry who patted Paula's arm and recommended, "Take as many naps as you can, honey, because the end may not be in sight. Andy hasn't slept decently since day one and he's four years old."

Fighting at bedtime and waking up during the night are problems that all parents of young children face, but parents of spirited kids are more likely to find their hassles bigger and their lack of sleep more enduring and draining. Considering their temperamental type, you can predict that you, the parent, are going to be spending a great deal of time and attention helping your spirited child settle down and fall asleep.

ORGANIZE THE SETTING

Think about how you prepare yourself for bed. Do you read a little, check the doors, change into your pajamas, or eat a snack? These are all activities you have developed to organize your setting. Activities and objects that help your body switch from being active to being at rest. They are cues to your brain to start slowing down, the props that tell you how to act.

By the time you are an adult these cues are so much a part of your routine that you may be unaware of them. When your first child arrives, you may simply put him to bed when you go to bed, or decide on a certain time you want to lay him in his crib and put him there, not realizing that he needs the same kind of cues that you experience every night.

Imagine your favorite setting in which to fall asleep. Is it warm, soft, and quiet? Most of us don't fall asleep in the middle of a conversation (unless you're two months' pregnant), while doing dishes, or with the radio blaring. We need the right setting to induce sleep. The same is true of our children. It's unlikely that they will easily fall asleep if the commotion level is high or if they are involved in an activity. We have to create a setting that encourages sleep. One that cues their body and brain that it is time to slow down and relax.

Watch closely. Where does your child fall asleep most easily and what props seem to help? If it is in the car, it doesn't mean that you have to drive him around every night, but take note of what makes sleeping in the car so easy. Is it the motion? Would rocking suffice? Is it the quiet? Can you turn off the television and stereo? Is it the drone of the motor? Can you turn on a fan?

You can choose any props or activities. Running water for a warm bath, dimming lights, playing tranquil music, touching a soft blanket, back rubbing, reading together, eating a snack, listening to a story tape, putting away toys, putting on pajamas, changing diapers, toileting, or brushing teeth all encourage your child to slow down and switch from active to rest time. The common factor is that they are soothing and calming and provide solid cues for your child.

Be certain as you select your props that some of them are portable. If your child wakes in the middle of the night you won't want to run another bath but you can give a back rub, or snuggle the soft blanket. These portable props allow you to easily cue your child that it is still sleep time no matter when she wakes or where you are at.

It takes time to establish a bedtime setting, especially if you haven't had one before, but it can be done. To avoid having to make frequent changes in your setting, include activities and props that will grow with your child. A warm bath relaxes a baby as well as a preschooler. Reading is enjoyable to small babies as well as older kids. A back rub is pleasant for any age.

You will want to avoid activities and props that encourage physical behavior during wind-down time. You might be tempted to try and wear your child out by wrestling with him, dancing, running, or roughhousing. But for spirited kids these activities are very stimulating. They create a setting of wind up instead of wind down. Rather than encouraging sleep, they can easily lead to overstimulation and a major bedtime battle.

When you are away from home, remember to bring along some of your props, the crib sheets, favorite toys, books, and baby blankets that look, smell, and feel familiar. The more similar the setting, the easier it will be for your child to fall asleep and get the rest he needs to cope in a new situation.

WORKING TOGETHER

There isn't one magical plan that will get all spirited kids to bed without a fight and keep them there all night. Bedtime settings and routines will look different for every family. There isn't one right way to prepare for bed and sleep, but from my perspective, effective bedtime cues and routines need to meet three criteria:

1. They provide the child with concrete bedtime activities that you the parent are comfortable carrying out repetitively for months and even years. Ultimately the child may take over herself.
2. The child feels calm, secure, and content as she goes to bed.
3. Both Mom and Dad agree on the routine and feel comfortable going through it.

Take note of what you are already doing that helps your child relax. Do more of it. If you're not sure, experiment to find what fits for your child. Here are some tools other parents have found to be effective.

1. IF YOUR CHILD IS INTENSE

Stay with her: It's eight o'clock. You know it's time for little people to be in bed and moms and dads to have a break. The problem is that babies and toddlers don't know what that means and preschoolers and school age kids want to know *why* they have to go to bed.

It's true some kids go to bed without a hassle. I've got one. I thought it was a miracle when my daughter was born. She was one of those kids I'd read about. The kind you laid down in the crib and who *stayed* there without *any* fuss. In fact, within about thirty seconds of laying her down she was asleep. I almost felt guilty. I had spent hours rocking her brother, but she didn't want to be rocked. She was tired and ready to sleep. The kid didn't even know what a curtain call was.

My son, on the other hand, fit no charts or studies and refuted all tried-and-true methods of getting kids to fall asleep. He has curtain calls down to an art form. To this day it takes him twenty to sixty minutes to wind down and fall asleep. As an infant and toddler he screamed bloody murder if you left him alone.

There are hordes of books on sleep problems that will encourage you to let your child cry it out. There is a flaw in this advice. Supposedly the child stops crying after a few minutes. Spirited kids don't. Left to their own devices, intense, spirited children become overwhelmed by their powerful reactions. They may be unable to stop, crying for hours instead of minutes. They get more upset as the minutes tick away. The bedtime battle is extended instead of shortened.

Some children react so strongly that they will vomit. Some experts raise a warning that to respond sympathetically is to be controlled by your child. "If they vomit," they advise, "clean it up and put them back to bed." But small children don't vomit to control their parents, they vomit because they are stressed. They also rarely vomit in a neat little pile. There is nothing worse than walking into a room sprayed with vomit on the walls, the carpet, stuffed animals, and each individual bar of the crib. If your child is prone to vomiting, go to him, help him to take deep breaths and calm down before he regurgitates. Your support at this point will save both of you a great deal of frustration and discomfort when you are much too tired to deal with it.

After living with the Yoruba and learning from them, I am very comfortable recommending that if rocking your baby or picking him up helps him to relax and fall soundly asleep, feel free to do so. Meeting your child's needs is not creating a bad habit. You won't be doing it forever. If your child is intense, he needs help staying calm during the transition to sleep time. When he is older and understands that you still exist even though he can't see you, he won't need you to be as close to him.

If your child is a toddler you might try pulling a chair into his room and reading the newspaper, folding the laundry, or reading a good book until he falls asleep. Gradually as he gets older you can set a time limit on how long you are willing to sit with him, because it can take him an hour to settle down.

"I'll sit here for fifteen minutes," you might say. Then you can shorten it to ten minutes and then five as the months progress. If he gets out of his bed, remind him that you will leave him alone in his room if he does not stay in bed. Allow him to read to himself or listen to tapes but do not allow him to talk with you after a designated "chat time." If he won't stay quiet, step out of the room then let him try again.

Preschoolers are old enough to keep the image of you with them even though you are separate. That's why we can expect them to begin staying in their room. But even with a child this age, it is better to respond to their tears before they go over the edge than to push for five more minutes.

To ensure that you don't feel trapped by this routine, invite your spouse to take turns with you and use a sitter on a regular (at least once a week) basis, so your child gets used to someone else supporting her as she falls asleep.

As we discussed staying with our kids at bedtime in class one night, Kathy groaned. "I don't *want* to sit with her. I've got other things to do and I need a break!"

All of us can empathize with Kathy. At the end of a long day we're tired too. I have a friend who had adolescents when my kids were little. "Part of being a parent," she told me, "is waiting. When they're little it's waiting for them to fall asleep. When they're older it's waiting for them to finish a dance lesson or an orthodontist appointment, but you'll always be waiting."

Intense spirited kids need our help settling down. You can expect it. Try to think of it as a treat for yourself rather than one more demand to meet, a time when you don't talk to them anymore, you just sit and think, read, or finish your needlepoint. Make it an enjoyable part of your day rather than a hassle—you know you'll be dealing with them anyway because they won't go to sleep. If you try to do something else you'll just be chasing them back into their beds and yelling at them. Rather than frustrating yourself, expect it and plan it into your day.

You may not mind staying with your child as he or she unwinds and learns to stay in bed, but you may be wondering what to do about the other kids. That's where creativity comes in. Not every child needs this much help unwinding. Some kids, like my daughter, hit the bed and are out. That child requires your time and attention at another time of the day. Give it to her when she needs it, after nap time or after school. You don't have to feel guilty if you sit with one child and not another at bedtime. You meet the needs of both of them but in different ways.

If more than one needs your help unwinding you may have to sit on the floor between their rooms, or take turns—Monday night one room, Tuesday night another.

Your bed or mine? With a child who does not fall asleep easily and wakes up frequently you will soon be faced with the question of the family bed. In most cultures of the world the family bed is not a question. It is an expectation. In our society, however, it is a question that needs to be answered or it can become a major source of contention.

Sometimes, out of the need to survive, spirited babies join their parent or parents in their bed. This is an acceptable solution if it works for you. In *Whose Bed Is It Anyway,* Dr. Lillian Katz wrote, "Not so long ago psychologists were quick to put sexual or romantic interpretations upon the child's demand to stay in her parent's bed and cautioned parents against permitting it. However, today, these concerns seem to be greatly exaggerated."

There isn't a right or wrong answer, it's whatever works best for your family. But talk about it, set limits with it so that it doesn't disrupt your intimate relationship with your partner. Some families put the crib right next to their bed, or a sleeping bag on the floor. Others insist that the child go to bed in his own room so that Mom and Dad can have time alone at bedtime, but they allow their child to join them in the middle of the night. The goal is to find a way to calm the spirited infant or toddler easily, quickly, and with as little stress as possible so all of you can sleep more peacefully.

As you make your decision about the family bed, realize that it's a decision you will be living with for months, maybe even years. As your child grows older you will be gradually weaning her from your bed to hers. This is very possible to do, but it does take effort.

2. IF YOUR CHILD IS PERSISTENT

Make sure your limits are clear: I once asked a colleague why some kids *always* seem to push a little bit more. She looked across the lunch table at me and asked, "Did you drive within the speed limit coming over here today or did you push it just a little?" I squirmed in my chair. "Spirited kids like to test the odds," she said, "and so do most adults."

Bedtime is a favorite place for persistent kids to test the odds. "I am willing to spend time putting Jessie to bed," Brad said, "but I get tired of her demands. She always wants one more drink of water or one more book." Bedtime is a matter of personal choice for each family, but be *clear* what it means in your family. If you read books during your bedtime ritual, decide *before* you start how many you are willing to read, who picks them out, and how long they can be. If you have a snack, clarify what foods are appropriate for the bedtime snack and which ones are not *before* making a choice. Once you set your bedtime, use a timer or a clock to *prove* that it is bedtime. If your child wants to talk with you set a limit of *how long* he can talk. And be clear about what bedtime means. Does it mean in bed? If so, whose bed, yours or mine? Does it mean anywhere in the bedroom? Is falling asleep on the floor acceptable? Does it mean lights out and no more reading or listening to tapes, or does it mean a light on, reading to yourself, or listening to tapes until you feel sleepy? You can select the limits that fit your family, just be sure you can enforce them consistently and that your child fully understands them.

3. IF YOUR CHILD IS SENSITIVE

Fighting over pajamas is not worth it: Forget about the cute pajamas with feet in them, elastic cuffs, and lacy collars. Sensitive kids can't stand pajamas that bind, scratch, or in any way irritate them. Consider letting your child sleep in sweats, an oversize T-shirt, baggy cotton shorts, or a loose nightgown.

Talk about feelings: Because they often worry, spirited kids also need to know why it's so difficult for them to go to sleep. I didn't realize this until one day a ten-year-old told me she gets sick at bedtime. "What happens?" I asked her.

"I have the sleeping sickness," she said. "I can never go to sleep like other people. There must be something wrong with me."

Spirited kids have vivid imaginations. If we don't give them factual reasons as to why they need time to unwind, they'll come up with their own. They need to hear:

You're very sensitive to noises, smells, sights, and feelings. It's challenging for you to shut them out at the end of a day.

You are full of energy. It is hard for you to slow down.

You don't need a lot of sleep but it is time for Mom and Dad to have some time alone so you need to stay in your room.

It is all right to lie here quietly. You will fall asleep soon. You are not sick.

A quiet, low-stimulation setting is critical for sensitive kids. They have to be able to block out noises, lights, and even smells to be able to fall asleep. If they need a night-light, be sure it is dim enough to avoid over-stimulation. If they listen to a story tape select one that is mellow rather than exciting.

4. IF YOUR CHILD IS PERCEPTIVE

Help him hear your messages: At bedtime our children have to follow many directions. They have to stop doing what they are doing, change clothes, have a snack, and whatever else you do to get ready for bed. Kids hear best when they are motivated to listen. Make getting ready for bed and sleep a comfortable time. Include cuddle time, back scratches, and things that feel good so your child is motivated to listen. Remember to turn off the television and get eye contact. Don't try to direct your child to get ready for bed while you're talking on the phone or doing something else. Focus on your child and the directions he needs to follow, then you can both stick to the task and finish it.

5. IF YOUR CHILD IS SLOW TO ADAPT

Allow enough time: There is a "Crankshaft" cartoon in which Mom and Dad are putting on their coats to go out. They turn to Grandpa and say, "Now the kids are supposed to be in bed by nine . . . you'd better start about six."

It takes time to get slow-to-adapt kids to bed. Trying to rush or skip part of the routine only extends the process as intense kids overload from too many transitions too close together. Plan bedtime into your day. Expect that it will take you at least an hour so you are not frustrated. If it takes less time, it will be a nice surprise.

Begin with closure: It sounds crazy doesn't it, start with closure? But one of the major reasons we can't get spirited kids into bed is because they don't want to stop their activities. A bedtime routine needs to start with closure on the existing activity. You can bring closure by an announcement such as:

It will be time to start getting ready for bed in ten minutes. You need to find a stopping point. If you can't find one, I will help you.

At the next commercial we will be turning the television off.

When the last block is stacked it is time to stop.

You can catch the ball five more times and then we'll quit.

It may be helpful to set a timer. Timers are a wonderful way to allow slow-to-adapt kids time to transition. Some families use a music box that plays for ten minutes then gradually winds down. The sound is more pleasant for noise-sensitive kids.

Follow a routine: When slow-to-adapt kids know what is happening next, it is easier for them to transition and comply. You may want to create a chart or picture book that depicts all of the steps you take during your routine. The child can check them off as he completes them. Bob and Joni used this method to stop their bedtime fights.

"Bedtime was really difficult until Brandon was three," Joni said. "Our biggest problem was getting him to stay in his room. He was our first child and we had never heard of a bedtime routine. We didn't even know what it meant. When we learned about it we decided to try it. We had him cut out pictures from magazines of things people did to get ready for bed. We glued the pictures on construction paper and made them into a book that we read at bedtime. Once we had gone through the book he would do the things he had seen, sometimes he would even do them on his own. Then we read another story and really tried to make bedtime a good time with our focused attention. It took about a week but after that he stayed in his room."

6. IF YOUR CHILD IS IRREGULAR: A BONUS TRAIT

Establish a bedtime: Dr. Richard Ferber, in *Solve Your Child's Sleep Problems,* wrote, "Many of the children I see have difficulty sleeping because their sleep-wake patterns are irregular. They fall asleep early one night, late the next, wake at odd hours and never have their naps at the same time two days in a row."

If your child falls asleep at a different time every night, it's hard to establish a bedtime because you don't know where to start. To take the battle out of bedtime for irregular kids, we have to look at the entire day. Dr. Ferber suggested, "Set up a daily schedule for your child so that he will have a regular bedtime, a constant time of morning waking and a consistent nap time. Children's daily rhythms can only become established and maintained in a regular twenty-four hour pattern if they are set each day by events that always occur at the same time."

The first few days, chart your child's sleep pattern. Get a feel for when he normally falls asleep and wakens. This is your starting point. If your child frequently falls asleep at nine thirty P.M., begin by aiming your bedtime for it. If you would like to change it to an earlier time, take note of when he normally wakens in the morning. If he awakens at nine o'clock A.M., wake him fifteen minutes early, at eight forty-five. The next day wake him at eight thirty A.M. When you do this know that slow-to-adapt kids *hate* to be awakened early and will cry for the full fifteen minutes they normally would have slept. Be ready for it. It is very *painful* to regulate a spirited child. Choose a time in your life when other stresses are at a minimum.

Once you are awakening your child thirty to forty-five minutes early move bedtime fifteen minutes earlier. Now your bedtime will be nine fifteen P.M. Keep moving up his wake time and bedtime in gradual steps until you get to a reasonable hour. Be realistic. You're not going to get a nine-year-old to bed at seven P.M. Kids really vary in their need for sleep. Some young infants will sleep twenty-three out of twenty-four, others will need only ten hours of sleep. The same is true of toddlers and preschoolers and school age kids. Some will need twelve to fourteen hours of sleep while others will only need eight to ten.

If your child is napping you may also have to move nap times. You can't expect a child to nap from three thirty to five thirty P.M. and then go back to bed for the night at seven or seven thirty. Dr. Ferber also advised that when you wake a child early don't let him add the fifteen minutes to his nap time, which is very tempting to do with a spirited child. Remember you want that fifteen minutes at bedtime. You'll also want to avoid the temptation to skip a needed nap entirely in order to tire him out for bedtime. An overtired, intense child is even *worse* to deal with at bedtime. Let him have his naps, just make sure they're early enough in the day and not too long.

To prevent your hard work from being sabotaged, mark the change to daylight savings time on your calendar. It can take spirited kids three weeks to adjust to this time change. Start the process of change at least two weeks in advance of everybody else. Otherwise the week of change will very likely be a disaster. Gradually move your child's bedtime and wake time fifteen minutes every day or two until you get them where they need to be. Adjust your schedule too. Mark the first Monday and Tuesday of the daylight savings time switch on your calendar. If possible, schedule no appointments before ten thirty A.M. That way if things are rough at home you can deal with them without feeling pushed. Otherwise get yourself up early enough so you have the time you need to help your child. (Tuesday is usually the worst because by then, they are really out of whack.)

You can't *make* an irregular child fall asleep but you can insist on a definite bedtime. Gradually, with a firm, consistent routine that is carried out *even on weekends,* your child will begin to adapt relatively smoothly. The good news is that parents of school age kids rarely complain about irregularity as a problem. Either the kids have adapted to a schedule or they are old enough to get themselves to bed!

7. IF YOUR CHILD IS ENERGETIC

Plan physical activities during the day not at bedtime: Many kids get *wild* at bedtime. They dash around the house, leaping, jumping, and wrestling. It is easy to get pulled into their energy and start rough-housing with them, but you can't wear out an energetic, spirited kid at bedtime. They'll only get more energetic until they crash in a flood of tears.

Make sure your energetic child has had physical activity during the day not at bedtime. At bedtime it is time for soothing, calming activities that help the body and brain slow down and relax.

ENJOY THE REWARDS

Reinforce cooperation: As you go through your routine let your child know how she is doing by saying,

You really did well getting out of the tub after fifteen minutes.

You remembered that we only read two books.

I only had to remind you once to stay in your bed.

I can tell you're growing up, you were able to get ready for bed by yourself.

You might even keep track of her accomplishments and plan a reward. Ask your preschooler what she would like to earn. Reward systems don't work unless the child wants the reward. I know a parent who once offered her five-year-old daughter a bicycle if she would stay in bed every night for the next month. "No thanks," the child replied, "I'll probably get one for my birthday anyway." After further discussion they ended up with a Happy Meal at McDonald's as her reward!

Kids can surprise you, so don't try to second-guess them. Help your child select something that is enticing to her but within your budget and abilities. Let her know that each night she goes to bed without fussing and stays in her room until she falls asleep she will earn a quarter toward her reward, a star, or whatever token you have decided on. The younger the child, the shorter the time before she gets her reward. A two-and-a-half-year-old may get her's the next morning. A three-year-old after two nights. The five-year-old after four or five. Once bedtime is going smoothly discontinue the rewards. Rewards are only used to teach a new behavior for a specific amount of time. Once she has learned it and has made it her own, you don't reward her anymore. It's expected behavior. But it is always appropriate to compliment her on a job well done.

Get your own needs met: Be creative in getting your own sleep needs met, knowing that your well-being is essential to the well-being of your child. We've all read the stories of prisoners of war being denied sleep to slow their thinking processes, drive them crazy, and make them confess to crimes committed or not. Sleep deprivation is a real torture. If you have survived or are in the middle of surviving life with an irregular, slow-to-adapt, persistent, sensitive, intense child you can easily empathize with prisoners of war. When you are exhausted you find yourself functioning in a haze, unsure how you got a meal on the table or how you found your way home from work. You drag yourself from one day to the next lacking the energy to experience any joy. Somehow you've got to get some sleep.

Lower your expectations: Housework can wait, the lawn can be mowed less frequently, the car will survive if it's dirty, and sick days can be used for sleep as well as for the flu. You can't make your spirited child sleep but you can create opportunities for yourself to sleep. When the baby naps, you nap. If you have other kids, hire a teen after school, go to your bedroom and sleep. If you're in a two-parent family, take turns getting up one night then sleeping the next. Do what you need to do in order to meet your own sleep requirements. You can't be an effective parent if you're too tired to get up and move or to even think. Make sleep a priority.

You don't need to worry: There isn't anything wrong with your child and there isn't anything wrong with you. Sometimes that's hard to believe in a world that makes sleeping through the night a sign of status. There is *no* sound research that demonstrates that a child's sleep patterns are related to the quality of parenting the child is receiving. If your child is not sleeping through the night you don't need to feel badly about it. It is not a reflection of your ability and unless wakefulness is associated with a high fever or other form of illness, there is no reason to worry that something is wrong with your child. The fact is, a child who is temperamentally irregular, sensitive, persistent, active, and whatever will arouse easily during the night. You can expect to be up one or more times but you don't need to worry about it. Just get some sleep, somewhere, somehow during the day so that you have the energy to meet your child's needs.

Find the routine that works for you and forget about the shoulds. Be sensitive to your unique child and kind to yourself. Pat yourself on the back when your child goes to bed calmly and safely and you are comfortable with the routine. Allow yourself to meet her needs without feeling guilty, yet set limits that respect you and other family members as well.

BEDTIME AND NIGHT WAKING: A SUMMARY

Bedtime and night waking are two of the most frequent and frustrating issues for parents of spirited kids. It is possible, however, to recognize why it is difficult for your child to call it a day and create a routine that encourages sleep.

Predict: Take a look at the temperamental traits. Knowing your child, predict which ones make it challenging for her to simmer down and fall asleep. Is she sensitive and easily overstimulated? Is she persistent and hates to take a break? Is she irregular, needs little sleep, and doesn't fall into a schedule? Are transitions difficult for her? Is she active and always on the move? Are her protests powerful because she is intense? Each of these traits makes relaxing and falling asleep more difficult to accomplish.

Organize the setting:

Provide props—activities and objects—that cue your child that it is time to sleep.

Make sure some of your props and activities are portable so that they can easily be repeated in the middle of the night or taken along with you when you travel.

Avoid bedtime activities and props that encourage physical behavior, instead use those that soothe and calm your child.

Work together:

Expect to stay with your child to calm her. Try to think of this time as an opportunity to catch up on your reading or favorite craft.

Take turns with your spouse putting your child to bed so that you don't get trapped by your child's insistence that only you can put her to bed.

Allow enough time to prepare your child for bed. Rushing or skipping part of the routine only extends the process.

Help your child to bring closure to activities before starting your bedtime routine.

Set a definite bedtime and expect your child to go to her bed, but do not expect her to fall asleep.

Enjoy the Rewards:

Compliment your child when he cooperates with you.

Get your own needs met so that you have the energy to help your child.

Find a routine that works for you and forget about the shoulds.

15

MEALTIME

*Heaven forbid if you take the Wheaties down for him. If you
do, you have to put it back up on the shelf and let him take it
down or he won't eat.*
—Martha, the mother of four

SPIRITED KIDS don't just eat their food, they experience it. The simple
act of eating a piece of bread can be entertaining or grotesque, depending
on your point of view. First they sniff it. Then they lick it. They'll stick their
tongue right through the middle of it and joke about their "doughnut" bread.
If you don't keep a sharp eye on them they just might hang it from their
ears.

Their sense of taste is keen. They can taste the differences in name
brands and the texture of meat may make them sick. They have defined
rules about what foods may touch each other or be mixed together. The
mere thought of the Jell-O salad touching the mashed potatoes and making
them red may be *absolutely* repulsive to them.

Getting spirited kids to the table, keeping them there, and ensuring
that they eat some semblance of a nutritional diet is a major source of
consternation for parents of spirited kids. By working with your child's
temperament, it is possible to make mealtime more tranquil.

PREDICT

What makes mealtime tricky for your child? For many spirited children their
sensitivity fosters strong opinions about what they will and will not eat.
Intensity makes their reactions forceful. Persistence results in little tigers
who want to do it themselves! Perceptiveness leads to "grazing"—eating,
playing, browsing, talking, eating—but never quite finishing anything. And

slow adaptability makes it tough to get them to the table in the first place. The bonus traits may also affect mealtime. Irregularity leads to erratic hunger pangs. High energy promotes a desire to eat on the run and a negative first reaction leads to frequent refusals.

Believe it or not your spirited child isn't really all that different from other young children. The developmental books will tell you that all young children are prone to food jags—insisting on eating one particular food—or food strikes—not eating at all. Other kids also dawdle, wiggle in their chairs, spill their milk, react negatively to new foods, and eat erratically or constantly. This is the picture of the *average* child. Add to that the greater temperamental strength of the spirited child and you have the potential for a very interesting situation.

Problems often arise during the toddler years when a normal reduction in appetite occurs. In *Your Toddler, Ages One and Two,* Dr. Richard Rubin writes, "Babies double their birth weight by four to five months and triple it by a year. But in the next year and a half, the growth rate slows way down; a toddler gains only six to eight pounds in eighteen months. It stands to reason that his appetite should become smaller too."

Many parents are not aware of this normal change in appetite. A sudden refusal by their toddler to eat sparks the beginning of the feeding wars—concerned parents pitted against toddlers with a declining appetite. Mealtime does not need to be a battleground. By predicting your child's typical temperamental reactions and understanding the natural and necessary reduction in appetite, you can respond in a positive manner.

ORGANIZE THE SETTING

In *How to Get Your Kid to Eat . . . But Not Too Much,* Ellyn Satter offered a guiding principle for maintaining a positive feeding relationship: "The parent is responsible for what the child is offered to eat, the child is responsible for how much, and even whether, she eats."

"This principle," she continued, "both charges you with what is your responsibility to do and lets you off the hook when you have done it. It is up to you to get healthy food into the house. It is you that makes sure the meals and snacks are nutritious. But once you have done that, you simply have to let go of it, turn the rest over to your child, and trust her to do her part."

In *Your Toddler,* Rubin describes an experiment done many years ago by Dr. Clara Davis that showed that young children, if given the chance, will choose to eat a healthful diet. Rubin wrote, "Dr. Davis offered a wide variety of nutritious foods to a group of babies between eight and ten months old and let them decide completely what and how much they wanted to eat. She found that, over time, these babies chose a combination of foods that any nutritionist would call a well-balanced diet. Each meal was not balanced, and often several meals in a row were not, but over several days each baby's choices added up to excellent nutrition."

Control the props: According to the U.S. Department of Agriculture, a nutritious diet includes food from the following food groups:

1. Breads, cereals, and other grain products
2. Fruits
3. Vegetables
4. Meat, poultry, fish, dry beans, eggs, and nuts
5. Milk, yogurt, and cheese
6. Limited fats, oils, and sweets

If you provide these foods for your child, you can trust even very small children to use good judgment. Your child can't fill up on cookies if they aren't in the cupboard. He can't drink pop if there isn't a can in the refrigerator. You get to control what food is available. If you want your child to eat fruit, leave it sitting out on the cupboard in an attractive basket ready to eat. If you want your child to drink milk, make sure it is sitting cold and inviting in the refrigerator. This is creating the setting—providing the props that allow the appropriate action to occur.

Make snacks self-service: Snacks are actually an important part of meeting the nutritional needs of children but can be a source of trouble with the child who wants to eat all of the time or sporadically. You don't need to worry about your child's snacking if you control what and how much is available for snack. To take the tussle out of snacks make them self-service.

Get out all of your small plastic containers and create a snack cupboard and refrigerator shelf for your child. Each morning fill them with whatever snack items you have planned for the day. Include things like dry cereal, crackers, fruit, pieces of cheese, raw vegetables, and other nutritious foods. Then just leave them on a low shelf in the cupboard or the bottom shelf in the refrigerator. You can also fill a juice cup and leave it there as well. Every time your child snacks she will be fulfilling one of her nutritional needs and won't be fighting with you because it's self-serve.

In our early childhood centers, the snack center is open all morning, and there is no designated snack time. A child can choose to go to this center whenever he is hungry. It eliminates a transition to snack time and also allows irregular kids to eat when they are hungry.

WORKING TOGETHER

Food isn't factual: It seems like it should be. You can see it, smell it, touch it, taste it. But it still means very different things to each one of us. What's amazing to me is how different the messages are. I grew up with a dad and grandfather who always grabbed a piece of pie and ate it *first*, declaring that they wanted to eat dessert while they still had room to enjoy it. I've run into a few others like them but most people have learned that dessert is eaten last and only after their plates have been cleaned up.

Before we can work with our child's temperament, we have to be aware of the messages we have received from parents, relatives, teachers, or friends about the *right* way to eat. Here's what other parents have said.

"In our house eating was very controlled. We had to try one bite of everything, eat very defined amounts, and not leave the table until we were excused."

"My mom had an aunt who always bugged her about how skinny she was. My mom hated it and as a result never said anything to us about food. If we were full and there was one bite left on our plate, it stayed there. There wasn't any pushing."

"Breakfast was our big meal of the day. Everyone had to be seated at the table at seven thirty A.M. It didn't matter what time you'd gone to bed, you were to be at the breakfast table. I am not a breakfast eater and never have been. To this day the sight of pancakes is revolting to me."

"Half of my mom's relatives were very obese and half were not. She was really worried that we would take after the obese side of the family and be discriminated against. She wouldn't let us eat any sugar and never allowed second helpings."

"We never really talked about food. We ate when it was served. Got ourselves a snack if we were hungry and that's it. It was never a very big deal."

Look at your food messages. Check to see if they are interfering with a sensitive response to your child's temperamental needs. Do they allow you to accept your responsibility to provide nutritious food and allow your child to decide how much he will eat? Your parents and grandparents did not have the information about health and diet that we have today. Make sure your messages are accurate and appropriate for today's life-styles. When your expectations are clear, it is easier to work with your child's temperament.

1. IF YOUR CHILD IS INTENSE

Teach him good manners: Cooking an entire meal only to have your spirited child sit down, take one look, and scream, "YUK," is a very frustrating experience. If you have a child who reacts intensely, tell him it is all right to refuse food but he needs to say, "No, thank you. I don't care for any." Even a young toddler can say, "No, thank you."

I offered this advice in class one day. A parent responded with a very serious frown. "You don't think it will work?" I asked, responding to her expression.

"I just hope it does," she answered. "Last week we had dinner at my in-laws. Mark is very intense. He didn't like the sweet potatoes my mother-in-law put on his plate. He screamed when she plopped them down, but she didn't seem to notice. He scooped them up in his hand and threw them against the wall. I was mortified."

"That's toddlers," I said. "They like to throw things, but let's get him to stick to balls. Tell him he can say 'No, thank you' or choose not to eat it, but make sure he knows it isn't all right to throw food."

A few weeks later she reported back. "I was really dreading going to dinner at my in-laws again. Especially after what happened last time. But I tried what you suggested. Before we went I told him he needed to say, 'No, thank you. I don't care for any.' He's very talkative so he could say it, but I didn't know if he understood me."

"Well, my mother-in-law tried putting zucchini on his plate. 'No, thank you,' he said. She paused and looked at him, almost shocked. He said it again, louder this time, 'No, thank you!'

"I thought oh no, here we go again, but she stopped, looked at me, and said, 'Well I guess he really means it,' and passed him by."

Intense spirited kids need to be taught good manners. They react strongly to situations and need to know the correct words to express their wants and needs. This is especially true for the serious and analytical child who sees the flaws. While it is fine for them to point out the lettuce is slightly brown, or the potatoes are cold, they need to do so in a tactful manner.

2. IF YOUR CHILD IS PERSISTENT

Satter advised, "Most struggles over feeding grow out of genuine concern for the child and bad advice. Parents are regularly encouraged to overrule information coming from their children, and impose certain foods, amounts of food, or feeding schedules. Whenever you impose rigid expectations, feeding will be distorted."

It's important to know that the amount a child needs from each of the recommended food groups is actually very small. Two cups of milk fill the dairy requirement for a day. One-half cup of cereal is considered a serving in the cereal/grain area. Mary Darling, an extension specialist in nutrition at the University of Minnesota, says, "Rely on your child's appetite. Start by giving her a quarter of an apple. Make more available if she wants it, but allow her to tell you when she has had enough." Permitting a persistent child who needs to hear yes to take the lead is a very important factor in developing a positive eating relationship.

Involve your child in food preparation: Did you know even one-year-olds can dip vegetables or fruit for you, scrub potatoes and carrots, and tear lettuce or snap beans? Two- and three-year-olds can wrap potatoes in foil, pour from a small pitcher, and mix and shake ingredients. Older preschoolers and young elementary kids can spread toppings, roll dough, beat with an eggbeater, peel with a vegetable peeler, cut with a table knife, and grate things. The more that spirited kids are involved in preparing their food, the more likely they are to eat it. You can't cut their toast the wrong way if you let them do it. The syrup is on their pancakes right if they pour it from a small pitcher themselves (you control how much syrup is in the pitcher). The jelly is the proper consistency on the peanut butter and jelly sandwich if they've spread it themselves.

It's true that in the beginning it takes you more time to teach them how to do it than to do it yourself, but it is time spent teaching rather than fighting. It feels better. In the long run kids who are proficient in the kitchen are proud of themselves and are more self-sufficient.

Involving any child in food preparation is also a great way to take the pressure off of the poison hour—that time of day when the kids need attention and you need to get a meal on the table. If they're standing on a stool at the sink washing the potatoes (to death) you know they're not beating up their brother. Baked potatoes taste great whether they've been washed for a few minutes or fifteen. Set a timer if you need to help the persistent child stop and get them in the oven!

Set clear limits: During the early years it is easy to follow Satter's principle of taking responsibility for serving nutritious food. You are the grocery shopper and the supplier of food in your household. If you don't want to fight with your child over junk food don't bring it into your house. This monopoly on supply ends much too soon, however, as your child moves out into nursery school, visits with friends, and enters elementary school. The world of junk-food heaven opens up to him. It is critical that he understands your nutrition guidelines, and the rules you are using to make healthy decisions.

Kids are not into complexity: Your guidelines have to be simple. Something a child can easily understand. One rule might be, for example, only one sugar food a day. Sugar foods are things like cookies, pop, sweetened cereal, or ice cream. Kids as young as three can identify a sugar food. The rule of *one* allows them a choice but helps them set a limit. Another rule might be that one snack has to be fruit. Again, they can choose when in the day they have it, but somewhere you know that they'll get it. These guidelines not only teach your child basic nutrition rules, they also prevent fights. When your child asks you if he can have pop at ten in the morning, all you have to say is, "Are you choosing that as your sugar today?" The child can then decide if that is his preference. You don't have to be the bad guy.

When the guidelines are simple and clear, even young children will monitor themselves. I was amazed one day when I overheard a preschooler at a Fourth of July parade inform a clown. "No, thank you, I don't care for any candy. I've already had my sugar today!" Clear, simple rules put the control inside the child. He can carry it with him wherever he goes. He doesn't need you to do it for him.

Avoid using food as a punishment or reward: When you provide a variety of good nutritious food in a positive manner your child will let you know when he is hungry and when he is full. Bribing him to eat or taking food away from him only disrupts his natural message centers. Once he has lost the ability to read his own body's messages he becomes more vulnerable to eating disorders. Research has shown that kids who are bribed to eat actually eat less and those who have food taken away from them eat more because they're afraid they won't get what they need. The two most important questions for you to be asking are "Are you hungry?" and "Are you full?" Let your child decide from there.

3. IF YOUR CHILD IS SENSITIVE

Serve a variety of foods at once: Spirited kids are selective eaters. They truly have a better sense of taste and smell than the average person. As a result they also have stronger reactions to the foods they eat. To avoid feeling rejected and unappreciated by their strong objections serve a protein dish, vegetable or fruit, milk, and bread all at the same time. If the smell of your hamburger makes them sick, they can quickly redirect their attention to the bread, fresh vegetables, or fruit cobbler you're serving. Understand that their response really is not an evaluation of your culinary skills. They truly are that sensitive to tastes and smells.

Be aware of food allergies: Experiencing allergies and being spirited are not directly correlated, but many spirited children do have food allergies. During an interview, Laura said, "Brad is very sensitive to some foods. It took us a long time to figure that out. We thought he was just being picky and stubborn. We would force him to eat. Now we recognize that he doesn't tolerate hamburger and spicy foods. He gets constipated and complains about not feeling well."

When you take the responsibility for serving nutritious foods and you allow your child to take responsibility for deciding which ones he will eat, you can feel comfortable respecting his judgment. He isn't necessarily just being picky.

If your child has "crazy times" after eating, start recording what he eats and how he behaves afterward. Be particularly observant of foods he craves. Often these are the foods to which he is most allergic.

I do not have scientific research to back me up, but many parents have also reported to me that their children overreact to medications. Closely monitor the dosage your child receives. He may actually need less than another child of the same age and size. It appears that because of their sensitivity, spirited kids are easily overmedicated.

Talk about feelings: Sensitive kids need to hear:

You have a very good sense of taste.

You are selective.

You'll make a great chef someday.

Sometimes you need to see a food more than once before you're ready to try it.

It's all right to say, "No, thank you."

It's all right to say, "I'm hungry."

It's all right to say, "I'm full."

Sensitive kids need the words to express the feelings and sensations they are experiencing. The more effective they are communicating with words the easier it is to work with them.

4. IF YOUR CHILD IS PERCEPTIVE What do you do with the child who chews every bite twelve times, takes tiny sips of his milk, and requires forty-five minutes to complete every meal? The answer depends on why it takes him forty-five minutes. Is he just enjoying his meal or is he distracted? Sometimes it takes kids forty-five minutes to eat because they're jumping up to look at a bird, give the baby a pacifier, or get the ball they left outside. They're not eating. They're grazing, moving around the table, picking up bits and pieces, and never finishing the food on their plate. The grazers need limits. For example, you might say, "If you leave the table more than once, you're telling me that you're not really hungry. If you want to eat, you need to stay here."

Limits alone may not be enough. You may also need to help your perceptive child stay focused by being sure to turn off the television and pick up stray toys and other distracters before you sit down to eat.

The pokey kids, who are enjoying every single bite, may need a reasonable time limit to stay within socially acceptable boundaries, and also an understanding family. If you have a slow eater, expect it, plan for it, and enjoy the time to relax yourself.

5. IF YOUR CHILD IS SLOW TO ADAPT

Establish a routine: Young children not only want to eat frequently but need to eat frequently. Their bodies are most comfortable taking in nutrition in small amounts every two or three hours. Nutritionists are actually beginning to recommend this approach for adults as well. Monitor your mealtimes carefully. When is your child typically hungry? Establish three specific mealtimes and a couple of snack times throughout your day. Make sure they fit your child. You might be running into trouble because you would like to eat dinner at six thirty but your child is ready at five thirty. You may have to move your meal to the earlier time until she is older and can last longer. If this is not possible, consider serving part of the meal as a five-thirty snack. It is not fun to eat a meal with a tired and hungry preschooler.

Slow-to-adapt kids need clear transitions: They don't easily stop playing and come in to dinner. You have to allow enough time for them to make the switch.

"I bring Todd in a few minutes early," Brenda said. "I have found that if I have him get the last few things on the table, it allows him transition time. Otherwise he is wiggling in his chair, grouchy, and downright contrary, because he is going through transition as he sits down at the table. By helping me beforehand he seems to work it out of his system."

Remember to clearly forewarn your child that it will be time to eat and help her to find a stopping point.

Let her know what's on the menu: "One of the biggest blowups I have ever had with my son," Kate told me, "resulted when I told him in advance that we were going to have tuna casserole for dinner. As I started to prepare it, however, I found I didn't have any noodles or cream soup. I decided to make hot tuna-cheese sandwiches instead. He was outside playing and I was enjoying the peace. As a result I didn't inform him of the change. I gave him the usual ten-minute warning then called him in to dinner. He washed his hands, sat down at the table, took one look at the food, and burst into tears. I had surprised him. He was counting on tuna casserole and the surprise of tuna-cheese sandwiches when he was tired and hungry was too much. It put him right over the edge."

Keep your child informed about the menu. When she knows what to expect, she comes prepared to eat. If you have to make changes, like Kate did, be sure to inform her *before* she gets to the table.

The time before dinner is full of transitions. Parents coming home from work. Kids coming home from school. Changing clothes, preparing food, and stopping some activities and starting others. Energy banks tend to be low at this time of the day and tantrums are more frequent. Providing a protein snack around three o'clock in the afternoon seems to give spirited kids the energy they need to get through the dinner hour without falling apart. A slice of cheese, peanut butter on crackers, or a piece of cold meat will do the trick. A lighter snack of crackers alone, juice, or fruit doesn't seem to fit the need. If a protein snack works for your child, be sure to inform your day-care provider and ask her to have one available for your child. You may notice a marked difference when you pick your child up.

6. IF YOUR CHILD IS IRREGULAR "My two-year-old won't eat supper with us," Sarah told me. "At most she'll sit at the table for five minutes, but won't eat. Two hours later, she wants cereal. My parents say we should spank her and make her sit down or take away all food after lunch so she's starving at supper. I'm not comfortable with either solution but I don't know what else to do."

One of the most common questions I am asked about spirited kids and mealtime is "What do you do with the child who won't eat the meal but wants to snack later?" People often view a child's refusal to eat as stubbornness, but the issue probably has little to do with persistence as most people seem to think. The real issue is irregular body rhythms—a child whose body does not easily fall into a regular schedule. If your child is hungry at different times every day, it's not because she chooses to be difficult but because of her natural body rhythms.

With an irregular child you have to look at the whole day, not just one meal, before you can decide whether or not you have a problem. Check to see if she is getting the nutritional food she needs over a period of twenty-four hours. Toddlers typically eat only one good meal a day. That's normal for this age group. Older children may also only eat one good meal a day, but if you watch carefully you will see that at that meal, and with snacks, they are getting the food their bodies need. There isn't really a problem.

If you are still concerned, review the growth charts. Is your child consistent with her placement on the chart? If at age two she was at the fiftieth percentile mark, is she still there at age four and six? If so, you don't need to worry. If there is a significant change, you should consult your pediatrician.

You can also monitor your child's activity level. If her energy levels are normal for her, you know she's getting what she needs. You don't need to get upset when she won't eat a particular meal.

Even if your child isn't hungry, it is still important to ask her to come to the table. Mealtime not only allows us to meet our nutritional needs, but is also a social time for family members to share the day's events. It is important for your child to learn these social skills. You can expect your toddler to come to the table and sit with you for five minutes. As she grows older you can extend the length of time you expect her to sit with you. This routine teaches her the social skills of the family meal—praying, talking, planning, and eating together. Often, sitting at the table will also trigger the hunger signal allowing her to enjoy the meal with you. Repeated every day, even an irregular child may fall into your family's routine.

You don't need to be a short-order cook: If your snacks fill part of your child's nutritional needs you don't have to hassle her about not eating a meal and then wanting a snack shortly afterward. It doesn't matter, because both the meal and the snack include foods that are essential for a well-balanced diet. To avoid feeling like a short-order cook, however, you need to teach her how to make that peanut butter sandwich herself.

7. IF YOUR CHILD IS ENERGETIC Toddlers don't sit easily for extended periods of time. Active toddlers sit for even shorter periods of time. In fact, active individuals—child or adult—don't sit for long periods of time in any kind of chair. Watch active adults in meetings. They wiggle their feet, tap their fingers, get up for a cup of coffee, excuse themselves for the rest room, and use numerous other socially acceptable methods to move. The need is very real.

If you know your child needs to move, make sure she has had exercise before she comes to the table. If you are traveling with her don't expect her to sit quietly in her car seat for three hours and then sit again while you eat in a restaurant. Plan for her success. Try stopping in a park or rest stop where you can picnic and she can run and jump. If that isn't possible let her walk around the restaurant lobby until the food is served rather than waiting at the table. In some way, find an acceptable outlet for her energy.

Staying at the table depends very much on the age of the child and the situation. For safety's sake and social acceptability you probably want a rule that says, when you eat you must sit at the table.

In Europe, most children are expected to stay at the table for more extended periods of time than their American counterparts. However, they are also entertained at the table. The adults involve them in the conversation. Books are sometimes brought to the table for the child to read until they are excused.

If you would like your child to stay with you at the table, plan to involve her in the conversation or to bring along some of her favorite table activities. Understand, however, that your child's need to move is very strong. A pressure builds when she is required to sit for an extended period of time. Make your expectations realistic. Even if you entertain her at the table, long and formal dinners may need to be saved for adult-only evenings out.

8. IF YOUR CHILD'S FIRST REACTION IS TO REJECT Kids whose first reaction is an initial rejection or withdrawal are likely to tell you they hate a new food no matter what it is. Don't be caught by that reaction. If you don't want food left on the plate, ask your child before serving if she cares for any. If she says no, respect it and leave her alone. You are free, however, to remark about how much you are enjoying the new food and to serve it again at another meal. A negative first reaction may make you believe that your child doesn't like a food when she really just needs time to get used to it. When you introduce a new food be sure to plan something in the meal that she will like. That way you can avoid the worry that she isn't eating anything.

ENJOY THE REWARDS

The most effective way of teaching appropriate behavior is reinforcing it when you see it. Let your spirited child know you are pleased when he says, "No, thank you." Comment on how well he has used his napkin or his fork. (He won't be very competent with a knife until around age ten.) Compliment him on trying a new food or staying in his chair. Enjoy how capable and independent he becomes as he learns to prepare foods himself.

Be realistic: If your child has been successful for five minutes and now wants to leave the table you can strongly consider letting her go. End the meal in harmony rather than screams.

If you are concerned about your child's eating consult your pediatrician. If your doctor's advice isn't working for you, talk with a licensed dietitian or read one or more of the nutrition books available. There are many re-sources to answer your nutrition questions and, most important, many answers that are flexible enough to meet the needs of your family.

Be kind to yourself: Follow Ellyn Satter's advice: provide the food and meals your child needs, then let yourself off the hook. When you aren't worried about controlling how much your child eats, you can enjoy the conversation much more.

MEALTIME: A SUMMARY

Getting spirited kids to the table, keeping them there, and ensuring that they eat some semblance of a nutritional diet is a major source of consternation for parents of spirited kids. By working with your child's temperament, it is possible to make mealtime more tranquil.

Predict: What makes mealtime tricky for your child? For many spirited children their sensitivity fosters strong opinions about what they will and will not eat. Intensity makes their reactions forceful. Persistence results in little tigers who want to do it themselves! Perceptiveness leads to "grazing"—eating, playing, browsing, talking, eating—but never quite finishing anything. And slow adaptability makes it tough to get them to the table in the first place. The bonus traits may also affect mealtime. Irregularity leads to erratic hunger pangs. High energy promotes a desire to eat on the run, and a negative first reaction leads to frequent refusals.

Organize the setting:

Provide a good selection of healthy foods, then allow your child to choose how much he or she will eat.

Make snacks nutritious and self-service; then you don't need to battle with your child about what he or she eats and when.

Work together:

Look at your messages about food and eating. Check to see if they are interfering with a sensitive response to your child's temperamental needs.

Let your child know that it is appropriate to refuse food, but he must do so respectfully and tactfully.

Involve your child in food preparation. The more that spirited kids are involved in preparing their food, the more likely they are to eat it.

Make your nutritional guidelines simple so that your child can monitor them herself.

Let your child know what's on the menu and inform him of any changes *before* he sits down at the table.

Look at the whole day, not just one meal, before you decide whether or not your child has an eating problem.

Even if your child's first reaction to a new food is negative, try serving it again. She may change her mind.

Enjoy the Rewards:

Be realistic. Know when to end the meal so you have harmony rather than screaming.

16

GETTING DRESSED

Can you love me as I am, or will socks keep us apart?
—Pastor Dave

THERE WAS a church bulletin lying on my desk. The bold type read "From the Assistant Pastor." Maybe one of my staff was trying to tell me something, I thought. I picked it up and started reading.

"It was 'one of those mornings,' " the article began. "Put on your socks, Ben," had been my command a few minutes earlier. You see, in our household, putting on Ben's socks is a ritual, an action never done with little thought. Socks must be carefully checked and rechecked for seams, for loose annoying threads or for anything that has the potential of bringing discomfort. The moment of truth comes when the socks are put on. Will they feel just right or should they be adjusted . . . or perhaps be removed entirely and switched to the other foot!"

I started to chuckle. I've never met Assistant Pastor Dave but we have something in common: children who find getting dressed a major venture. I read on.

"As I said, sock placement is a ritual, and this morning things were not going well at all. I was angry. I didn't want to be angry, but I was. 'How can socks be so difficult to put on?' I asked. His response was a shrug of uncertainty. 'Get your socks on right now!' I yelled. I thought I would be challenged and confronted by my strong-willed youngster, but I was wrong.

" 'I need you to help me, Daddy,' were his simple words to me. Ben's tears and his need presented me with a question of enormous significance. Can you love without condition? Can you love me as I am, or will socks keep us apart?"

227

I stopped reading, struck by the impact of Pastor Dave's words. "Can you love me as I am, or will socks keep us apart?" Socks—white cotton tube socks, brown socks with blue rings, dress socks, old socks, new socks, whatever shape or form they take, we begin and end most of our days putting on and pulling off socks. It may seem insignificant to most people but in the family of a spirited child putting on socks can be a divisive event, parents pitted against wiry little bodies, dashing across the room to escape tags that scratch, elastic that's too tight, and fabrics that hurt their skin.

Getting dressed is a major challenge not because the kids want to be stubborn, uncooperative, and free spirits but because of their temperament.

PREDICT

"Check your child's temperament picture," I said to the group. "What temperamental traits make dressing troublesome?"

"Definitely sensitivity," Bob responded. "Anna will only wear pants because she doesn't like the feel of dresses."

"That's funny," Kathy remarked, "because I would say sensitivity too, but Sarah will only wear dresses because pants are too binding."

"Energy is the issue at our house. Jonathon gets one sock on and then he's gone," Barb added.

I continued writing as the list grew. Kids who wanted to wear sweaters in July because of slow adaptability. Intense kids who threw fits because they got stuck in their turtleneck or couldn't get their shirt buttoned. Kids disrupting mornings and making parents scream, not because of a desire to drive their parents crazy but because of their temperament.

Check your child's temperament picture. Do textures bother her because she is sensitive? If changing styles or type of clothing is difficult, is it because of adaptability? Is it hard for him to focus on directions because he is perceptive? Is she opinionated about her clothes because of persistence? Is she easily frustrated because of intensity? Whatever your child's temperamental picture, you can predict how she will react to getting dressed. Then you can begin to plan for success. Nobody needs to start *every single day* with a fight.

ORGANIZE THE SETTING

Our goal is to get kids to dress independently, appropriately, and in a reasonable amount of time. That means they need a setting that allows them to stay on task, listen to direction, and to have available clothing that is easy to work with and fits the weather and occasion.

CREATE A SPACE TO DRESS.   Think about the things in your setting that make it difficult for your children to get dressed successfully. What vies for their attention?

Kathy immediately said the television, and she's right. Television disrupts communication with spirited kids because it sends out its own "listen to me" messages and frequently leads to overstimulation. Avoid television in the morning. In fact, consider making it a rule that there isn't any television in the morning—it truly helps the routine go more smoothly.

Detractors can be anything. You will have to figure out what hinders a smooth morning at your house, but the parents in my classes tell me the chief culprits in their homes include the following.

Windows: "Mica dashes to the window to watch the birds and the cars. He gets so excited, he makes me excited. Then we're both watching. If I really need to get him dressed, I've got to keep the shades down until we're finished."

Open doors: "Jeff runs away, not to be a brat, but because he loves to run. The only place I can get him dressed is in the bathroom with the door shut. To him, an open door is an invitation to run away."

Toys and other "things": "It's a joke in our house. The only place Katie can get dressed is in a barren wasteland. Every toy and object has to be put away or she starts fiddling with it."

Look carefully at your setting. Anything that sabotages your child's efforts to stay on the task needs to be dealt with or done away with. Don't tempt your child to misbehave, when you can help him cooperate simply by changing the setting.

Once you've gotten rid of the things that prevent success, look for those things that help. Here's a few I've learned.

a. Appropriate clothes. If you want your child to dress appropriately you have to have the right clothes available. If you don't want your spirited child wearing shorts anymore, get them out of his room.

b. Good organization. Arrange your child's drawers so there is a "dress-up" drawer, a "school" drawer, and a "play" drawer. Your child can help you decide what goes in each. Choices are then limited to the appropriate drawer.

c. An indoor/outdoor thermometer. Use a thermometer as a guide for clothing that fits the weather. Place a thermometer that tells you both the inside and outside temperature in your child's room. Make sure it's big enough to glue a picture of shorts at 70 degrees, a swimming suit at 80 degrees, a sweatshirt at 60 degrees, and a warm jacket at 35 degrees. With these guidelines even a three-year-old can let the thermometer tell her what kind of clothes to wear today. She can't argue with a thermometer like she can with Mom and Dad. Take the steam out of the battle by letting the thermometer do the work.

d. A mirror. Help your child to stay focused and happy by providing a mirror for him to watch his progress.

e. Easy clasps. Purchase clothing that slides on easily, has big buttons, Velcro or easy-pull zippers in the front. Avoid clothes that are difficult to get on and off.

You can create a setting that encourages your child to dress independently, appropriately, and in a timely fashion. Take a look at your child's setting and make the changes necessary to help your child be successful. If your child is three or older be sure to include her in the process.

WORKING TOGETHER

Differences in expectations are often the cause of conflict when it comes to getting dressed. Although we want our kids to dress independently we still want them to meet our standards. Our standards and theirs may not match.

"Jeff is one of those kids that wants to wear shorts in January and his winter jacket in June." Charlotte said. "For a long time I really fought with him over it, but finally I just decided to let him find out for himself, within reason, of course. Now, I let him step outside with the shorts on, or I let him wear the jacket. Within minutes he is asking to change."

"I wanted a little girl I could dress up," Patti told me. "When I got one that wasn't interested at all in dresses, I realized it was me that had to deal with the issue of what I wanted my child to look like and what I was willing to let go of."

As we work together to get dressed, we need to look at our own expectations. Are they realistic for this child? Do they fit this situation? We can choose how to adapt the script to each individual. My experience tells me it's tougher to do when your spirited child is a girl.

1. IF YOUR CHILD IS INTENSE

Teach her to use words: Spirited kids seem to fall into two camps when it comes to dressing themselves. One group has a mind-set of "I do everything myself"; the other, "I can't do anything without help." The can't-do kids have to be motivated—we'll talk about them when we discuss perceptiveness. The can-do kids can get frustrated and intense!

Tara is a do-it-herself kid. She can be exasperating to her parents. "It always happens when I'm late for work," her dad told me. "Inevitably the baby is in his high chair crying to get out. My seven-year-old needs breakfast before he goes to school, and Tara is insisting that she will dress herself. It would be fine if she'd pick something she could get on herself, but, of course, on those days she wants to wear the knit dress with the attached T-shirt. The one with two neck holes and four arm holes that is impossible for her to get on by herself. I wait, banished to the sidelines as she grunts and groans. She gets her arm through one arm hole, but the dress twists around so the other half is behind her. If I attempt to help her she screeches and slaps at my hand. She works and works until finally in exasperation she pulls it off over her head, throws it down on the floor, and kicks it across the room."

Tara is actually doing what we want her to do. She is attempting to dress herself. She is very motivated and independent. The problem arises when her coordination doesn't match her drive. She needs the words to express the frustration she is experiencing, appropriate outlets for that frustration, and help breaking the task down into parts that can be accomplished more successfully.

If your child is like Tara, talk with her about intensity. Give her the words for frustration and anger. Let her know she can stomp and yell, or she can ask for help. Then help her break the process down into small steps that are easier to accomplish. If you're not sure how to do this keep reading until you reach the section on perceptiveness and dressing.

Use humor: Humor helps reduce frustration, diffuse intensity, and win cooperation. After participating in a class Barbara wrote to me, "Today started with Brett refusing to let me wipe his buns. It wasn't even eight A.M. yet and I could just imagine what the rest of the day would be like if this was how it was starting. Normally I would have demanded that he let me do it and we both would have started screaming. Our lives had seemed like one big battle since the day he was born. This time, however, I decided I wasn't going to fight with him. I was going to figure out how to work with him. We had talked about using humor to avoid a blowup so instead of demanding, I started sniffing the air. 'Whew, stinky buns!' I exclaimed. I pretended to look behind the shower curtain for those 'stinky buns' and then under the sink. He was amazed. He started laughing and looked under the soap dish himself. Finally we both found them on his backside, finished the job and happily walked out of the bathroom. Before your class I would have been furious. Humor is helping both of us appreciate his spirit."

Getting dressed doesn't have to be a serious event. If you and your child frequently disagree, or find yourselves getting upset, play with your intensity. Laugh about your strong reactions. Use your child's sense of humor to make light of a difficult situation. Underwear tried on as a hat or a sock on a hand instead of a foot eases the tension. Shaking your head with a smile on your face reminds both you and your child that you've gone through this before and you will survive.

2. IF YOUR CHILD IS PERSISTENT *Shopping is a key ingredient to dressing without fussing.* When it comes to clothing, we want as many yeses as possible with persistent spirited kids. Persistent kids like to choose what they will wear. They don't like to take no for an answer. That means it is very important that you and your child agree about what clothing is available to wear.

Purchase clothing that is easy to get on, matches any other piece in the dresser drawer, and *feels* good. You can avoid fights over mismatched plaids, flowers, and checks by not buying them or only buying patterned pants and plain T-shirts.

If your spirited child is an infant or toddler this is easy to do. You can just consider his need for soft, nonbinding clothes and pick them out yourself. Soon however, he will become verbal and very clearly state his opinion about what he will and will not wear. Then it's time for what I call "consensus clothes."

Consensus clothes allow spirited individuals to wiggle their necks freely and stretch their arms. They are clothes that can rub against a body without any irritation, weird sensations, or pain. But you can't stop there. If you did, you would have a closet full of baggy sweat pants, oversize cotton T-shirts, loose-fitting sundresses, and well-examined (for lint and strings) tube socks. Consensus clothes include clothing that also allows the parents of the spirited individuals to hold their heads high in pride, smile at people passing by, and freely admit that the child standing next to them is theirs.

Consensus clothes help to take the battle out of getting dressed every morning. The trade-off may be five hours of shopping for a month of relatively painless mornings. Because shopping with spirited kids isn't all that exciting either you can decide which is more valuable to you. Personally I choose consensus clothes because I can mentally prepare myself better than hitting it cold turkey every morning. The key elements to shopping for consensus clothes are the following:

a. I will listen to you. Let your child know you are about to take on an arduous task. Arduous always throws them off, so you start with a definition instead of an argument. Inform him that you are going shopping. When the uproar has settled (most of them hate shopping) ask him to listen carefully and tell him, "I *will not* make you buy anything you hate. I *will* expect you to be flexible and try on things I suggest." By agreeing to work together you can both be satisfied that an outfit doesn't fit, looks horrendous, scratches like crazy, or is just what you both want.

b. Expect to make several shopping trips. Trying to get an outfit for tomorrow's event is asking for big trouble. Many spirited kids have a negative first reaction. That means the first time they try something on, they will probably hate it. Leave it at the store, pray it doesn't sell quickly, and then talk about it on the way home. Look for things that are similar to old favorites or things to which they are already accustomed. You might say, "That blue outfit really looked nice on you. It reminded me of your favorite pink outfit. Remember how you didn't like that one at first either? Now you love it and are sad that it is getting too small for you. Think about it and maybe we'll go back and look at it again." Then *be quiet*!

c. Take a break. Consensus shopping takes tremendous patience, strong self-control, and a tough skin to avoid letting the piercing gaze of sales clerks penetrate your skin. Never shop on an empty stomach. Shop for an hour then stop for a snack. The kids won't mind it even though you're the one who really needs it.

d. Know when to quit. At my house, it's actually my spunky daughter who far surpasses her spirited brother in her strong opinions about clothing and style. Recently we were out on our fourth attempt to find an outfit for her to wear to a wedding. We'd been to JCPenney, Carson Pierre, Hauglands, Jack and Jill, TJ Maxx, Somersaults, Kids "R" Us, and were now in Daytons. We tried on at least fifteen outfits, most of them of my choosing. There was a dress that looked darling. She hated it—wrong color. A pink culotte outfit with a T-shirt overblouse was all wrong because the material underneath was stiff and scratchy. She didn't like the way it felt! A black pants outfit with cummerbund and short jacket met with the same reaction. I tried to tell her to pick one and take it home to show Dad. It didn't work—she started to cry and reminded me I had promised her I wouldn't buy anything she hated.

I was losing it, but I hadn't started screaming yet. The clerk gave me "that look" and asked, "How do you deal with this?"

I smiled sweetly as I said, "We shop a lot." And when the clerk wasn't looking we snuck out of the dressing room and left the store. It wasn't nice but it felt good.

I wanted to get angry. I certainly was frustrated that we couldn't find anything that was acceptable to my daughter and yet I realized it was very important to her. She wasn't saying no to see how far she could push me. She was saying no because to her the outfits we had tried truly didn't feel good or she didn't feel attractive in them. Still, two and a half hours into the fourth shopping trip my tolerance was wearing thin.

"You're getting frustrated, Mom," she said.

"Yes, I am," I admitted. "Shall we stop at Hauglands one more time?" I interjected, determined to get this job done!

She looked at me carefully. "I think we'd better go home," she said. "By the look on your face I think your temper needs a break!"

She was right. My temper did need a break. We went home, no one screaming, still friends, and fortunately six more days until the wedding.

e. When you find it, buy it. It wasn't until our sixth shopping trip that we finally found our consensus outfit. This was a record-breaking venture. Usually two or three times out is all we need. I was lucky—the outfit was even on sale. There are times I spend more money on her clothes than I would like, but I know that if we finally find the right thing she'll wear it every day—if I let her. In the end we'll get our money's worth. If we're shopping for play clothes, I look for the other colors and buy multiples. So what if the style is the same? It feels good to her, looks all right to me. A different outfit is not worth another five hours of our time and energy.

The important thing about consensus clothes is it respects the feelings of both the parent and the child. It is exhausting but it feels good. You have worked together. The last thing you want to do is to set up a win-lose situation with your child, where losing means wearing an outfit that Mom or Dad likes. How much better for your child to wear the beautiful dress or sharp sweater by choice than to feel coerced. Consensus clothes build a working relationship that has the chance of surviving a spirited adolescence. The long-term value is great. The short-term dividend is peace in the morning.

When they change their minds: During the toddler and preschool years especially, you may go through all the steps of shopping for consensus clothes only to find your child has changed his mind. *Never* allow your spirited child to wear anything immediately. Keep the tags on and let him try the clothes on again at home before you take a scissor to the tags. Then, and only then, do the tags come off. If you've done all of these things and he still refuses to wear it, you have definitely earned the right to one full-fledged Tarzan scream of frustration.

After you've got that out of your system, sit down with him and together closely examine the outfit. Find out what is wrong with it. Does the collar come up too high? Is the elastic too tight at the waist? Are the sleeves too short or binding? Take note of these for next time. Be sure that you listen carefully to your child, and do not ignore his complaints. Tuning in will limit the number of outfits that sit in the drawer or closet unworn.

Because spirited kids are so persistent, if an outfit is deemed unwearable you may even consider giving it away to someone who can use it. When it sits in the drawer or closet unworn you may be tempted to cajole them into wearing it. Frequently these efforts end up in frustration and fights. Even in families where the clothing budget is very tight parents have used this solution. Is it wasteful? Carried to the extreme, yes. Respectfully done, however, it recognizes that all of us sometimes make mistakes. We can learn from them and make a better choice next time.

SOMETIMES THERE ARE situations when we must demand that our child wear something that is important to us. It is appropriate to do so, especially at times when our child may not want to wear adequate clothing for the weather or doesn't understand the social norms for a particular situation. As you make your demands however, be careful that you don't back yourself into a corner like Jeanne did.

Jeanne had just completed a class called "Children, the Challenge." In the class she learned about natural and logical consequences. The child suffers the consequences of his own decisions. She decided to use this method on her son, who at the time was three. They were scheduled to be at a picnic for his nursery school in thirty minutes. Cory was not getting dressed. Putting natural consequences into effect she said, "Cory, if you're not dressed when it's time to go you will go in your pajamas."

What Jeanne hadn't learned is that three-year-olds don't understand the social norms of parties. He didn't get dressed and so she felt compelled to take him in his pajamas. He had a ball. It was Jeanne who was mortified. Make sure your ultimatums don't backfire on you.

3. IF YOUR CHILD IS SENSITIVE

Be aware of textures and fit: Sensitive kids can really feel the lint, threads, and bumps in their clothing. They aren't trying to be difficult. Be creative as you work with them. Leggings and tights can keep legs warm for the child who hates pants. There are beautiful pants outfits that can fit even dressy occasions for the girl who hates dresses. Beaded moccasins can replace stiff patent leather shoes. Cotton sweaters look as nice as wool. Look for an imaginative solution.

As you purchase clothing, be sure to look inside as well as outside at each piece. It's the inside that touches sensitive skin. It needs to be soft and pleasant.

Talk about feelings: Spirited kids need to understand why getting dressed is so difficult for them. It's important to tell them:

You react to changes in temperature.

You are sensitive. Your shoes never feel quite right at first, but wear them for a few minutes and see if they feel better.

You are very perceptive. That makes it difficult for you to get dressed because you think of other things to do.

You are full of energy. It's hard for you to stand still long enough to put your clothes on or to have your diaper changed.

You are very persistent. You like to get dressed yourself. It's all right to ask for a little help when you need it.

I think it is the tag that is bothering you. We can cut it out and it will feel more comfortable.

The more extensive your child's vocabulary, the better she can explain to you what she is feeling and what she needs from you. Good communication prevents misunderstandings.

Believe them when they tell you they're hot: Spirited kids are intense and energetic. The blood surges through their veins, making them hot. You might feel negligent letting your child wear a short-sleeved T-shirt when you've got on a turtleneck and wool sweater, but it may be all she truly needs. Trust that she will let you know if she's cold. Carry the sweater in your bag so you know you've got it, if it's needed. Remember the Ann Landers gem of the day. "A sweater is something you put on when your mother is cold."

The same is true of pajamas. The spirited child may be comfortable in a lightweight T-shirt and boxer shorts in January when the rest of the family is wearing their flannel pajamas and socks to bed.

Know when to take it off: If you get your child into that special outfit, know when to get her out of it. It is much better to put the frilly, lacy dress on your daughter, take a quick picture for Grandma, and get her out of it while she is still happy. If a special outfit is required for a holiday dinner don't forget to take the sweats along. Clothing that constantly irritates exhausts your spirited child. When she's exhausted she stops coping and the tantrums start.

4. IF YOUR CHILD IS PERCEPTIVE   "Jason is seven years old and still begging me to dress him every morning," his mother complained. "He lies on his bed or slides off it like slow-moving lava until he's on the floor—a lifeless object, incapable of lifting a finger. Fortunately, his three-year-old brother dresses himself, so I can help Jason if I want to, but quite frankly I've had it, I'd rather just yell at him."

When it comes to getting dressed, Jason is a can't-do-anything kid. Like the marketing director of Coca-Cola we talked about in chapter 9, we have to motivate him to want to get dressed.

Use your imagination: Spirited kids have wonderful senses of imagination. You can use this to motivate them to dress. Ask them what they would like to be this morning. How about an astronaut, a firefighter, Teenage Mutant Ninja Turtle, or even Santa Claus. Once they've chosen their characters pretend the clothes you are putting on them are their costumes. As you put on their socks, make them astronaut socks. Slide on a sweater that is an oxygen pack. Pull a shirt over their head that is a space suit. Have fun with it. Becoming an astronaut is much more motivating than putting on old brown corduroys.

Compromise: You can also motivate the can't-do kid by agreeing to put on one sock, then insisting that your child put on the other. You put on the T-shirt, he puts on the sweater. Gradually you will want to pull out of this process doing less and less until your child is dressing on his own. You may still have to sit in the room while he dresses, but at least he is getting the clothes on.

Well-guided verbal instructions can help: As you direct your child, be sure your instructions are clear and concise. You might say, "Lay your shirt on the bed. Now put your head through the head hole, now your arm, now your other arm." Break the process into little steps that are easily accomplished. By helping your child to see the steps involved you keep him on task.

5. IF YOUR CHILD IS SLOW TO ADAPT   Dressing is full of transitions. It requires a child to stop doing what he was doing, possibly move to another room, and then switch clothing. It is ripe for conflict for a slow-to-adapt child.

Allow time: You may wish you could dress your child in ten minutes but the fact is it may take forty-five. He really isn't trying to sabotage your efforts to arrive at work on time. He is simply attempting to get the right "feel" and to make the transition from one outfit to another. It takes a great deal of time and effort for everyone involved. Plan the time you need into your schedule so you don't feel rushed.

Set up a routine: It is important to set up a consistent pattern that you follow each morning. Your routine might include a seven A.M. wake up, twenty minutes to lie in bed listening to the radio or ten minutes to be rocked by Mom or Dad. Don't expect a slow-to-adapt child to wake up, immediately jump out of bed, and start on a task. He can't do it. Allow another thirty minutes to get dressed and perhaps forty minutes to have breakfast, brush teeth, get backpacks, coats, etc. ready to go at eight thirty. It doesn't really matter what the activities are, or what order you carry them out in, just be sure they are consistent and calm.

Choose ahead: Spirited kids like to have time to get used to ideas. Select the next day's outfit the night before. If it is a transitional time of the year, be sure to pick out a warm outfit and a cool one then let the thermometer make the choice in the morning.

"I've got four kids," Brenda remarked, "and I can tell you, choosing what they will wear the night before is the only way I can get them all out in the morning. We lay out everything—even their mittens and boots. Seeing the pieces laying there seems to help all of them be prepared and more cooperative—even the ones that aren't spirited."

Prepare for change in seasons: I remember greeting a group of parents with "Happy first day of spring." I was met with a huff.

"Happy, my eye," a parent threw back at me. "The last week has been a torture trying to change clothes from one season to the next."

Spirited kids don't like any kind of change—including changes in clothing demanded by different seasons. Used to long winter pants, they'll pull on the hems of shorts trying to make them longer. They'll scream and throw fits over bulky snowsuits and down jackets. You can ease them into the change by getting the new clothes ready a few weeks early. Lay some of them out in their bedroom and let them play dress up with them. By the time they're ready to wear them for real, they will have adapted.

6. IF YOUR CHILD IS ENERGETIC

Let her do as much as possible: Even a five-month-old baby can pull off a sock if you loosen it over her heal and then let her grab the end and pull. The more involved in zipping, buttoning, pulling on, or pulling off your child is, the less energy she'll have to roll or run away. As soon as your energetic kid can stand, dress her standing up in front of a mirror. You'll be respecting her need to move, but the mirror will grab her attention.

ENJOY THE REWARDS

Once you've gotten your child dressed, cheer. Cheer for yourself, your own patience and ingenuity, and for your child and her continued growth. It does get better. After a recent workshop, a woman came up to me and said, "My daughter is now twelve. When she was a preschooler, getting her dressed was a three-hour venture. She couldn't stand lint in her socks. I would find myself sitting there at seven in the morning pulling out minute balls of lint from her socks, knowing that if I didn't she would scream for the next hour or tear them off her feet. Today she puts on her socks without a fuss. Her dad asked her if she remembers throwing fits about lint in her socks. She said, "Of course, I do, and it still drives me crazy. I just tolerate it now."

Repetition brings success with spirited kids. The more they do something, the more they become comfortable. The old battles fade away, replaced by those of the next stage of development. Instead of socks, it's hair that won't lie right or makeup that smears—but at least they have their successes to fall back on and remind them that this too they shall resolve.

Let other people help: Our spirited classes were a great success *except* for the very end. Every session ended up in tears as parents tried to get coats on tired kids who were coping with a transition. It felt awful. Our solution was to make getting on coats the last classroom activity for the kids. The teachers, rather than the parents, helped each child get ready to go. It was a miracle cure. The kids thought it was great fun and all the parents had to do was throw on their own coats and walk out the door. The only stumbling block was making sure parents were ready to go too so kids didn't get overheated. Spirited kids save their biggest battles for their parents. They're most comfortable with you. So whenever you can, let someone else help out. The kids won't mind and it's a break for you.

GETTING DRESSED, eating dinner, going to bed at night, and other typical tough times don't need to be a daily battle. You can plan for success. You can prevent problems or at least the number of problems by respecting each other's temperaments and adapting your responses accordingly. Dare to be different. *Don't let socks keep you apart.*

GETTING DRESSED: A SUMMARY

It may seem insignificant to most people, but in the family of a spirited child putting on socks and getting dressed can be a divisive event—parents pitted against wiry little bodies, dashing across the room to escape the tags that scratch, elastic that's too tight, and fabrics that hurt their skin. Getting dressed is a major challenge not because the kids want to be stubborn, uncooperative, and free spirits but because of their temperament.

Predict: Check your child's temperamental picture. Try your best to figure out what temperamental traits make dressing troublesome for your child. Sensitivity is often a major issue. Adaptability and intensity may be factors too.

Organize the Setting:

Create a space for dressing that helps your child focus on the task at hand. Remove toys and other attractive items that may distract your child.

Avoid power struggles by allowing an indoor/outdoor thermometer to help your child decide what is appropriate to wear for the day.

Purchase clothing that is easy for your child to put on and take off by himself.

Provide a mirror to help your child stay focused.

Work Together:

Teach your child the words to describe the frustration she experiences when she is getting dressed so she can say it rather than scream it.

Purchase clothing that is easy to get on, matches any other piece in the dresser drawer, and feels good.

Shop with your child in order to select clothing that is acceptable to both of you.

Expect to take several shopping trips before you find the right clothes.

Believe your child when she tells you she is hot.

Allow time for your child to dress without feeling rushed.

Prepare ahead for changes in seasons.

Enjoy the Rewards:

Remember repetition brings success. Over time dressing will become less of an issue.

Let other people help. If your child goes to day care let the teacher help her with her coat before you arrive. If you are in a two-parent family take turns helping your child dress.

PART FOUR

SOCIALIZING WITH SPIRIT

17

GETTING ALONG WITH OTHER KIDS

Mother, do you think you'll ever be able to socialize her?
—Megan, the sibling of a spirited child

THE MOMS and their babies had been lounging on the floor in the early childhood room. The bright rainbow-colored parachute stretched out underneath them. They'd rolled balls, dangled rattles, gooed and gurgled at their reflections in the mirrors, and made faces at each other. The teacher started to sing, "Make a circle. Make a circle, everyone."

A sixth grader standing next to me at the observation window asked, "What is she doing that for? Babies don't know what a circle is."

"That's right," I responded. "They don't. We have to teach them about circles and how to act when a group sits in a circle. Right now we are just exposing them to the idea, but in a few years we'll expect them to know what coming to the circle means."

Social skills and protocol are learned. They are the life skills that we all need for working cooperatively in society. Without giving up dignity or identity, spirited children have to learn how to adapt and accommodate to the group. They have to learn how to manage spirit on their own, without us always troubleshooting for them.

The journey your child takes as she moves out from you to interact with others in the neighborhood, at school, and on the team may be an easy one. For many spirited kids, an understanding and acceptance of their style is all they need to be successful. Others, however, may stumble. They might not be welcome in the neighborhood because they are punching and tackling the other kids. They may burst into tears if someone at the bus stop teases them, or they may never want to invite anyone over to your home. Watching your child struggle as he tries to figure out how to get along with others can be a very painful experience.

"I just don't know what to do." Betty sighed. "It has gotten to the point that when I see a group of kids I start to cringe. Kevin will barge right in to a group and end up destroying the game. He's only four, so I know he isn't doing it on purpose, but it always ends up with him in tears and the other kids furious. I can feel the icy glares of the parents, silently demanding me to control my 'brat,' but I'm at a loss. I don't know what to do."

RECOGNIZING BOUNDARIES

Although many children and adults seem to pick up social skills without guidance, spirited kids who are drenched in their perceptions and fired by their intensity may miss the cues—the simple body actions that inform them that they have crossed one or more social boundaries—the guidelines that tell them their voices are too loud, their bodies are too close, or their intensity is penetrating. As a result, they are unable to move into a group and function within it harmoniously. If this is the case for your child, you will have to help him identify and honor boundaries, then back out and let him go.

LEARNING TO ENTER A GROUP

I stood at the observation window with a group of parents. "Watch carefully as your child joins another child," I told them. "Tell me what you see."

"Tommy is arguing with Terry over a chunk of Play-Doh. He just grabbed it away from him," said Kari, her words sharp with frustration.

"Mica is standing back and watching the kids in the housekeeping area. He isn't joining in," Sue remarked, her voice dropping in disappointment then rising as she exclaimed, "Now he is. He waited for an empty chair and then sat down. Now he's chatting with Laura and Brad."

Why was Mica successful in joining a group and Tommy wasn't? Research shows that kids who move into a group without drawing immediate attention to themselves, ask relevant questions, and avoid disagreeing with other group members are more successful than kids who don't.

This is important information for serious and analytical kids who are prone to make evaluative comments the minute they enter a situation. Teach your child to reserve his suggestions for change until he has become a part of the group.

Whether a child is analytical or not, if he is experiencing difficulty entering a group, you may have to teach him to *stop,* make eye contact, say hello, and *listen.* By listening, he can size up the situation and ask relevant questions, or find something to which he can agree. When he is tuned in to what is going on, he can enter successfully.

"I've tried that and it doesn't work!" Sarah stormed. "I've told that kid for years to stop, but he still barges right in. He's six now and I think he's doing it because he knows he'll get his own way."

"Louie is a high-energy kid, isn't he?" I asked.

"Yes, but what does that have to do with anything?" Sarah questioned.

"High-energy kids learn with their bodies. If you want them to stop, look, and listen, you can't just say it with words. You have to show them with their bodies."

Sarah's eyes lighted. "You could be right. He always listens to his hockey coach. When the coach says stop, he stops, but it's his whole body sliding to an ice-shaving halt."

The younger the child and the higher your child's energy, the more you will have to help him stop, look, and listen. At first exaggerate your movements. Slap your hands to your sides and stomp your feet together in a great big stop. Then you might say, "Check to see where they need a helper. Look for a toy no one is using. Watch quietly before you join in."

By teaching your child to stop, look, and listen you will help him to discover the subtle social cues that will inform him when and how to move into a group successfully.

BE AWARE OF SPACE

Once your child is working within a group, the boundaries that determine personal space become important. Individuals need a certain amount of space to feel comfortable and work effectively. The extraverted, and especially the high-energy, extraverted spirited child is notorious for invading the space of others because he is so anxious to share his ideas.

In the classroom one day I observed Rachel and David playing with a train. Each had a locomotor with six cars attached and were whirling their trains around and around the track. Rachel was so anxious to catch up with David and show him her train that she rear-ended his cars and derailed them. David burst into tears.

"Rachel, look where your locomotor is," the teacher said. "See how it is touching David's train. He is telling you that he doesn't like it. You need to keep your train a few inches behind David's so you both can use the track." She then showed Rachel where her train needed to be. Rachel paused, waited for David to straighten his train on the track, and then rolled again. She did her best to stay three inches back, jerking to a stop, but stopping.

Rachel wanted to play with David. She didn't mean to make him angry, but the thrill of the motion and the desire to share her excitement had blinded her to the limits. She needed help getting the picture—an awareness of the invisible limits—but once she had it, she was successful. She could honor the limits, when she could see them.

Whether it is telling your child to look where her feet are so that she can see when she is standing too close, or where her hands are so that they aren't in someone else's face or touching someone when they don't want to be touched, you are helping your child to learn about the space needs of others. This awareness is important to keep her from invading someone else's space and potentially offending them.

Intense spirited kids can also cross social boundaries with their voices. Mia was the loudest kid in class. She snarled, snorted, squealed, giggled, and stormed like no other. The other kids cupped their hands over their ears when they saw her coming.

"Mia, I love your enthusiasm," I heard her teacher explain, "but sometimes it is overwhelming to others. Look at the other children. They are cupping their hands over their ears. See how they back away from you. Notice how they flinch when you shout. Your voice is hurting their ears. I know you don't mean to hurt their ears. Listen to your voice, and try to speak softly." The teacher's voice demonstrated the level. "They won't back away from you when your voice feels comfortable to them."

Over several weeks I watched as the teacher worked with Mia, catching her not when she was loud, but when her voice was appropriate. "What a nice, comfortable voice, Mia," she would remark. "That's the voice your friends like to hear." Frequently a child doesn't know what an appropriate voice sounds or feels like. Catching her doing it "correctly" is the best way to teach her.

Spirited kids are perceptive. By making use of this ability, they can learn to discriminate the subtle cues others send them. The signals that clarify boundaries. Once learned, it is not unusual to find spirited kids in leadership roles and as popular group members. It just takes a keen eye and a little help from you.

RESOLVING CONFLICTS WITH WORDS INSTEAD OF FISTS

Studies on brain functioning detailed in *The Brain* by Richard Restak show that when individuals become very angry or frightened, their brains move into a lower level of functioning. They stop thinking and move into a survival reaction—fists flying, teeth biting, nails scratching. Intense kids have to learn to control their intense reactions in order to keep thinking and performing appropriately in social situations.

During class one morning, Todd, Peter, and Ben were pretending to be camping. A picnic of plastic french fries, hot dogs, and grapes was spread out on the table. Peter picked up a hot dog. Without warning, Ben snatched it out of his hand bellowing, "*Mine!* You can't have it. It's *mine!*" Peter lunged for the hot dog. Ben slugged him. The blow glanced off Peter's cheekbone and sent him sailing over the top of the table.

Spirited kids are intense, but accepting intensity does not imply that we allow them to be aggressive. We can demand that they use their intensity appropriately.

As I watched Peter and Ben, the classroom teacher moved in front of Ben. Bending down to his level, she commanded, "Stop. I will not let you hurt Peter. The rule is no hitting. No matter how angry you are you may not hit."

Ben almost looked relieved. Peter definitely appreciated the support. Spirited kids need to know that we, the adults in their lives, will take charge when there is a possibility of injury or harm. We will enforce the rule. We will not allow one child to hurt another. Stopping potentially dangerous behavior doesn't mean placing blame. It clarifies the rules and sets the stage for more positive problem solving techniques.

"I think you are very angry," the teacher responded to Ben, "but you have to tell Peter with words. Are you ready to talk to Peter or do you need a time-out, a chance to cool off?"

Ben continued to swing at Peter who was now standing, leaning against the teacher. The teacher stroked Peter's back and Ben's arm attempting to calm both of them and to restrain Ben from hitting again.

"Ben, listen to your body," she stated firmly, then continued more softly. "You are very tense. Look at your hands, see how they are fisted? Do you feel your eyes squinting? You are very tight. Come and sit over here."

She propelled him gently to the corner, talking quietly to him. "When your hands unbend, and your eyes open wide, we will go back and talk to Peter," she said. She stayed with him, not saying anything, letting her closeness and soft body language tell him she was there to support him and that she cared. Peter came too, but after a few comforting strokes he moved back to the "camp."

Spirited kids have to be taught that it is acceptable to pull out of a situation when they are frustrated or upset. When a young child is overwhelmed by his intensity as Ben was, he needs help figuring out what happened and what went wrong. In the video "On Their Own with Our Help," infant specialist Magda Gerber advises that when two children are in conflict, you need to address the aggressor more than the victim. The aggressor is more frightened. He doesn't realize what has happened. He doesn't know what to do about it unless he has been taught.

Ben's body slumped against the teacher's until he gradually climbed into her lap. "Let's go talk to Peter," she advised. He nodded and allowed her to lead him back to the "campsite."

"Tell Peter what you want," she said. "Tell him with words that you were angry." Ben tightened, and the teacher gently placed a hand on his.

"I don't want to share," he said. "I had it first."

"Peter, what would you like to say?" the teacher asked, turning to him.

Peter responded, "It was my turn. You have had all the hot dogs and now I want a turn."

When kids fight, especially intense, sensitive kids, we've got to talk about the feelings of everyone involved. Spirited kids have to learn how to express their own feelings and also to *listen* to those of others. Empathy has to be learned. By talking about feelings we also allow kids to express their emotions and diffuse their intensity. This is a time for sharing, not an opportunity to determine blame.

Seems simple, doesn't it? Of course, it doesn't usually work as smoothly as it did in this classroom.

"My kids would just turn around and scream, 'I hate you,' " Andy remarked, when I began sharing this story with the group.

"Yea, Betsy wouldn't have anything decent to say," Marsha added. "Last night she told her brother that she would like to rip his face off and run it through the blender."

If the physical abuse turns to verbal abuse, your child is not ready to talk yet. His words tell you that he needs to continue his time-out. You might tell him, "I can see you are still too upset to work this out." Then insist that he return to time-out. But later, when he is ready, bring him back to resolve the issue. Too often spirited kids are removed from the conflict and never brought back. As a result they don't learn how to express their feelings appropriately or to solve the problem with words instead of fists.

In chapter 7, I talked about looking for yeses. Dealing with conflict in a positive, healthy way means coming to a resolution that all can accept. Once the kids have talked about their feelings, it's time to explore their interests.

"Well what happened with Ben and Peter?" The group asked, wanting to know the end of the story.

I continued. The teacher said to both of them, "It seems like you both wanted that hot dog. How could you work this out?"

As I watched, the two four-year-olds faced each other. I waited, wondering what their response would be. They both squinted and hopped on one foot. It was Ben who said, "I'm full. You can have the hot dogs. I'm going to take a nap." He crawled into the sleeping bag, a loud snort escaping as he snored in his "sleep."

"It does work," Bev offered. "It's hard to believe but it does. Yesterday my kids had the day off of school. They are each so different. It's difficult to find something everyone is willing to do together. Tasha is a strong introvert. Megan is an extreme extravert. I thought I would take them both to the zoo but they immediately started complaining. They didn't want to go to the zoo. I didn't care, so I said what would you like to do? Tasha wanted to stay home. Megan wanted to invite three friends over and go roller-skating. Neither one of them is old enough to be left alone, so we had to come up with something that everyone could agree on. We obviously had a problem!

" 'Tasha, you want to stay home, and Megan, you want to go roller-skating,' I said. 'Is that really what you want?'

"Tasha nodded her head yes. Megan started to complain that Tasha never wants to do anything that she wants to do.

" 'Do you really want to skate?' I asked Megan trying to distract her.

" 'No, but I want to be with my friends,' she insisted.

"That was a little easier. 'All right. You want to be with friends and Tasha wants to be at home. What could we do?'

"We made a list of things to do: putting up the badminton net and having a game, baking, renting a movie, and hosting a video game competition. They each moaned and groaned during the process, but I insisted that they not evaluate until we had a long list. Then we went back through all of the ideas.

"We decided that Tasha and I would bake and Megan would invite three friends over for badminton. They had a great time playing and by the time they were done Tasha and I had a snack prepared and ready for them. It wasn't what I had expected, but it didn't cost anything and everyone had a good time."

Looking for yes teaches kids to respect different points of view. It allows persistent kids to unlock and work cooperatively. It reduces frustration because everyone knows they will be heard. Many books will advise you to remove yourself and let your children work their own problems out. With young children, especially intense spirited children, you have to teach them how to problem solve, before you can leave them to their own devices. Otherwise it's like leaving them at the pool and saying, "I'm sure you can figure out how to swim."

When you first begin helping children find yes with their peers, they may have trouble coming up with ideas. You may have to offer suggestions, but soon, with practice, they'll be able to do it themselves. By four or five years of age, you will hear kids starting to look for yes on their own. They'll run into the house to grab a timer so each person can have a five-minute turn on the swing. They'll make up a rhyme that allows each child a turn at the jump rope. If one activity isn't working, they'll think of another. They'll recognize that different interests drive the choices and look for ways to make everyone happy.

Understanding how to find yes, to work cooperatively with others to solve problems, is a critical social skill. It can be used to stop the battles between persistent kids and their parents. It works in the classroom, and it can work at home with siblings and friends too.

LEARNING TO HANDLE TEASING

Siblings tease, children tease, lovers tease. Learning to handle teasing is an important social skill, but a potentially touchy lesson for spirited kids.

"My son has teasing down to an art form," Frank remarked in class. We waited to hear his story.

"One night," he began, "Al and I were driving in the car. I was pre-occupied about some things at work so I wasn't paying any attention to him. Out of the blue I heard him question, 'Dad, do you know how many boy-friends Krissa has?'

I ignored him, my blood pressure rising. Krissa is six years old.

" 'Dad, I saw her chasing Brian around the house kissing him,' he insisted.

" 'Al,' I snapped. 'Krissa isn't even in the car. Why are you saying these things? You can't bug her when she isn't even here.'

" 'Because, Dad,' he responded coolly, 'it always gets your atten-tion.' "

I roared. Perceptive spirited kids know right where to get us. They are fully cognizant of everyone's most vulnerable spots and can go for the kill. Without really meaning to, however, the perceptive child who senses the vulnerable points of others can really hurt them. He needs to learn to use his ability in a positive rather than a negative way. Expect some good-natured teasing to go on, but teach your child to pay attention to the facial expressions, words, and body language of others that indicate the limit. Just like other social boundaries, the limit for fun and appropriate teasing may have to be taught. Make sure your child understands that statements that shame, ridicule, or hurt others are not allowed. Teasing cannot be an excuse for verbal abuse. Kids don't know what *verbal abuse* means. You have to teach them. When one child starts to call another "stick legs," "stupid," or any other deriding name, you have to say, "Stop. That is verbal abuse. It is not allowed in our family."

When spirited kids are on the receiving end of teasing, their intensity can make them a susceptible target. If they are embarrassed or angry, their reactions may overwhelm them.

During an interview, I asked eight-year-old Sokim about the last time someone teased her.

"I was just roller-skating," she told me. "I had on headphones so that I could listen to music. I just wanted to be alone. Lindsey kept bugging me. She was saying, 'Your butt sticks out,' and Allison was calling me names. I wanted to kick and swear at them. I wanted to beat them up. I knew I was going to cry because they hurt me. They really made me mad. I didn't do anything. They didn't have any right to say what they did."

"What did you do?" I asked. "Did you beat them up?"

"No," Sokim, replied shaking her head. "I knew I wasn't supposed to hit them, even if I felt like it. I needed my mom to tell them to leave me alone, but she didn't hear them, so I just went in the house. If I can get away a few minutes I can stop how mad I am. I watched TV. It helped me cool down."

Sokim had learned to take it, to cope with being teased. Even though she reacted very strongly to the antagonizing words of the other children, she had learned to keep her cool. She went in the house and stepped away from the abuse.

It isn't always possible to step away, but the more options a child knows to stop the flood of emotion created by teasing, the more successful she will be. Talk with your child about teasing. What is acceptable for her to do. Can she walk away? Can she ignore the teasers or tell them to stop? Can she talk to someone else? When should she ask an adult for help? Make sure your child has identified her options.

LEARNING TO SHARE

Sharing is one of the most challenging social skills for all children to learn. The limits are so unclear. Moms and dads don't share their cars with the neighbors, and yet kids are supposed to. Mom takes a sip of Dad's pop but a toddler isn't supposed to snitch a drink from someone else's bottle. We share some things but not everything. It is all very confusing.

The younger the child the more difficult it is to share. Toddlers are just learning what ownership means. They don't want to share. They are actually going through a developmental stage in which they are learning what's MINE.

"Well that's good to know," Steve said. "At Christmas we gave our eighteen-month-old son an engineer's dream. A child-size locomotive for him to ride. The whistle tooted, the bell rang, and if you pushed the red button 'smoke' escaped from the chimney. I loved it and so did he. In fact he loved it so much that he was dragging his cousin off of it and bellowing every time she came near."

To protect your toddler's reputation, save the locomotor until the cousins go home. When other kids are invited over, pull out several cars, a whole pile of Duplos, or any other toys that come in multiples. Avoid toys that require toddlers to take turns. Toddlers aren't developmentally ready to be very gracious. In fact, you may find that for a few months, sharing may be so difficult for your toddler that the only place he can play successfully with another child is in a neutral location—a local park, playground, or other setting where no one owns the toys.

Older kids can be expected to share some, but sensitive spirited kids, especially introverts, are very protective of their possessions. Teach your child to put away the things she does not want to share, before other children come to play. Help her select items she is comfortable letting others use. Talk about her feelings. Respect them, but let her know that sharing and doing nice things for others is an important part of friendship.

When you see her being successful, compliment her. You might say to her:

Mica was thrilled that you let him ride your bike. I think you really made him feel good.

You did a great job sharing your new ball with Todd. He seemed to enjoy playing with you.

I know it was hard for you to let Sarah have a turn, but you did a good job of sharing with her.

Reinforce those social skills! Help her to recognize those she has and encourage her to use them more.

SURVIVING TRANSITIONS

Social interactions include many transitions. When someone enters or leaves a game, it is a transition. Winning a game or losing a game is an ending. A change in the rules or in an activity demands a quick response. Putting away toys, going outside, greeting a friend, or saying good-bye all require an adjustment. For a child who is slow to adapt coping with these transitions can be very challenging.

"Maybe that's what happened to Ted," Terri remarked. "He and Bobbie were playing catch in our front yard. Jeff called asking to play with Ted. I was busy with the baby and didn't feel like walking outside to get Ted for the phone call so I just told Jeff, 'Come on over, he's outside playing ball. I'm sure you can join the game.'

"Jeff rode over on his bike, and because I had given permission to do so, immediately joined the game. I realize now, this was all a surprise to Ted. Within minutes I heard the bickering. 'You can't play. He's not out. It's my turn.' When I walked outside Ted was in a rage. The peaceful ball field was now a battleground."

"Your hunch is probably correct," I responded. "Ted is a slow-to-adapt kid. I suspect he was surprised and couldn't cope. He probably didn't know what hit him. All he knew was that a rush of anger stung him and he reacted with angry words."

If you can, warn your child about upcoming changes in social situations but if you can't, teach him to recognize them himself. When he understands that he is upset because someone unexpectedly joined his game or that he is experiencing discomfort because a change has occurred, he is better able to cope. He can step back, take a deep breath, or do whatever he needs to, in order to manage his feelings. He'll release his frustration appropriately. The outbursts will stop and the number of his successes in social situations will increase.

Losing a game is an especially painful transition for the spirited child because it is an undesirable transition that he didn't plan for or expect. Slow adaptability combines with an intense frustration for a potential blowup. Spirited kids need help learning to win or lose in style. Sit down with your child and explain to him how a good winner acts. Let him know that you expect him to shake hands, set the ball aside, and be respectful of the losing team's feelings. Talk too, about what it feels like to lose. Teach him that it is not all right to throw a ball down on the court. It is not okay to refuse to shake hands. It is not appropriate to whine and complain about the referees. Kids don't necessarily know the appropriate protocol—you have to teach them. If you aren't sure how to help your child cope with the transitions involved in social situations see chapter 10 for more ideas.

PRACTICE WITH YOUNGER CHILDREN

Social skills are learned. Social skills are critical for a spirited child to fully utilize his or her strengths. If your child is experiencing difficulty with peers his own age, try inviting slightly younger children to your home. Research has shown that practice with younger children can be a very effective way to learn social skills. You'll want these sessions to be successful so keep them short. One hour may be enough. Plan a variety of activities, including soothing, calming ones. Sharing is one of the toughest skills to learn so at first include toys that are multiples. By doing so, your child will be able to practice the other social skills before he has to tackle the complexity of sharing.

Stay tuned in as your child plays with others so that you can reinforce what your child is doing well. Avoid interrupting the play but when the moment is right compliment both children on what they have done well. You might say something like:

Great job cooperating, guys.

Good listening.

You did a super job of taking turns.

You used words to tell Amy you wanted a turn.

You allowed Pete to join the game.

Remember success builds on success. By emphasizing your child's strengths you build his confidence—a confidence that will carry over to other social situations.

UNDERSTANDING THE DIFFERENCES BETWEEN INTROVERTS AND EXTRAVERTS

Oftentimes when I talk with parents who are worried about their child's social skills, I realize the real issue is understanding the differences between introverts and extraverts. It is important to remember that popularity or social skills cannot be measured by the number of friends your child does or does not have. In chapter 5 I explained how introverts and extraverts interact with others. Introverts are frequently not given full credit for their social skills because they are more selective with their friendships. If you are an extraverted parent, you may worry that your introverted child doesn't have friends, because he is not eager to invite other children over to play. Remember that introverts form deep, long-lasting relationships with a few good friends. Their social skills may be excellent, they simply are more particular and take longer to form their relationships. If your child is playing successfully with at least one other child, you probably don't need to worry. He has social skills. He is just being very selective in how he uses them. Remember introverts enjoy and need time alone. Being alone and being lonely are not the same thing to an introvert.

CELEBRATING SUCCESS

It does take energy and a keen eye and ear to help your spirited child develop his social skills, but over time you will be rewarded as you listen to him skillfully resolve a problem, get elected student council representative, or negotiate a group decision. Spirited kids can get along with others. By learning to use their intensity, persistence, and perceptiveness well, they often grow up to be outstanding leaders and politicians.

In a recent *Minneapolis Tribune* article, Susan Feyder described Tom Gegaz, Tires Plus CEO, by saying, "If you looked up the word *intense* in the dictionary, you probably would find Tom's picture beside it. Intensity has served him well, particularly when he was struggling to get his tire business started."

In *Fortune* magazine, Walter Guzzardi wrote, "At least one of [John] Deere's contemporaries tinkered with adding steel to plows but only Deere had the wit to persist with the idea, to take the product to the farmer, to preach its virtues and to price it right."

I'll bet my bottom dollar—they're spirited!

18

HOLIDAY AND VACATION HOT SPOTS

So lively and quick. I knew in a moment
it must be St. Nick.
—Clemont Clarke Moore

I NEVER EXPECTED to spend my son's first Christmas hiding in my mother-in-law's bathroom, but that's where I found myself. I was doing my best to soothe my infant son's wails, while his cheeks stretched taut, tinged purple under the stream of tears. I didn't remember any of my older sisters and their babies hiding in the bathroom. Yet as I sat on the throne nearly drowning in my own pity, I realized that I had spent most of his first holidays right there—restraining myself from flushing both of us down the tube. It had started with his baptism and continued right through Grandma's birthday, Halloween, Thanksgiving, and now Christmas.

The day never began that way. He'd flash his big blues at anyone and gurgle and goo to their hellos. Perched on my lap he was Mr. Charm, a politician working the crowd. Then it would happen. I could feel his body stiffen against mine. The cycling of his legs and arms became jerky like a washing machine off balance. His hands fisted, knuckles whitened. The smile slipped from his face as he erupted into fire-engine wails. The only way I could calm him was to take him outside or to sit in the bathroom (the one quiet room in the house) with the lights out, softly talking to him and stroking his face. Sometimes I cried too.

Holidays, birthday parties, family gatherings, vacations, and special celebrations can prove to be a virtual mine field for spirited kids and their parents. They are filled with hot spots—the people, places, and things that rub against the grain of spirited children's temperaments and drive them wild.

Close your eyes and think about your child's last birthday party. Now try Halloween, Thanksgiving, and vacation. What hot spots did you hit?

"Santa Claus," Tom remarked. "She is scared to death of him."

"Shopping," Claudia added, and the others joined in.

"My mother's living room. It's full of glass."

"Presents—they weren't hers."

"Bedtime—she couldn't sleep and then she was exhausted."

The list grew. Each hot spot was unique and yet there were commonalities—temperamental traits. Surprise triggers lurked at the dinner table, in crowds, and at the theater because of sensitivity, in the presents and at nap time because of slow adaptability. High energy levels made sitting quietly in the church or synagogue, at Grandma's house, or in the car a major effort. A hotel, a strange pillow, and numerous other seemingly insignificant situations brought discord simply because they were new and different.

The special challenge of this mine field of holiday and vacation hot spots is for your child to learn to negotiate it with friends, relatives, and hundreds of strangers. To be successful he needs your extra support and instruction.

ESTABLISH REALISTIC EXPECTATIONS

Marilyn's steps scraped across the threshold, her gait restricted by two-year-old Stephanie, plastered to her right thigh. Their eyes scanned the ground in front of them instead of the faces around them gathered for the "Holiday Hot Spots" class. Good cheer was not in evidence. I pulled them aside, my hand reaching out to touch Marilyn's forearm.

"Looks like it's been a tough week," I began, attempting to voice my concern, yet allowing her to take the lead.

Her voice was quiet, tired as she spoke. "The issue is really more mine than the kids. I'm exhausted with the holidays. I get up, go to work, come home, and then I need to shop, bake, and decorate. I know Stephanie is spirited. I'm aware that she is more excited, more sensitive than the other kids. I understand that she needs me, but sometimes I just don't have it in me."

During holidays and vacations spirited children need us more than ever to help them cope. It takes energy to provide that support. Unfortunately we are often drained by baking, shopping, entertaining, cleaning, driving, or other activities. When our kids need us the most we're not available. Sometimes in order to bring joy to holidays and vacations we have to let go.

Traditions are supposed to be fun—an opportunity to come together as a family and celebrate. We collect them as we go along, gathering some from the family we grew up in, from our spouse's family, and from friends.

The result can be an *overload* of traditions. Too many shoulds that lose their joy. That's what happened to Marilyn. Her list grew every year. She had not allowed herself to factor in the energy drain of caring for a young child, especially a spirited one. As a result she and Stephanie zinged through the holidays like two pinballs bouncing from one score to the next.

When you plan your celebrations or vacations, make your plans then cut them in half. Don't sabotage yourself thinking that you can do it all or that only if you were more capable you would be able to handle this. You have a spirited child. You are working harder. You are exploring more feelings, teaching more skills. You are preparing a child who is more for life.

Permission in hand, Marilyn went home to slash her shoulds. She told me later it began with sugar cookies.

"Every year we *must* make sugar cookies." she said. "It's a family tradition. I was rolling them out. The kids were bawling, my husband was yelling at them to shut up, and the dog was peeing on the floor at the door. This was supposed to be fun? I don't even like sugar cookies and my husband isn't supposed to eat them. I threw the dough in the garbage, sat down with this tablet [which she emphasized by waving it in my face], and made two columns: 'what's fun' and 'what isn't.' Then I started yelling out the things we do: 'Go to Aunt Vera's.'

"The kids responded by chanting, 'No, no, no. We won't go.'

"I agreed, but for the moment had the sense to keep my mouth shut. 'Making sugar cookies,' I continued.

" 'I like the frosting,' my husband said, 'but making the dough and rolling them out is too much trouble.'

"I concurred. We kept going through all the traditions we have collected. It was quite a list. But now I have this list. The things that are fun! This year we're staying home and having Aunt Vera come to our house. We're not making sugar cookies, but we did buy some at the bakery and let the kids frost them."

When you are honest with yourself and accept the reality of what it means to be the parent of a spirited child, you can grant yourself permission to go home rather than to one more store. To say no to lunch at one grandparent's house and dinner at the other. Everything doesn't have to happen this year or during this vacation. As your child grows and becomes more skilled, you will be able to expand your journey. This year Grandpa and Grandma need to come to you, but maybe a year from now you and your child will both be ready for that trip. Enjoy the stages and grow with them—gradually. You don't need to work at having fun. By setting realistic expectations for yourself, you will have the stamina and forethought to help your child learn to negotiate the hot spots smoothly.

CHECK YOUR CHILD'S EXPECTATIONS

"I dreaded carving the jack-o'-lantern this year," Tim said, "Nissa always gets so upset when it doesn't turn out the way she expected. This year I decided to be a little smarter. I suggested that she get a piece of paper and draw different jack-o'-lantern faces on it until she found just the one that she liked. She worked about twenty minutes until she had the right one. Then she took an erasable marker and drew the face right on the pumpkin. When she was done, we started cutting.

"First I cut out the eyes following the lines she had drawn—no problem. Then I started on the nose. She had drawn a round nose with two dots in it for nostrils. I cut it out leaving the dots like an *i*—again no complaints. I couldn't believe my luck. I moved on to the mouth and cut just as she had drawn it. She loved the results! There wasn't even one outburst."

Spirited kids never forget their favorite traditions. Their excitement builds for days until they can hardly stand it. Their imaginations run wild creating an image of what the holiday or vacation should look and be like. To prevent a major blowup or letdown, talk with them about what they remember from last year's celebration or vacation. What did they enjoy? What are they looking forward to again this year? You may not be able to meet all of their expectations—that's fine—but at least you have discovered them at home, in private, and not in a room filled with other people.

Talking ahead will also help you prevent the tears of disappointment when you cut the jack-o'-lantern the "wrong" way or forget to cut the cranberry gel into turkey shapes. It will also give your child time to figure out how she could do it herself. Of course, there will still be disappointments and surprises but the fewer the better.

SHARE INFORMATION WITH RELATIVES
AND STRANGERS

"Eva is the first grandchild. It really is wonderful all of the attention that is showered on her, but the relatives grab her the minute we walk in the door. She reacts by hiding behind us, clinging to my leg or hitting them if they keep pushing. She absolutely detests being kissed. She'll wipe it off, sneer, and say, 'Oh, yuk!' It hurts my dad. I'm embarrassed, my husband gets angry. What a mess!"

Helping relatives and strangers understand and work with your spirited child is crucial to her success. They need to know she wipes off their kisses because she is a sensitive introvert, not because she doesn't like them. She refuses to take off her coat when she arrives and doesn't run to Grandpa like her cousins do because she is slow to adapt.

Most people want to build a relationship with your child, but they may not be sure how to go about it. All they have are the techniques they have learned in the past and what they observe and learn from you and your child. Share with them what you have learned. Talk about the techniques that work and don't work and explain why. If they question your new-fangled ideas think of the quote from an IBM advertisement in *Fortune* magazine: "What made a company great 40 years ago would kill it today." Times have changed. Techniques have changed in business and in parenting. Learning new skills keeps us on top.

Celebrations and vacations require individuals to adapt to one another. Spirited kids need to learn the skills to be successful in these situations. Other people need to treat the spirited child respectfully and allow him to practice.

"But what if they don't?" Marsha asked. "At Thanksgiving we met my parents at a hotel. My dad took Joe in the pool. Joe doesn't swim but he loves the water. Dad put him in an inner tube and started pulling him through the water. It scared Joe and he yelled, 'Stop,' but Dad ignored him and kept whirling him around the pool. I finally had to jump in and 'save' Joe."

Sometimes as the parent of a spirited child you have to directly step in and help your child. You might have to tell your father to stop—which isn't always very easy. Use it as an opportunity to teach. You might say, "Dad, Joe is asking you to stop. Please listen to him. He is just learning to swim and needs a chance to practice. He'll feel more comfortable and have more fun if you work within the shallow end." Or "Dad if you let him watch first he'll join you in a few minutes."

"But what if you tell the other person and he won't listen?" groaned Brenda.

"Don't go there very much," drawled Frank.

If the other people are not listening to your suggestions and your child is not being successful, you may need to make some choices. You can choose to visit less frequently or shorten the length of your visits. You can invite people to your home where you have more control of the situation.

As children mature and become more capable of managing their temperament they will be able to handle more difficult situations. Limiting your visits when your child is a toddler doesn't mean you will always have to do so. But it is better to keep the interactions short and successful rather than long and dreadful. Help your child be successful—a little bit at a time.

PREPARE FOR ENTRY

Teaching your child how to greet exuberant relatives and friends can enhance relationships. If your child gets off to a good start, the whole event
is likely to go more smoothly. Greeting people can be tough for a spirited
child especially if he is an introvert, slow to adapt, and experiences a
negative first reaction.

When greeting others, your child needs your support. Don't let her
tears or reluctance embarrass you. With your words and with your actions
send her the message that you are there to help her. You understand. You
know she can be successful.

If your child is an infant or toddler plan to hold her on your lap. If
possible sit with her on the floor when meeting or greeting people for the
first time. When you are on the floor with her, she can freely move out from
you to the others without having to go through the experience of being put
down. It is much more comfortable for a young child to move out to others
and run back to you to check in when you're on the floor.

If your child is older teach him to say hello, shake hands, and then find
a comfortable place from which to observe until he is ready to participate.
The big overstuffed chair in the living room may be a perfect place or the
stool at the kitchen counter might work. Any place is fine that allows him
to pull out of the action a little bit, but not appear antisocial.

Talk to him about his need to check things out before entering a new
situation. Teach him to let others know that he learns best by watching and
will be very happy to play with them after an initial warm up. Even the New
York Knicks get a warm up before they play the game and show us their
stuff. Remind him of successes from the past like the first time he met
Santa Claus, his day-care provider, or teacher. Let him know that he is
more experienced and skillful at greeting people than he might think.

If you know there will be a crush of people arrive early.

"That really works for us," Anne remarked immediately when I offered
this suggestion in class. "It takes Christopher a day to warm up. If we're
only visiting for a weekend, it's half over before he's ready to roll. We now
do our best to arrive earlier than anyone else—if possible, an entire day
early. That gives us time to go through the issues of a new table, a new
bed, new house, all that stuff before the crowd hits."

Allowing your child time to become comfortable with new surroundings
before having to cope with new people as well reduces the energy drain on
him. It helps him to be successful.

Entry time can be shortened by showing your child pictures. Kids from
toddlers on up can benefit by a preview of Uncle Jim's portrait, or a look at

Grandpa and Grandma's house. Check out books from the library that describe the new places you will be going. Talk about the things you will see and do and the people you will meet.

WATCH OUT FOR CROWDS

Holidays and vacations are often filled with crowds. People in lines, packed in stores, in the parking lots, and at Grandma's house. Everywhere there are crowds. In a crowd spirited kids are blasted with a barrage of sensations. The odors of turkey and mashed potatoes mix with perfumes and sweat. Twinkling and flashing lights; blaring music; tinkling bells; and singing, swearing, and chattering voices are all absorbed by spirited children. Within minutes they can become overwhelmed by the sensations flooding their bodies. Some simply crumple, whimpering at your feet, others let loose screeching and howling or running wildly.

"We all know you can't spend your life avoiding crowds," I said to the group. "So how you can you help your child cope?"

"Actually we have learned to avoid some crowds," Mike offered. "We found he can be successful if there aren't crowds day after day. When we went to Florida we planned one day at Disney, the next lounging at the pool. One day at Epcot, the next at the beach. The beach was crowded but because of the open space it wasn't overwhelming. As long as we gave him those breaks he did fine—and so did I."

"I just called my aunt and said, listen, the boys are going to go nuts if they are cooped up all day. You've got to clean up your basement so they can play," Bev stated.

The others listened to her, mouths hanging open in amazement. "You called your aunt and told her to clean her basement? Didn't she get angry?" Patti questioned incredulously.

"My aunt is a good lady. She just forgets what it is like to have little kids so I reminded her. I told her she didn't have to do it, but if she didn't we were coming late and leaving early. It worked. She cleaned it up and we were able to send them down to the basement to run around, scream and just get away from all of the other people. Everyone had a great time. She even invited us back next year.

Patti shook her head in amazement. "I haven't got Bev's guts, but I do have a backpack ready to go with us next week for Thanksgiving dinner at my sister's. In it I have packed four of the kids' favorite books, one bag of Play-Doh, and one of Silly Putty. If the kids start to get wild, I'm ready."

"During the holidays I never take my kids shopping," Jane offered.

"How do you avoid it?" Martha questioned.

"I wait till my husband can watch them, sometimes I get a sitter, trade off with the neighbor or whatever, but I don't take them. The displays are more abundant, closer together, and just beg to be grabbed. The stimulation drives me nuts, and I have no patience with them. They are much better off at home without me."

"I guess we're brave," Bob remarked. "We do take ours shopping. I hate to shop though, so we only go for about an hour. They seem to handle that amount of time all right."

Every situation and child calls for a different approach but next time you and your spirited child will be exposed to crowds, think about what you can do to help him be successful. It may mean not going, as it did for Jane, or limiting your exposure like Bob and Mike. It could be creating an introvert or time-out space like Bev did or bringing along soothing/calming activities like Patti. Whatever you decide to do is fine, just think about it ahead of time and take the actions necessary to help your child be successful.

Introverted spirited children especially need quiet breaks from the crowd. Talking with people, listening to them, answering their questions is draining to the introvert. When you know that you will be spending an extended period of time with a group, you need activities that allow your child to escape from the crowd without appearing unsocial. Teach him to ask for them. If you are an introvert you will need them too.

If you or your child is an extravert, understand that you are enjoying the group more than the introverts in your family. Respect their limits. Stay tuned in to stimulation levels. When you are having a good time it is easy to miss the cues that stimulation limits are being hit.

BEWARE OF GIFTS

How can gifts be a hidden trigger for spirited kids? Every emotion for the spirited child is intense, whether it is happiness or disappointment. Gifts either excite us or dash our dreams. Gifts also include an element of surprise. Slow-to-transition kids hate surprises. Serious and analytical spirited kids get into trouble because they are not effusive with their praise. This can be disappointing for gift givers, who have spent hours shopping, searching for just the right gift only to have it opened by a straight-faced kid, who has to be reminded to say thank you. Are spirited kids ungrateful brats? Are they spoiled? No, but they do need help learning to handle gift giving gracefully.

Set your child up for success by buying gifts that encourage the kind of behavior you want. A Big Wheel received during a Minnesota winter begs to be ridden through the living room. If you don't want your spirited child to be tearing through the house, don't give him a Big Wheel when it is 10 degrees below zero. Wait for spring or summer. If you don't want him shooting at everyone, don't give him a cap gun. Make sure any books or tapes you buy, you like. Persistent kids will demand to hear their favorites over and over again. If you can't stand them you are liable to suffer needlessly.

Most spirited kids like toys that allow them to use their imagination. Items such as little toy people, blocks, Legos, Fisher-Price play houses, musical and story tapes, and dress up clothes are favorites. These are all toys that can be used in many different ways. There isn't one correct answer. Most spirited kids won't look twice at toys that have one "right" way to play with them. This includes puzzles, many board games, cards, and peg boards. If your spirited children enjoy puzzles, watch how they actually use them. In most cases the pieces are being employed as pretend food, space ships, and other inventive creations!

Spirited kids also enjoy active toys like Big Wheels, trampolines, bicycles, and jungle gyms. Make sure you have a place to use them and to store them. Physical toys need to be monitored closely to prevent rev up. When actions start to get wild, it is time for soothing/calming activities.

It's not uncommon for spirited kids to get into trouble with gifts because they want to open them *now!* All kids get excited about gifts but intense kids can hardly contain themselves. You may want to consider opening a few gifts early to diffuse the excitement. Perhaps gifts could be opened first and other activities could follow. Whatever you decide, let your child know what to expect. Help him to find a way to diffuse his excitement.

Remember that although a key element of gift giving is surprise, a surprise is a transition and slow-to-adapt kids don't like transitions. You can help your child manage the surprise of gifts by giving her hints. Little tidbits of information that help her prepare herself and work through her feelings.

Eight-year-old Sarah had desperately wanted a tape recorder with a microphone for her birthday. She loved to sing. All she could think about was recording her own voice like a real tape. In order to keep her off guard, her mother told her a tape recorder was too expensive. She would not be getting one.

Unknown to her mother, Sarah was devastated, wallowing for days in her disappointment. Gradually though, she worked through it and by her birthday was prepared to receive something else. Her mother beamed at her as she handed Sarah the box containing the recorder. Pleased with herself that this time she had something Sarah really wanted.

Sarah opened the box, took one look, burst into tears, and fled from the room. Her mother gasped first in surprise and then anger. Annoyed and disappointed that no matter what she did, it never seemed to please Sarah.

What she didn't understand was that Sarah wasn't ungrateful. Sarah was overwhelmed. Forced to transition much too quickly, she was unable to recover, and fled to hide her intense feelings. If you know you will not be able to give your child an anticipated gift, be honest with her. If there just might be a special package don't lie. Hint that it might be there. Don't force her to deal with her intense disappointment or surprise in front of others.

Of course, there are times you don't know what's in the box or under the tree. You can't avoid all of the surprises but you can help your child by playing "what if." "What if you feel like crying," you might ask. "What would you do? Where could you go. Could you run into the bathroom, sit on my lap, or go to your bedroom? If thrills are racing through your body, can you whoop and holler? Can you run around the kitchen, or do you need to head for the basement or out the door? What happens if your brother gets a gift you think is better than yours? What if only Susie has presents? How will you feel?" "What if" helps your child deal with the possibilities and prepare for disappointment. When she is prepared she is much more likely to behave well.

Finally, when it comes to gifts, analytical spirited kids need to learn about manners. They have a keen eye for quality, style, and quantity. This comes in handy when you're shopping for a major appliance but can be a bit embarrassing at a birthday party. Without thinking analytical kids make comments like: "Oh, yuk! Look at that trim," "What an ugly shirt," and "I already have that tape"—the kind of comments that can pull you, scarlet-faced, right under the table. If you want your child to be respectful and tactful teach her the exact words you want her to say such as, "Aunt Georgia, what an interesting blouse" or "Grandma, this is one of my favorite tapes." Don't let your analytical child loose without some guidelines and practice.

As your child learns to handle gift giving gracefully, look for the things she has done well. Remark about her enthusiasm, her success in waiting for a turn or the nice thank-you hug she gave Grandpa. Highlight her gifts within.

BE READY FOR CHANGES IN CLOTHING

Holidays and celebrations often call for dress-up clothes. Binding, stiff, scratchy, and expensive clothes that aren't worn every day. For spirited kids who adapt slowly and are sensitive to textures, dressing up can be a nightmare, a trap, locking us into a huge battle. But it doesn't have to be that way.

Don't let Christmas morning, Halloween night, or Thanksgiving day be the first time your child sees his new outfit. Remember spirited kids need time to get used to things. Leave your child's clothes out several days in advance of the event, allowing him to look at them, smell them, even try them on and wear them. Set a timer so there isn't a fight over how long he can wear them if he decides he loves the outfit and doesn't want to take it off. Practice helps to ensure that on the day of the event the outfit won't feel brand new anymore. Once he has worked through his first negative reaction you can expect a more cooperative child.

If it is a costume he'll be wearing, use the words "dress-up clothes" with him. All preschoolers are learning the difference between what is real and what is not. Spirited preschoolers with their rich imaginations may be uncomfortable with costumes because they might not be quite certain whether or not they will become Batman or a Teenage Mutant Ninja Turtle, if they are dressed as one. Even if they've figured out that they aren't really Batman they may still act like him. Select costumes that encourage the kind of behavior you want!

As you select dress-up clothes, consider your child's style. Spirited kids are creative thinkers. Their ideas of style and yours may be quite different. You can allow yourself to say, "My child is her own person. I can teach her basic standards and then I can step back and allow her to have her own style without feeling embarrassed." A nice thing about spirited kids is that they prepare us early for adolescence. While others fight with their teenagers over clothes, we will have already resolved those issues years ago.

Stepping back and allowing your child her own style isn't always easy. At least it wasn't for Nancy and her daughter Carolina—a modern young woman, even at age five.

"From the time she could talk, Carolina let it be known that she *hated* dresses," Nancy told me. "I literally had to wrestle her into one, and then she would pout. I couldn't stand the fights, so I began backing off, only insisting on a dress for very special occasions. At Easter we were going to be visiting my parents. Carolina was five and had picked out a dressy pants outfit that she wanted to wear. I really mulled this one over. Do I let her wear the pants? I worried. Will it embarrass my parents if she walks into church dressed like that?

"Finally I decided that it was a nice outfit. I would let her wear it, because she felt so much more attractive in it than in a dress.

"I was still a nervous wreck on Sunday morning. That's when my mother walked out of her bedroom dressed for church—in pants!

" 'Do I dare wear this?' she asked, turning to me. 'It's so much more comfortable than a dress and nylons.'

"Carolina burst into applause. 'Grandma, are you spirited too,' she squealed, grabbing her around the waist and hugging.

"I laughed. Appreciating spirit seems to be benefiting more than just Carolina."

HELP THEM SLEEP

Dealing with bedtime can be one of the most frustrating hot spots on vacation or during holidays—at least it has been for Ellen.

"It takes David hours to unwind at a hotel or at someone else's house. It's always been that way. Of course, my sister has the kid you just lay down in the crib and he goes to sleep, no matter where he is. She's out chatting with everyone and I'm stuck in the back bedroom with a wailing kid. It doesn't seem fair. Worst of all it makes me feel so ineffectual, but I can't make him sleep. The only thing I can do is to help him unwind. The older he gets, the shorter it's been, but it has been a long, embarrassing haul."

Getting enough sleep is so important during the holidays and on vacation. When your child is well rested he has the energy to cope, but spirited kids often have trouble sleeping in new and different situations.

Plan to give him more support at bedtime than you have to do at home. The younger the child, the more challenging it will be, because you can't explain to him what is bothering him. Expect it to take him longer to wind down and fall asleep. You may need to sit with him or rock him to keep him from becoming overwhelmed.

Be sure to bring along your props—his favorite bedtime books, his own pillow, and any other items that help him feel more comfortable and cue him that this is sleep time. Try to maintain a schedule similar to that at home. Avoid skipping naps or changing bedtimes from one day to the next.

As your child grows talk with him about the need for wind-down time in new situations. Encourage him to read to himself, breath deeply or to take a warm soothing bath before retiring. Let him know he is all right. He is just excited.

IF YOU TRAVEL—PLAN FOR THE JOURNEY

Traveling adds another whole dimension to holidays and vacations. Long hours spent in a cramped automobile or airplane can leave you with a migraine before you ever arrive at your destination. That's why you have to plan for the journey.

I've always admired my friend Vickie for her energy and skill as a parent. But the day she called me and told me she had put five kids—two spirited, three spunky—ages two and a half to thirteen in a station wagon and driven eleven hundred miles to Washington D.C., I began to doubt her grasp on reality. In telling me about the trip, she even used the term *vacation* to describe this trek. (I asked politely if she was calling me from a hospital, but she assured me that she was great and beat me to my next question by stating that "the kids are alive and well.")

How did she survive? She planned for success. It wasn't chance. It wasn't luck. She was *prepared*. She set up a reward system for good behavior. Driving down the highway screaming at kids in the backseat is not a relaxing journey—better to set up a reward system that encourages good behavior and allows you to focus on the road.

"I took an egg timer and a bunch of poker chips," Vickie told me. "I told the kids that for every fifteen minutes in the car that they did not fight or fuss, played quietly, and stayed in their seat belts, they would get a poker chip."

At this point I doubted the intelligence of her children, but she wasn't done yet.

"When they had four chips they could turn them in for a dollar." Now there was something I could identify with.

"Even the two-year-old loved it," she exclaimed. "I'd set the egg timer for fifteen minutes. When it went off, anyone who had been good got a poker chip. I experimented a little going twenty to thirty minutes between chips, but that didn't work. It had to be every fifteen minutes. All I had to do when voices started rising was to say, 'Are you earning your chip?' and things quieted down fast."

"How much did this cost you?" I asked.

"Twenty-one dollars apiece," Vickie said. "And that was their spending money for the trip. It was great, no nagging for this or that. I'd just tell them it was their money and they could spend it however they wanted. It really helped them understand the value of a dollar. The eight-year-old would ask me how much is this or that—he came home with fifteen dollars because he wanted to save for something special. My four- and six-year-olds pooled their money and bought a stuffed animal."

Rewards set a tone of cooperation. They are encouraging and focus on good behaviors rather than bad. When I was first introduced to this idea, it sounded like bribery to me, but my husband reminded me that my boss tells me that if I do my job I'll get a paycheck. Rewards provide a positive incentive.

Rewards alone are not enough though. An egg timer, poker chips, and dollar bills aren't all you need to buy you hours of peace in the car. Vickie did admit there had been more. She had stopped every two hours to let everyone out of restraints and a chance to run around. They had avoided restaurants and eaten picnic lunches in parks and rest stops where the kids could run, climb, and play with the balls she had brought along. Each child had a plastic bucket of paper, crayons, markers, books, and simple games. They sang songs and played trivia games, asking questions about familiar nursery rhymes and stories the older kids knew. The nights were spent at motels with a pool.

To ensure that you do not arrive at the resort or Grandma's house frazzled, plan for the journey. Bring along activities, expect to sing and tell stories, and know when it's time to pull off the road and take a break. Many times the greatest joy of a celebration or vacation is the journey there.

CREATE A TRAVEL HUB

Last year you rented a quaint little cottage and for two weeks basked in the sun. Your spirited child swam in the lake, dug in the sand, and after the first night, slept soundly. It was a wonderful vacation.

This year you decided to add more excitement. You toured the East Coast by car, a new hotel, a new city each night. It was a disaster. Your child was a wreck and so were you.

What happened? A child who is slow to adapt and one that experiences a negative first reaction can't cope when the changes and new experiences come too fast. To help your child be successful consider establishing a travel hub—one hotel, one relative's home, or campground that you stay at and move out from for two or three days before moving on to another hub. By establishing hubs you allow your child time to adapt to new places. He has a chance to check things out and feel secure. He'll sleep better and have more energy to cope.

You can also extend your hub by buying groceries and having a picnic in the park or mall or by eating at chain restaurants rather than trying all of the local restaurants. Sensitive kids react to new foods and changes in the water. The more familiar the setting and the food the easier it will be for them to adapt.

The younger the child, the more important the hub. Over time and with many successes under her belt, the older child will become more flexible and the hub less important. If your child is two and you decide to spend a week at a familiar cabin because you know he will be more successful there, don't think that you'll have to spend the next ten years there. He will grow and change. Success builds on success. Soon he'll be ready for a trip across the country.

PLAN FOR THE LET DOWN

Spirited kids tend to fly high during celebrations and vacations and crash afterward. They truly can go to extremes. Be prepared. Don't push yourself so hard that you don't have the energy to help your child transition back to a normal routine. Older kids can make their own plans. Eleven-year-old Kerry told her mother. "I love how I feel at Christmas, but I hate how I feel afterward. I'm saving this present to open when I feel rotten"—and she did.

Holidays, celebrations, and vacations do require more planning when you are the parent of a spirited child. At times it can feel like a great deal of work. But when you've done your job well, these events with a spirited child are full of special delights. They are enriched by their enthusiasm, zeal, and exuberance. Just think of that little man of spirit— the one who made so much clatter, everyone rose from their bed to see what was the matter. The same one who was lively and quick and whistled and shouted. Why, of course, St. Nick! It wouldn't be the same without him!

19

SUCCESS IN SCHOOL

I didn't want him to be "discussed." I wanted him
to be treasured.
—Kathy, the mother of two

WHY ISN'T IT EASY to send kids off to school? You'd think we'd be happy—appreciative of the break. And perhaps you are, it is a relief, a milestone. Still you may find your eyes filling, your vision blurred as your son or daughter mounts the school-bus steps for the first time—alone—or releases your hand and enters that preschool classroom—leaving you behind. She's on her own to face the world. You gulp, hoping that she will be treasured by those she encounters, rather than discussed as an oddity or a troublemaker. But you don't know and you stand there praying that he will be successful, that he will enjoy school, make friends, and bring a smile rather than a frown to his teacher's face.

Spirited kids can prosper in school. You can find them serving as student council leaders, in the starring roles, on the winning teams, and in the enhanced learning programs. They can be successful in a Montessori school, in a local public school, in a parochial school, or in a private school. The type or location of the school doesn't really matter. What does matter is that individual differences are respected and that parents, teachers, and kids are working together. In a school where this is happening you can see, feel, and hear things that let you know spirit blooms here.

The challenge for spirited kids is that they make up only 10 to 15 percent of the population, that means they need a classroom that has a rich smorgasbord of teaching techniques and a flexible structure, or they will always be pushed to adapt, to fit a style that isn't their own. Kids who are constantly forced to adapt become exhausted and frustrated and as a result act out, or give up. Fortunately spirited kids don't need perfect classrooms that fit their temperament 100 percent of the time—just a majority of the time. That's true of all kids. When children can work within their preferred style most of the time, it isn't a major issue to work out of their preferred style when it is needed in order to function within the group. If you have a choice in schools you can look for one where spirit blooms. If you don't have a choice you can help create that kind of atmosphere.

WHEN YOU HAVE A CHOICE

If you live in a metropolitan area, you probably have a choice of schools your child might attend. Use it! It feels much better watching your child march off on her own when you not only know where she's going but you feel good about it. So how do you find the right school for your child? You've got to get in and observe.

A loud groan dropped into the room, when I made this statement during class one night. I turned to Sherry, a young single mom. "What am I supposed to look for?" she asked. "I don't have a master's degree in education. I don't know a good curriculum when I see one. I'm not even sure I know a good teacher."

"It's easy," I responded, "because you know your child."

You don't need a master's degree to select a good school. Forget about analyzing the curriculum. I've seen written brochures that describe wonderful cooking, science, and art activities for children. In reality the teachers cooked and the children watched—that's not a good curriculum. You don't even have to bother with the written discipline policy. What's described on paper may not be a reality in a given classroom. All you have to do is go into a classroom and pick out a child who reminds you of your own, then sit there and watch him.

Sherry looked at me quizzically. "Really," she said, "but what will that tell me?"

"It will tell you how a child like yours, a child with spirit, feels and acts in this classroom with this particular teacher," I responded. "Watch how he uses the materials. How he responds to the instructions and to the rules. Do they seem to fit him? Is he happy, and excited to learn? Listen to what he says to the teacher and how she responds to him. Do they appear to be comfortable with one another or are they afraid of each other? Do the other kids seem to appreciate one another? Is it possible for each child to be successful? Is each individual treasured?"

"I'm checking out a school this week," Sherry replied. "I'll try it."

The next week I was anxious to hear about Sherry's experience and so were the others in the group.

"It was fantastic," she blurted out before we had even had a chance to sit down. "I observed two classrooms in the same school. What a difference! In both I could find a kid who reminded me of my son Marc. One even looked like him, and they both liked to bounce around the room like Marc does. In one classroom the teacher seemed very comfortable with the kids moving around the room to different tables and learning centers. She was up and down, moving with them, joking, laughing. She really seemed to like all of them. I heard her ask the little boy I was watching how his new baby brother was and then she asked another if his dad was still in Japan. She knew about the new puppies at one kid's house and about someone else's sick grandmother. It felt so nice. Nick, the little boy I watched, ran across the room to show her a picture he had done. I waited for her to yell at him for running but she didn't. She just looked at what he had done, smiled, patted him on the head and off he went again.

"When there was a break I asked her about Nick. She smiled and said, 'He's my best errand runner and he's got a great sense of humor.'

"In the second classroom, I picked out Alex, another boy that reminded me of Marc. In this classroom the kids were in their chairs much longer. Alex was absolutely squirming in his chair and biting his pencil. The teacher was pleasant. She didn't say anything mean, but you could see she lit up the most when she was working with a little group of very quiet girls. With the boys, especially the 'movers' she was much more stern and serious."

Like Sherry you can identify a classroom that fits your child. You can feel and see it by simply observing a child like yours functioning in that room. Believe your gut and your eyes. Don't let reputation or hearsay blur your vision or block your intuition. A great classroom for one child might be a disaster for another because their temperaments are different. That's why you can't rely on your neighbor's suggestion, especially if your child's personality is nothing like the kid's next door. You've got to get into the classroom and find the one that fits your child.

The nice thing about focusing your observations on the kids rather than the teachers is that it is less threatening for the teachers you are observing. You're not there to judge them as a good or bad teacher, you are there to find the best match for your child. As you watch, keep in mind your child's temperament. If he is slow to adapt watch for the transitions. Do you see an agenda for the day on the board so that everyone knows what to expect? Do you hear a forewarning before a transition occurs? How many transitions are there and is the child like yours moving through them comfortably, or is he stumbling? If your child is intense, check to see what activities are available to diffuse the intensity and how frequently the kids are rushed. Intense kids hate to be rushed. If your child is perceptive, listen for the directions. Are they clear? Whatever traits are important for your child, look to see how they are managed in this particular classroom.

"What do you do after you have found it?" Sherry broke in. "I know I want Marc in Mrs. Jensen's class, the first one I saw, but the school policy says that parents can't pick their child's teacher."

"Schools create policies like that," I explained, "so that fifty parents don't request Mrs. Jensen and then get angry that they don't all get her. It is a protective device."

In reality school principals and teachers want to work with you. They want your child to be successful. It is perfectly all right and very advisable for you to write a letter to the principal describing the qualities of your child and the type of teacher you think he would be most successful with. For example, Sherry might write a letter like the following.

> **Dear principal,**
>
> My son Marc will be entering your school in September. I would like you to know a little bit about him. He is very energetic and athletic. He loves to play soccer and basketball. He seems to learn best with a teacher who is comfortable with activity in her room and offers lots of opportunities for movement. He is also very sensitive and responds best to someone with a soft voice. Loud voices frighten him.
>
> Recently I visited your school. Mrs. Jensen seemed to have many of the qualities that would match well with Marc. I hope you will consider this when determining Marc's classroom placement. If it is not possible for him to be in Mrs. Jensen's classroom, I would appreciate it if you would place him in a classroom with someone of similar style.
>
> Thank you. If you have questions for me I can be reached at . . . .
>
> **Sincerely,**
>
> **Sherry Engstrom**

To the best of their ability the *majority* of principals will honor your request. They want you and your child to be happy. They really will respect your input. Write your letter in the spring, while the principal still has a lot of flexibility for placing children. The later in the summer your letter arrives, the more difficult it is to place your child in a specific classroom. Keep your letter concise and to the point. Let the principal know the *one,* most important thing for your child.

By taking the time to find a classroom that fits your child *before* he starts, you will have alleviated many potential problems. You will have found a setting that you believe will nurture your child. You'll trust it and so will your child. The lines of communication will have been developed before any problems arise.

PREPARE FOR SUCCESS

Even if you can't choose which classroom your child is in or what school she will attend, you can still plan for her success. Talk with your child about school. What is she excited about? What is he worried about?

"With Mica, our oldest, I found out quite by accident that he was scared to death to ride the school bus," Charlotte responded. "I never thought of that as a problem but it really was for him. Fortunately our neighbor drove the bus, so she took Mica with her one day and let him get inside one."

If your child is going to ride a school bus, make sure that the first time she ever looks inside one isn't the day she is expected to get on it and ride by herself. Find out where the bus garage is and go look at a school bus. The folks who work in transportation departments for a school district take their jobs very seriously. They are proud of what they do and will usually be more than happy to let you take a look at a bus.

You can also check with your local park or community education departments, church groups, or other programs to see if they are planning any field trips that include a ride on a school bus. Register for it and let your child's first bus ride be with you, the person she trusts the most.

If your child will be walking to school, rather than riding a bus, practice walking the route with her.

"Sarah was really worried about who her teacher would be," Bob added, as our discussion continued. "She also wanted to know what her room looked like and where the bathroom was located."

Many schools post classroom assignments before school starts, but if your school doesn't, call about a week before the starting day and find out who your child's teacher will be and her classroom number. You can also ask when the teachers will be setting up their classrooms. Then go to the school with your child, visit her classroom, check out the bathrooms, the drinking fountains, the lunch room, playground, media center, and gymnasium and meet the teacher and the principal. This relaxed, comfortable visit can alleviate a great deal of stress for the child who is slow to adapt or experiences a negative first reaction.

Whether it is riding buses, finding out what other kids are in the classroom, picking out clothes, or meeting the teacher, do what your child needs to do in order to feel comfortable on the first day of school. By alleviating or reducing her stress she will have more energy to focus on the tasks at hand and get off to a good start. You may even want to consider reducing all outside commitments for the entire month of September. This allows your slow-to-adapt child to focus her energy on getting used to her new classroom.

GET INVOLVED

Research discussed in "What Principals Should Know about Parent Involvement," by Joyce L. Epstein, principal research scientist at the Center for Research on Elementary and Middle Schools at Johns Hopkins University, shows that children whose parents are involved in their school and education are more successful than children whose parents are not involved. Take advantage of every opportunity you have to participate at your child's school. Obviously this may be limited by other demands, but to the best of your ability attend conferences, open houses, and performances. Volunteer to work in the classroom or to help with a party. The more involved you are in your child's school the more likely you are to develop good lines of communication. A few hours spent at a spaghetti dinner talking with your child's principal, or meeting the other kids in his class and their parents, may help you to prevent problems from ever happening. If issues do surface, those friendly spaghetti dinner conversations may carry over and allow you to solve problems much more quickly and cordially.

SHARE INFORMATION

"Should I warn the teacher?" Ben joked. "Seriously, what should I tell Christopher's teacher? Should I keep quiet and let her find out by herself or do I tell her what he's like at home? I don't want to bias her, but I want to help if I can."

You don't need to warn your child's teacher, but you do want to inform her. The first day of school the teacher meets her class, a group of kids assigned to her. She has to learn quickly what is special and unique about each individual. You can help her by sharing information. As you do, remember our discussion about labels in chapter 2. Use words that highlight your child's strengths and minimize her weaknesses.

"Hey, I did the right thing then," Kathy piped in. "The school where Eric goes has a morning where parents come with their kids. When I talked to his teacher that day, I simply mentioned what he was like. I told her that just starting school might be difficult for him. I asked her to let me know if she wanted me to work with him on anything. I also found out that 'a clown' would be taking school pictures the next week. I let her know that he was afraid of clowns and that it was perfectly acceptable with me if he didn't have his picture taken. The next week I called her just to check in on how things were going. She said, I was right, he didn't like the clown and because she knew it was all right with me not to have a picture she hadn't forced him. He did, however, participate in the class picture—of course, he stood right next to the teacher, but he's in it."

"I let Lindsey's teacher know that she is a very strong introvert," Patti added. "I think she was relieved when I told her it was all right with me if Lindsey pulled her desk slightly back from the rest of the group."

By describing your child's typical reactions, sharing effective techniques for working with him, and explaining your expectations, you give your child's teacher the information she needs to be effective. Everyone gets off to a good start as the teacher realizes you support her and are willing to help her educate your child.

WHEN THERE IS A PROBLEM

I couldn't help noticing Trisha glaring at me as we talked about schools. "Go ahead, Trisha," I indicated by nodding my head.

"I've done everything we've talked about," she began. "And last year it worked but this year. . . . We just went to Tommy's first conference. The teacher spent the first five minutes describing how he lifted, climbed, and leaned on his chair. 'He is going to break that chair before the year is out,' she said. Both my husband and I sat there gritting our teeth. Smoke was coming out of our ears. Unbelievable—five minutes about a lousy chair. I wanted to say, well lady, does that tell you the kid needs to move around a little more or what? The teacher wants him to sit down and do all the workbook, writing, and reading. I want him to have more opportunity to get up and move around. The only recess he gets is after lunch and on too many days, it's cold, wet, or sloppy and they have to sit in the cafeteria instead, playing with paper and pencils. This is not how Tommy handles life!"

"Have you tried—" my words were cut off before I could finish.

"Yes," Trisha snapped, obviously very frustrated. "I have tried to talk with the teacher, but it feels like she thinks I'm just making excuses for him. I swear whenever I'm talking she's thinking up replies rather than listening to me."

It hurts when our kids experience problems in school. It hurts a lot. It can be embarrassing and it can also remind us of our own school experiences where we felt powerless or in pain. These emotions can create barriers that put everyone on the defensive. Teachers know when you're angry, but teachers are people too. They have stresses at home and they have twenty-five or more kids to educate each day. If we aren't thoughtful in our approach to them our demands may feel overwhelming and they will back away from us. At the same time you shouldn't have to take a course in assertiveness to be able to talk to your child's teacher.

Our time was up that night. "Next week," I announced, "A lesson in how to talk so teachers will listen and how to listen when teachers talk."

Trisha shot me another glare, but as she departed she quipped, "I'll be back—and it had better be good!"

HOW TO TALK SO TEACHERS WILL LISTEN AND HOW TO LISTEN WHEN TEACHERS TALK

I borrowed a huge floor puzzle from the children's room. Each piece was painted in vivid hues of red, green, blue, and yellow. There were notches in each and bumps too. I handed one piece to every parent in the group.

"Tell me about your puzzle piece," I said. "What do you like about it? How is it unique and special?"

"Mine is a splash of red," Ben began, feeling a bit silly, but willing to play the game. "It has three notches. I think it's looking for friends."

"I must be your friend," Betty joined in. "My piece has a notch that looks like it fits one of your bumps. It's red on that side, but smears from red to orange then yellow."

They laid their pieces on the table and sure enough they fit together. We continued around the table, describing each different piece. Some with flat edges, others with bumps and notches. We connected them together one by one. Slowly a picture of a smiling dinosaur formed in front of our eyes. It had not been there when we each had held a puzzle piece in our hands.

"This is what it is like to send your spirited child off to school," I said. "From your hands you release one piece—a child—that joins with others to form something entirely different—a class—a group of children. The picture in the classroom that the teacher views may be very different from the piece you see at home."

It's important to remember our different perspectives when we enter a conversation with our child's teacher. She may see the picture of her entire class first and then the individuals that make it up. You, on the other hand, see your child first and then the class as a whole. In order to truly listen to one another we must consider both points of view—the individuals and the class as a whole.

"Trisha," I said, "last week you told us that Tommy's teacher wanted him to sit in his chair. You on the other hand, wanted him to be able to move around more. Now try to imagine the teacher's point of view. Think about twenty-five to thirty kids all moving around a room you are supposed to be in control of, what happens to your gut?"

"It clinches," she admitted. "But," she retorted, "that's how Tommy feels when he can't move."

"That's true too," I responded. "You are both right. You both have legitimate points of view. The challenge is to find a solution that works for everyone."

In chapter 7 I presented to you the PIECE model, a way to solve problems by finding common interests. The same principles apply in this situation. Trisha wants Tommy to be able to move. The teacher wants him to sit down and do his workbook. They're both locked in their positions. "What are the real concerns?" I asked.

Trisha replied, "I want Tommy to be comfortable and to be success-ful."

"What do you think the teacher is concerned about?" I questioned.

Pam, a first-grade teacher, answered. "She is probably concerned about losing control of the whole group, or what other kids will say if one child is allowed to walk around. Maybe she just wants him to get his work done."

"What solutions are available to them?" I continued.

"She could use learning centers, like Mrs. Jensen did," Sherry offered. "At different tables kids were working on experiments, connecting blocks for patterns, reading books, writing. Kids were all over the room. Some were lying on the floor. One was even in a nest of pillows under a table."

"What about letting him run errands?" Tom said.

"Make sure he gets exercise before school," Sarah added.

The potential solutions seemed limitless, yet Trisha still felt stymied. "You're right. I think these are all great solutions, but how do I get the teacher to listen?" she demanded.

When you want someone to listen to you, start by finding a point they have made that you can agree with—anything. For example, Trisha might have said, "We find Tommy to be active at home too" or "I'm sure many children find sitting in a chair and doing their workbook very effective." Even if you have to turn a negative to a positive you can—like the mom who responded to the teacher who called her son stubborn, "Yes, we find him to be quite tenacious too." By finding a point to agree on you have set a cooperative tone. Minds will be open for listening.

Agreeing doesn't mean that you don't honestly address your concerns. It is important that you let the teacher know what your *interest* is, not your *position*. For example, Trisha might have said, "My interest is to find ways for Tommy to be able to move and still get his work done" or "That technique doesn't seem to be working for Tommy, what else could we do?" By focusing on interests you avoid blaming. This takes down the defense barriers and lets you move to creative solutions.

If you can't figure out what the interests are, review the temperament traits to help you identify where the problem may lie. Is your child crying at the beginning of school because it is a transition? Is your child fighting in line because he is an introvert who needs more space? Is he being distracted because he is perceptive and his chair is next to the aquarium? Discover the issue and you can find your common interests.

As you talk, don't assume that the teacher is familiar with temperament. The temperament research is relatively new and, as a result, you may have information she doesn't. Share this book with her. Let her know that this information has been helpful to you. She may not have even thought of linking behavior problems to a misunderstanding of temperament.

Listen carefully as your child's teacher talks, and to the best of your ability, set aside your own interests while you try to discover hers. If she makes a statement you don't understand, ask for an explanation. For example, if a teacher tells you your child isn't getting her work done, ask her to give you an example. Is this an issue in every class or is it only on math worksheets? Is it happening on certain days, or times of the day, or every day, all day? Getting to the facts will help you find interests.

Education, like other professions, is full of jargon, and without meaning to, educators can leave parents in the dark as they converse in "educationese." If an abbreviation or an acronym is used with which you are unfamiliar, ask for an explanation. It is nearly impossible to define an interest if you don't know what EBD or ECSE means.

Once you have clarified the interests you can move on to exploring possible solutions. The best place to start is right in your child's classroom.

If you have been in the classroom to participate or to observe point out what the teacher is already doing that works for your child. For example, you might say, "I noticed when you let Tommy lay on the floor he could really concentrate." The best solutions are those things that the teacher is already doing—she just needs to do more of them. The second best are things she is already doing, but would be more effective if they were presented in a different order. For example, you might say, "I noticed that when you did exercises in the middle of circle time Tommy sat still afterward. Would it be possible to start circle time with exercises?"

If things aren't going well in the classroom and you can't seem to find anything that's working, look for successes from the past. You might say,

"Last year Tommy was able to complete his work when Mrs. Jensen used learning centers. Would it be possible for you to use this technique also?" or "Tommy seems to do his spelling words best when he can work with a partner." Another possible source of solutions is ideas that work at home, but make sure these will work in a group setting.

Remember as you offer solutions that teachers have temperaments too. They may experience a negative first reaction, be slow to adapt, or lock in easily. Don't force a solution. Offer your ideas then give them space. Agree to talk again later after you have both had time to think.

Be aware of your own temperament as well. If you are intense realize that your intensity may burn through your calm demeanor. Take a friend or spouse along, who can talk and listen too so you can pull out of the conversation and take deep breaths if you need to. If you experience negative first reactions, remind yourself to think, then decide how you feel about the possible solutions. If you are an introvert and need time to process information, ask for another meeting.

If you are trying very hard but find yourself unable to communicate with your child's teacher, use your other resources. Ask the principal, school psychologist, or social worker to meet with you and the teacher. If you have a day-care provider, grandparent, or someone else who knows your child well, they might also be helpful.

"That worked for me," Alice remarked. "The teacher and I just couldn't communicate. It was her idea to bring in the principal. I had met her before and remembered her as being pretty open. I agreed. The principal was very knowledgeable. She knew about temperament and development and I could tell the teacher would listen to her. The principal was able to offer a solution we could both accept."

When your child experiences a problem expect to find a solution. The majority of teachers are very committed to their profession. They want your child to be successful in their classroom and to work with you. Be flexible and creative as you work with them and remember spirited kids don't need perfect classrooms that fit their temperament 100 percent of the time—just a majority of the time.

WHEN THE PROBLEMS PERSIST

"What do you do when it doesn't work?" Dave sighed softly. His body sagged in his chair and he slowly rubbed the palms of his hands together as he talked. "Kara is now missing more school than she is attending. At first we thought it was a flu bug, but I know it's more than the flu. We think she's afraid of her teacher. She's never had a man before and this one tends to bellow. He's not yelling at her, but she's so sensitive, just the thought of someone possibly getting angry makes her apprehensive. We've talked with the teacher, nothing seemed to change. We brought the principal in, but all he would say was, 'She's going to run into difficult people in life and she needs to learn to deal with it.' There's a kernel of truth to that you know, but my little girl is hurting—bad—can I expect an entire institution to change for one kid?"

Dave's pain was real. We all felt it. The hang of his head and the slump of his body spoke of a parent's pain, the deep gut-wrenching twist that strangles your belly and makes you gulp for air when you fear that you can't protect your child, when you don't know what to do to help her.

"Sometimes," I assured him, "despite our very best efforts our child's problems in school may persist. In order to find a solution, you, the parent, are going to have to advocate for your child. You are going to have to ask the questions, and seek the answers and the support you need to help your child be successful. It isn't easy to be an advocate. It takes a great deal of time, energy, and emotional stamina. At times you may feel powerless, but you aren't. There are definite things you can do as a parent to help your child.

"Think about it," I said to the group, "what can you do to advocate for your child?"

"Don't assume one negative experience will carry to another," Cal responded. "Last year I just couldn't work with the principal at my son's school. I tried, but I couldn't do it. I started getting upset with the entire system, but then someone told me to talk to the principal's boss. I did. The guy was great. He gave me written information, talked with me about the issue, and then sat down with the principal and me and helped us resolve the problem. To this day, I'm grateful to that man."

When your child experiences a persistent problem at school you may find a scream building in your chest, a ferocious charge that wants to find someone—something—to blame. But this isn't a time for assigning blame. Now more than ever you need to use your good communication skills to work with the school personnel and other resources. Don't let a negative experience with one individual sour your feelings for an entire school or school district, just look a little further and you will find that caring, committed individual who will be willing to work with you.

"You also need to find out if there is a medical problem," Ben added. "Michele experienced severe stomach problems too. We thought it was stress, but the school made changes for us and the pain persisted. It ended up that she had a severe kidney problem that required surgery."

Temperament is a key factor in school success and an important one to explore. It is not, however, a panacea. If your child encounters problems at school that persist it may be due to a mismatch of temperament, but it could also be the result of learning disabilities, poor health, or many other factors. Schedule your child for a complete physical and psychological examination. Get the information you need before deciding how to proceed.

"We had to lighten up at home," Brenda offered. "Ricky was throwing a fit every morning about going to school, but once he got there he was fine. I realized I'd seen this behavior before when he started nursery school, but that was only three days a week, half days, and the fits weren't as explosive. It was his teacher who suggested that he needed warm-up time and maybe we just had to support him as he transitions into first grade. I started spending more time helping him to get ready in the mornings. That extra support seemed to be all that he needed. The fits stopped after about three weeks."

Your first inclination when your child is experiencing problems in school may be to clamp down at home, to get stricter, or to make more demands on him. But if your child is already stressed at school, or about school, he needs his home to be a haven, a safe place to regroup. It is appropriate for you to look at his responsibilities and outside commitments. Perhaps this is a time to release your child from some responsibilities rather than adding to them. It is also important that you are available for him. Plan to spend more time with your child, to be available to talk with him, help him with his homework, and get him off to a good start in the morning.

"We ended up going for family counseling," Bob offered. "Sarah was letting loose at school but the real issue was that my wife, Barbara, and I were experiencing problems in our relationship and Sarah was acting them out—at school. It really had nothing to do with what was going on in the classroom."

Remember spirited kids are the emotional barometer of your family. If you are experiencing major stresses within your family relationships you may have to address them before the problems at school can be resolved.

Involve your child's school counselor. He or she can work with your child, to help him cope with a divorce, death, or other issues. Some schools even have support groups for kids who are experiencing pain in their relationships.

As our discussion continued, the list of things a parent can do when advocating for their child grew. It included:

Requesting a different teacher, which is very feasible if there is another person available or the class sizes won't be pushed grossly out of balance by moving your child.

Hiring a tutor, someone to boost your child's skills and self-esteem. If you can't afford an adult tutor consider a high-school student, or a

Big Brother or Big Sister who can help your child feel good and strengthen her skills.

Involving the child with other teachers through music, gymnastics, or special programs. Sometimes if your child is experiencing difficulties in one classroom but is treasured in a music class or a particular math group, the good feelings from that class and that teacher may carry over to the less ideal situation, providing him with the energy he needs to cope.

Barbara listened intently to the conversation, but didn't offer any suggestions until the end. Then she blurted out, "Move." The others turned and looked at her, awed by the power of her word and the magnitude of her suggestion. "I've been sitting here listening," she said, "mulling through every suggestion. My son Brandon has been experiencing problems and I've done all of those things and now I realize it is time to move. He needs a different school. Everything inside of me has been fighting the idea. I'm worried that we can't afford it, but now I realize that I can't ask him to go back there. I can't ask him to go back every day to a place where he feels like a failure."

If you live in a metropolitan area it may be relatively easy for you to find another school. This is not a sign of failure, it is merely the recognition that people are individuals and that their needs are met in different ways. If you live in a small community and there isn't another school you may have to consider moving. It is a big step and a drastic one, but may be critical to your child's well-being. The cost of a move may seem insurmountable but the price your child will pay if she isn't successful in school may be much greater. Check your resources, think creatively, find a way to find a school where your child can be happy.

As our discussion drew to a close, I turned to Dave, who was now sitting straight up in his chair. "Well I certainly am not the only one who's experienced this, am I?" He smiled weakly. "Thanks for the ideas." The others nodded and patted him on the shoulder as he walked out the door. They'd been there too.

Advocating for your child can be a very draining experience. You need to remember that you are not the only parent who has faced this challenging task. Take care of yourself. You need to remind yourself that you are a good parent and that progress not perfection is our goal. Take time for exercise and other stress-reducing activities, and find others who understand. In the end your efforts will be beneficial. You will know that you have advocated for your child to the best of your ability and that you have helped her be successful.

It was two weeks before I saw Dave again. He strode confidently into the center, the stoop in his shoulders gone. "We went back to the school ready to advocate," he said, "not to blame." He emphasized the words expressing his discomfort with them, yet realizing they had been helpful to him. "I tried to figure out how to explain my concerns," he said. "I was sitting at swimming lessons when I realized we don't start the kids out in the deep end. We start them out in the shallows, where they can be successful. I went back to the principal and agreed with him. I said, 'You're right, she is going to meet people she doesn't get along with.' He liked that, then I said, 'But you know, when we teach kids to swim we don't put them in over their heads and I think the same thing is true when we teach kids how to get along with other people. I think Kara is in over her head and drowning.' He listened! He called the teacher in and we all sat down. Together we decided to move Kara, not because he was a bad teacher, but because it wasn't working for Kara. It felt all right to everyone and the results were immediate. Kara hasn't missed a day in the last ten."

Spirited kids can be successful in school. By working together, parents, teachers, and kids who understand spirit and know how to manage it well can make school a positive and fun experience—a place where individual styles are appreciated and spirit blooms. If you haven't found it this year, try again, keep working on it, don't wait. It is there! I know it. I've seen it. You can believe it.

PART FIVE

ENJOYING SPIRIT

EPILOGUE: THE ROSE IN MY GARDEN

And every time I held a rose
It seems I only felt the thorns . . .
—Billy Joel

I WISH THAT I could say that after reading this book you will live happily ever after, no pain, no hassle, in perfect harmony with your spirited child. I have been truthful with you throughout this book. I have shared with you only real emotions and tried techniques. I won't lie to you now. I can't promise there will be no hassles. There will be. Change takes time. Building a relationship is a process that occurs over years and every stage of development brings new challenges that force you to stretch, learn, and grow in different ways. Remember our motto is PROGRESS NOT PERFECTION.

There will still be days when you think you are wasting your time waiting for your slow-to-adapt child to adjust. When you huff and puff and pull at the reins ready to move on, feeling tethered by your child. On those days reread this book. Use it as a friend, a guide from those who have been there before you. As you review the material, you will find ideas that didn't seem to apply when your child was four but are extremely effective now that he is six. Grab them and use them.

On the good days pat yourself on the back, recognizing and appreciating what you are already doing well. Sometimes improving your relationship with your spirited child is merely a matter of doing more of what you already do well.

Do not fear intensity. Don't let it scare you. Intensity is passion, zest, and vitality. It's true that there will be days it will wear you out. Then kiss your child good-bye, go for a walk, and take a break.

As you learn about your spirited child learn about yourself. Become more aware of how stimulation, transitions, and new situations affect you. Be more cognizant of your energy level. Your own need for routine. Your joy in change.

Love your spirited child for who she is. Let her make you laugh. Let her share with you how she sees, hears, and experiences the things around her. Allow her to enrich your life. Because she is more, she will make you more.

Spirited kids are like the roses in my garden. They need more attention. Throw a little water on the other flowers and they grow. Not the rose, it needs special treatment. It has to be pruned and guided in its growth.

Other flowers can be plucked, pulled, and mauled by a preschooler and still last for weeks on your dining room table. If you treat a rose roughly it will wilt in your hands or stab you, make you bleed.

But there is not another flower like the rose in my garden. Its rich perfume fragrance titillates my senses. Its satin soft petals tickle my fingers. Its blooms are so vibrant they stir my soul. Spirited kids are like roses—they need special care. And sometimes you have to get past the thorns to truly enjoy their beauty.

RECOMMENDED READING LIST FOR PARENTS OF SPIRITED CHILDREN

DEVELOPMENT

Ames, Louise Bates; Ilg, Frances L.; and Harber, Carol Chase. *Your Two Year Old: Terrible or Tender.* New York: Dell, 1976, $8.95.

———. *Your Three Year Old: Friend or Enemy.* New York: Dell, 1977, $8.95.

———. *Your Four Year Old: Wild and Wonderful.* New York: Dell, 1978, $8.95.

———. *Your Five Year Old: Sunny and Serene.* New York: Dell, 1979, $8.95.

———. *Your One Year Old: The Fun-Loving, Fussy 12- to 24-Month-Old.* New York: Dell, 1982, $8.95.

TEMPERAMENT AND TYPE

Budd, Linda. *Living with the Active, Alert Child.* New York: Prentice-Hall, 1991, $19.95.

Chess, Stella, and Thomas, Alexander. *Know Your Child: An Authoritative Guide for Today's Parents.* New York: Basic Books, 1989, $12.95.

Kroeger, Otto, and Thuesen, Janet M. *Type Talk: The Sixteen Personality Types that Determine How We Live, Love, and Work.* New York: Dell, 1988, $9.95.

Turecki, Stanley, and Tonner, Leslie. *The Difficult Child: A Guide for Parents,* rev. ed. New York: Bantam, 1989, $9.95.

SELF-ESTEEN

Clark, Jean Illsley. *Self-Esteem: A Family Affair.* New York: Harper & Row, 1980, $8.95.

DISCIPLINE

Dinkmeyer, Don; McKay, Gary; and Dinkmeyer, James. *Parenting Young Children*. New York: Random House, 1989, $10.95.

Dodson, Fitzhugh. *How to Discipline with Love*. New York: New American Library, 1987, $5.95.

Faber, Adele, and Mazlish, Elaine. *How to Talk So Kids Will Listen and Listen So Kids Will Talk*. New York: Avon, 1982, $7.95

————. *Siblings Without Rivalry: How to Help Your Children Live Together So You Can Live Too*. New York: Avon, 1987, $7.95.

Weinhaus, Evonne, and Friedman, Karen. *Stop Struggling with Your Child*. New York: HarperPerennial, 1991, $7.95.

EVERYDAY TOUGH TIMES

Ferber, Richard. *Solve Your Child's Sleep Problems*. New York: Simon & Schuster, 1986, $8.95.

Satter, Ellyn. *How to Get Your Kid to Eat . . . But Not Too Much*. Palo Alto, Calif.: Bull Publishing, 1987, $14.95.

SUCCESS IN SCHOOL

Rich, Dorothy. *MegaSkills: How Families Can Help Children Succeed in School*. Boston: Houghton Mifflin, 1988, $8.95.

INDEX